To Flora:

All the best to two very special longtime friends.

Best Wishes —

Murphy Martin

Front Row Seat

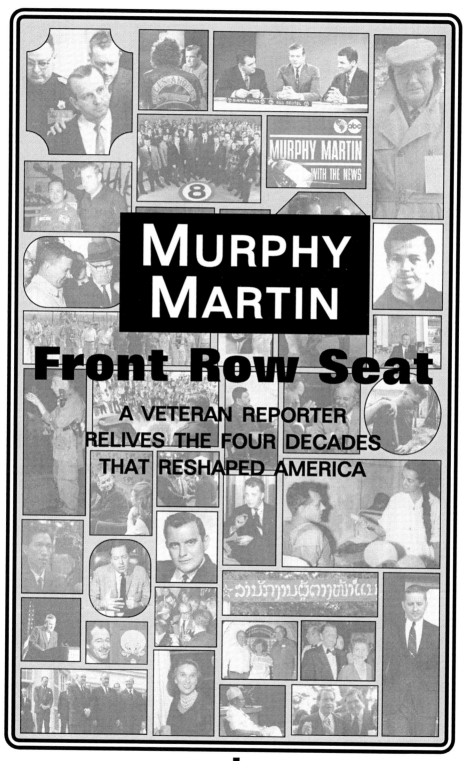

MURPHY MARTIN

Front Row Seat

A VETERAN REPORTER RELIVES THE FOUR DECADES THAT RESHAPED AMERICA

EAKIN PRESS ⬥ Austin, Texas

For Joyce—
Without your unparalleled devotion and support,
this book would never have been completed.
Thanks for being my best friend, my love,
my wife for forty years and counting!

FIRST EDITION
Copyright © 2003
By Murphy Martin
Published in the United States of America
By Eakin Press
A Division of Sunbelt Media, Inc.
P.O. Drawer 90159 ◻ Austin, Texas 78709-0159
email: sales@eakinpress.com
◻ website: www.eakinpress.com ◻
1   2   3   4   5   6   7   8   9
1-57168-813-7
Library of Congress Control Number 2003114081

Contents

Foreword by Hugh Aynesworth   v

Acknowledgments   ix

Part I // The '60s: Covering Tragedy and Turbulence

1 The President Has Been Shot in Your Town   1

2 Bizarre, Unbelievable, Unreal:
     The Trial of Jack Ruby.   18

3 The Kennedy Assassination: Fact or Fiction   38

4 The Violence of the Times.   54

Part II // More Than Just a Story

5 The Most Rewarding Moment.   91

6 Perot's Plan B in Iran 112

Part III // Ross Perot: A Professional Private Citizen

7 What's $100 Million, More or Less? 137

8 In and Out of the Race for President 149

**Part IV // From Truman to Cosell:
Fascinating Folks Along the Way**

9 Presidents and Would-Be Presidents 175

10 Never a Dull Moment. 200

11 Fame, Faith and (Mis)Fortune. 221

Part V // The Media: Beware the Power

12 Television: Then and Now 253

Afterword: That's My Time; Thank You for Yours 262

Foreword

Murphy Martin grew up in the small town of Lufkin, Texas, and probably never in his wildest dreams envisioned some of the things he later would encounter. Friends often mention that though he moved on to become an influential network newsman and correspondent and even later a well-known political adviser and motivational speaker, he never strayed far from his simple East Texas roots there.

I've read a lot of memoirs written by famous people, politicians, giants of the business world, actors, and con men. Even a few newsmen. Some relate how they accomplished this or that. Some expound on their personal tenets and beliefs. Some praise God. Often the more humbler credit luck or good family upbringing. A few tell you they did it all themselves. And there's an occasional "almost" or "what if?" tome.

In this refreshing book, long overdue, Murphy Martin weaves the story of how he got into journalism, how he refined his reporting skills, honed his perceptiveness, and compiled a strong network of contacts—all the while retaining an incredible work ethic and building trust with those with whom he dealt.

He doesn't tell you all this, but as one peruses his finer moments and accomplishments, one understands full well that an average reporter, editor, or broadcaster might not have been quite as successful, not quite as able to accomplish what Murphy did in his more than thirty years as a journalist. We seldom came head-to-head over the years journalistically, but I saw what he did and respected him immensely. Somewhat later we became real friends.

I was privy to his several years in public relations, after he left television news to get involved in Ross Perot's dedicated effort to free our prisoners from Vietnam prison camps. Even later as a key adviser to Perot in his 1992 presidential campaign.

A newsman's evaluation of a public relations practitioner often depends on the journalist's trust in that PR person. Once again, Murphy passed the test. Though he worked for a most demanding and mercurial gentleman in Mr. Perot, I never heard anything but praise during those years for his competence and professionalism.

In *Front Row Seat* you will meet many characters Murphy encountered along the way—some you've heard about, some whom you might have even forgotten, but folks that dodged in and out of Murphy's often-exhilarating career.

One of the more intriguing areas in this obvious labor of love is where Martin explains how faith played a role in many of his decisions and how he, slowed by numerous medical problems the past few years, kept his spirits high and his work continuing.

Reporters daily have access to folks that the average person would never encounter. But some never manage to elicit or explain that special aura or mood that makes the famous person remembered far beyond his ordinary shelf-life.

The author takes you through some of the early civil rights struggles, to covering the assassinations of the 1960s, to a bevy of behind-the-scenes political scenarios. The reader will meet such people as Ross Perot, Mickey Mantle, Tom Landry, John Wayne, Richard Nixon, Gerald Ford, John Connally, Harry S. Truman, Chet Huntley, Howard Cosell, Nelson Rockefeller, and others.

You'll see a twinge of Lyndon Baines Johnson that offers new insights, glimpses of Ted Kennedy, the Rev. Martin Luther King, Jr. Murphy knew and worked alongside Peter Jennings and Ted Koppel at ABC-TV when they were pups.

So very timely at this time, the fortieth anniversary of the JFK assassination in Dallas, are Murphy's chapters recounting those chaotic days when the world virtually stood on its head—eyes and hearts connected to Dallas.

Rushing to Dallas quickly that weekend, Murphy's reporting was exemplary over the next months, obtaining exclusive interviews with the assassin's widow, Marina Oswald, as well as his brother, Robert. He had known the press junkie Jack Ruby and reported special insights from his trial, where Judge Joe B. Brown offered Murphy daily advice and information.

A test of a successful and respected man, I think, is counting the lasting relationships—the real friendships—he accumulates in an often strange, constantly shifting world.

Guess who has often sat by Murphy's hospital bed during his several bouts with heart disease? Quietly and assuringly whispering encouragement to Murphy and Joyce. It's a man who certainly doesn't lack for ways to spend his time.

Ross Perot.

Guess who drives from Wichita Falls to see Murphy when he encounters a setback? One of the quietest, most gentlemanly men I've known, Lee Harvey Oswald's brother, Robert.

And the list goes on and on.

When you read this book, I believe you will understand why.

—Hugh Aynesworth
Dallas Bureau Chief
Washington Times

Acknowledgments

The idea for this book originated with the late Larry Grove, a very fine journalist with the *Dallas Morning News*. We met several times in 1980, talked about subject matter, even made an outline of what we thought some interesting chapters would be. After preparing a few abbreviated sample chapters, Larry and I talked more than we wrote and the next thing I knew doctors were set to open my chest for something called a quadruple bypass. Until a week earlier, a bypass was something I used to avoid traffic tie-ups, but that was before I discovered something called angina pains.

The surgery by Dr. Lonnie Whiddon at St. Paul Hospital in Dallas went well, but it took a while for me to regain my health despite the wonderful subsequent healthcare provided by Dr. Paul Wade, my internist for more than twenty years. It also took some time—several years—before I fought through procrastination and again thought about the book. By then, I had lost my good friend Larry Grove.

My procrastination in not completing the book earlier may have been a blessing in disguise because so much more happened after 1982. *Front Row Seat* is much more compelling and interesting with behind-the-scenes looks at more years of association with Ross Perot, culminating with his run for the presidency in 1992 when I was his television adviser. Also, the book offers a penetrating look-back on the fortieth anniversary of the assassination of John Kennedy, revisiting with those closest to the story.

This book was finally completed after I had my umpteenth heart procedure, a couple of more bypasses, and times when I got close enough to shake hands with the Man Upstairs on a couple of occasions. It was after one of those in 2001 that I asked Him to get me well enough to complete a book I started twenty-three years earlier. In a few months I was able to resume work on the book, and with the help of more wonderful people than I deserve, I finished *Front Row Seat* in July 2003.

I found a very talented editor/writer, Mike Farris, who was also an attorney. His judicious editing, plus his spot rewrite work, added greatly to my final product. Mike Farris was extremely valuable to my project.

People who helped me live the American Dream through journalism are numerous, and there is always danger you will omit a name that should be mentioned. Those indelible in my mind include Bert Shipp, my mentor when I arrived at WFAA-TV in 1961. The late Nick Archer, director of Basic News at ABC-TV, steered me through the network maze, and we remained friends until his death in 2002.

Hugh Aynesworth, author of several books (the latest out in November 2003 is entitled *JFK: Breaking the News*) and the number-one authority on the JFK assassination, was very helpful in organizing my work.

Carlton Stowers helped me early on and again after I renewed my efforts to conclude this project. Stowers has many successful books on the market, and the knowledge he shared with me was helpful.

John Sparks, a former news producer at WFAA-TV and NBC-TV in New York, was available as his schedule permitted. He was most helpful.

John J. Nance, author/pilot/lawyer/ABC-TV aviation reporter, was a writer in the newsroom at WFAA-TV while attending SMU. His subsequent success proved helpful in my making the right calls along the way.

Cheryl Hibbitts spent many extra hours typing early transcripts of interviews of many people who are in the book. Professional, dependable, valuable was Cheryl.

Research has to be double-checked. Some of those who always took the time to provide information, proof information, or just give their needed valuable judgments about different names, dates, and places of subjects in *Front Row Seat* include former Dallas County

Assistant District Attorney William Alexander. His recall of November 22, 1963, was invaluable. Also, the planning behind the prosecution of Jack Ruby he shared with us added much to the story.

Retired FBI Agent Robert Gemberling, who was made supervisor of all Oswald material after the assassination, offered his perspective then and now, and his thoughts about retired FBI Agent James P. Hosty proved very enlightening.

Priscilla Johnson McMillan, who interviewed Lee Harvey Oswald in Russia after serving on Senator John Kennedy's staff and wound up writing Marina Oswald's post-assassination book, was very frank and open with her thoughts forty years after the assassination. We are also appreciative of Ms. McMillan's availability and help in locating others pertinent to our work.

Numerous people with whom I had worked at one time or another during Ross Perot endeavors helped me check the facts, names, and dates. I am appreciative. Among them are Tom Marquez, Tom Meurer, Merv Stauffer, Sally Bell, Sharon Rae, and certainly Ross Perot himself, who always made room in his busy schedule for added interviews or answering telephone questions. The four chapters involving Perot are much more interesting because of the information we had carefully put together down through the years.

Our thanks to WFAA-TV for granting us the use of any of our work while there, including pictures.

Other pictures in the book come from my personal files, ABC-TV, United We Stand files, Warren Commission handouts, Gamma, '92 Perot Campaign, and numerous photographer friends.

This book relied heavily on selected material from hundreds of interviews I have done, in the form of tapes and transcripts of tapes. Journal entries and story notes derive from my pack-rat philosophy of never disposing of story material. Some material used is from memory and indelibly embedded recall of stories I will never forget.

The urgency that Virginia Messer and her staff at Eakin Press placed on this book is appreciated. The diligent editing of Melissa Roberts of that staff helped make a good product better.

Much has been written in this book about television interviews. They were important to the bulk of the work recalled here. But radio also played a significant role to my living the American Dream through journalism. Among the radio stations where I delivered the news along the way were: KTRE in Lufkin, Texas; KSPL in Diboll, Texas; WFAA Radio in Dallas; KRLD in Dallas; and WABC Radio in New York City.

Many other people provided inestimable skills that projected me to success in journalism. You know who you are, and I thank you. Without you it would have never happened.

I owe all those who made this book possible a deep debt of gratitude, but to no one do I owe more than my wife, Joyce. She helped me coordinate my research, helped me remember long ago details to weave with transcripts and tapes too numerous to mention. Her support during challenging times brought on by health problems makes her my nomination for the All-Florence Nightingale-Team of the last two decades.

And yes, I hope my son Michael, my grandchildren Angela and Clay, and my great-grandchildren Lauren, Walker, Ashley, and Ty Zachery, as well as my nephew Randy Odom, find a special meaning attached to this book.

Front Row Seat is a book by an anchorman/reporter, not a scholar. All of the material used here resulted from having been an observer at close range of the people, places, and subjects we covered during the last four decades. It is my hope that *Front Row Seat* will provide you with your own front row seat. If it does, this project is a success.

Thanks to all who kept me properly focused through forty years of television news changes. Just remember, as my friend Benny Binion always said, "Don't ever holler whoa or look back in a bad place!" Enjoy!

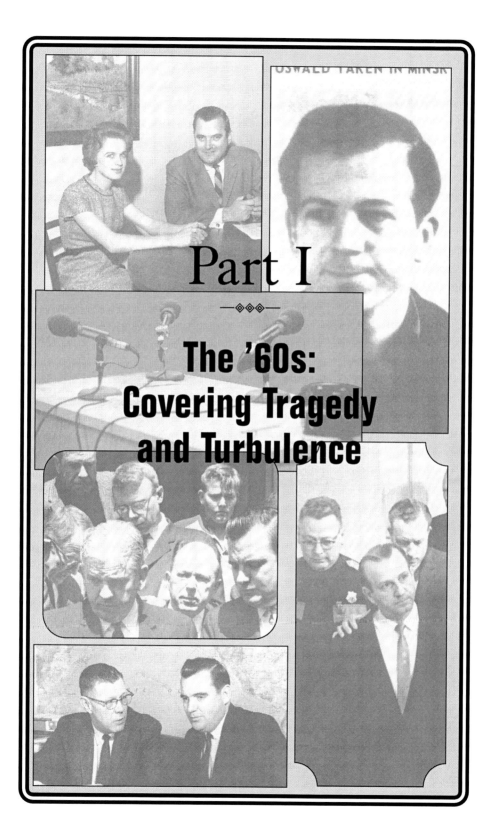

OSWALD TAKEN IN MINSK

Part I

❖❖❖

The '60s:
Covering Tragedy
and Turbulence

The President Has Been Shot in Your Town

"I am satisfied that it has been very well covered entirely and leaves no room for doubt in my mind that Lee actually did assassinate the president of the United States and kill Officer Tippit."
—ROBERT OSWALD,
BROTHER OF LEE HARVEY OSWALD

"The president has been shot in your town!"

It took just a second for the words to sink in that November day in 1963. I knew that President Kennedy was in Dallas, the city from which I had moved to New York just ten months earlier to take over the nightly news on ABC-TV, but was it really possible? *Shot?*

"Get to the studio as quickly as you can." With that, my producer, Walter Pfister, hung up the phone.

A chill coursed through me and I suddenly felt short of breath. I exchanged looks with my wife, Joyce, and nodded dumbly. Wally had just confirmed what we didn't want to believe minutes earlier when Joyce's mother had called from Dallas with the same message. Being in the news business, I understood the importance of confirming stories and corroborating sources. Well, I now had that confirmation and corroboration.

And I didn't like it.

It was just a little before 2:00 P.M. I wasn't due at the studio for hours, but that would have been under normal circumstances. This

1

was most decidedly not a normal circumstance, so I rushed into the bedroom of our Central Park South apartment to get dressed.

As I began putting on my suit, my mind raced into overdrive. Random lines, spoken in that distinctive Massachusetts accent, echoed in my ears:

"Let the words go forth from this time and place, to friend and foe alike, that the torch has been passed to a new generation of Americans."

"*Ich bin ein Berliner.*"

"I believe this nation should commit itself to achieving the goal, before this decade is out, of landing a man on the moon and returning him safely to earth."

Familiar scenes of touch football games on the White House lawn flashed across the movie screen of my mind. Could it be true? Was all that now in jeopardy?

Within thirty minutes, I was sitting at my desk above Studio TV-C on West 67th Street, glued to the television monitors, as was everybody else. ABC had started "live" studio coverage at 2:00 with Don Goddard, Ed Silverman, and Ron Cochran reporting and ABC correspondent Bob Clark on the line from Parkland Hospital in Dallas. Details leaked in slowly about what had happened. Just as the president's motorcade had turned off of Houston Street in downtown Dallas, by the Texas Schoolbook Depository, shots rang out. No one knew for sure how many, or from where. All anyone knew was that the president had been rushed to Parkland Hospital with a massive head wound.

As Secret Service Agent Clinton J. Hill would recall just a week later: "I jumped onto the left rear step of the presidential automobile. Mrs. Kennedy shouted, 'They've shot his head off,' then turned and raised out of her seat as if she were reaching for something that had blown out. I forced her back into her seat and placed my body above President and Mrs. Kennedy."

Almost lost in the shuffle was the fact that Texas governor John Connally, riding in the limousine with the president, had also been critically wounded. Frankly, no one seemed to care about that. All focus was on John Fitzgerald Kennedy.

Then, at 2:33 P.M., we heard the words no one wanted to hear, no one wanted to believe: President Kennedy was dead.

So much promise gone in an instant, leaving behind a demure

First Lady in a blood-spattered pink suit, who would become the most famous widow in the world. Leaving also a nation in mourning.

For the next seventy-two hours, Ron Cochran, Bob Young, and I anchored coverage in New York of the frenzied activity in Dallas, some 1,600 miles away. With the help of an incomparable staff at WFAA-TV, the ABC affiliate in Dallas which had employed me as news anchor less than a year earlier, we provided millions of mourners every tidbit of information about the story that had driven America to her knees.

And the news didn't stop with the assassination of a president. There were reports that a Dallas police officer, J. D. Tippit, had been shot and killed in Oak Cliff, just across the Trinity River from downtown Dallas, and that a young Texas Schoolbook Depository employee named Lee Harvey Oswald had been arrested in the nearby Texas Theater. The nation's attention riveted on Dallas as Oswald became the prime, and only, suspect in the assassination, as well as in the murder of Officer Tippit. The media circus was just beginning.

Sunday afternoon, November 24, I was sitting at the anchor desk when I was handed a bulletin at 12:37 P.M. that said Oswald had been shot in the basement of Dallas Police headquarters downtown. You can't imagine how hard it was to appear calm as I assured viewers we would provide more details as soon as they were made available— details as to how a murder could be committed in police headquarters among a sea of police and reporters. As I gave those assurances, I had no idea how stunning one of those details would be to me. It came just moments later when the gunman was identified as Dallas strip club owner Jack Ruby.

Jack Ruby! He was more than a familiar name to me. *I knew Jack Ruby personally*. During my tenure anchoring the news for WFAA-TV, Ruby had been a frequent visitor to the newsroom, looking for free publicity for the strip clubs he owned. To give him credit, he was creative, trying to convince us the goings-on at his clubs were newsworthy. Of course, if we ran a news story about his clubs, he wouldn't have to pay for spot advertising or an ad in the Dallas papers.

He appeared one day and announced: "I have something I *know* your viewers would want to see." As he explained it to me, I had to agree that our viewers might well want to see a stripper who used snakes in her act.

"Unfortunately," I told him, "we don't think that will go over very well as 'news' at the dinner hour."

Undaunted, he came back in about a week or so with another idea. He had developed a "twist" board—something you could stand on and "twist" along with Chubby Checker and lose weight. Maybe he was just ahead of his time, but we had to pass on that "story" idea as well.

That was the Jack Ruby I knew. As I described him on the air, "Jack's the kind of guy who may have five grand in his pocket and not a dime in the bank." I knew that he was not the kind who would stick a gun in the ribs of a handcuffed man and pull the trigger. But as I watched the video feed from WFAA-TV in Dallas, there was no mistaking the man with the gun. Ruby finally got his free news story.

By now, it had become obvious at ABC that we needed more personnel on the scene in Dallas, even as plans were being made for coverage of the president's funeral at Arlington National Cemetery. Because of my contacts in Dallas, I was an obvious choice to go to Texas. Unfortunately, the network had already used all its available cash dispersing reporters to cover the story, and the banks wouldn't open again until Tuesday. This was before the days of unlimited expense accounts and a corporate credit card in every wallet, and it posed a very real problem.

"We need cash," Steve Riddleberger, vice president of ABC News, told me.

"Have you asked Paddy McGlade?" I asked. Paddy owned and operated a bar and restaurant just a block away and had a large customer base from ABC.

"We need *real* money," Riddleberger said.

A fair point, but we were desperate. Without cash, our grand scheme to cover the rapidly diversifying angles of the assassination could be delayed for days.

"Can't hurt to ask," I said.

Riddleberger thought for a long moment. "Call him."

I did, then relayed his response to Riddleberger. "He wants to know if five thousand's enough."

Needless to say, network executives took on a new appreciation of their favorite neighborhood bartender after that.

And by that night, I once again found myself in Dallas, reunited with my good friends at WFAA-TV. One of those was Bert Shipp, now retired, who still retains more news contacts in the Dallas area than anyone else in the market. Shortly after the assassination, Bert discovered that Tom Alyea, a WFAA photographer, remained inside the Schoolbook Depository even after the police had sealed off the building. Following instructions from Bert, Alyea continued to shoot film from inside, tossing each exposed roll out the window to a waiting co-worker below. The wealth of footage from inside the Depository gave WFAA and ABC considerable footage no other network had.

Looking back, I still believe that ABC's coverage of those four indescribable days is an example of professional journalism at its best. For that, credit is due to a host of people, including Jay Watson, Bob Walker, Bert Shipp, and others at WFAA, as well as a list of ABC correspondents that reads like a Who's Who in broadcast journalism: Bill Lawrence, John Scali, Bill Lord, Bob Clark, Frank Reynolds, Roger Sharp, Paul Good, Bill Beutel, Jules Bergman, Dick Bate, Lou Cioffi, Bill Sheehan, Lisa Howard, David Jayne, and Merwin Sigale.

———◈◈◈———

"How would you like to be a radio announcer?"
—DARREL YATES, OWNER OF RADIO STATION KRBA IN
LUFKIN, TEXAS

As Joyce and I descended the steps to the tarmac at Love Field Airport to begin my assassination coverage in Dallas, the lights of the downtown skyline loomed just a few miles to the south. I thought back on my journey as a newsman that had taken me from the Piney Woods of East Texas to this same city just two years earlier.

I hadn't intended a career in broadcasting. And I certainly hadn't planned to go into radio. Not many did in those days. I was among many of my contemporaries I have met through the years who landed in broadcasting by sheer accident. My "accident" happened during the summer of 1942.

Growing up in Lufkin, Texas, a town of fewer than 15,000 set slap-dab in the middle of the Texas Piney Woods, my ambitions were much loftier. I wanted to join the Army Air Corps and become an ace in the air war overseas. Barring that, there was always work to be found at the huge paper mill in town or at one of the two large foundries. And there was plenty of excitement on summer evenings spent hanging out with friends. We didn't have malls in those days, so standing on the main downtown corner under old-fashioned streetlights had to suffice. We talked about school, sports, girls, and the war that raged in Europe and in the Pacific. Some of our buddies were already over there, and we couldn't wait until we were old enough to go. But, for the time being, we had to satisfy ourselves with standing on the corner and watching the world, as we knew it, go by.

The scent of pines would ride in on fresh breezes, washing away the heat of the day, almost making the odors from the paper mill and the foundries tolerable. You could almost feel the collective thrill that coursed through us as neon signs would begin to pulse with the coming of darkness. Who needed New York?

On one of those evenings, gathered with my friends, I saw Darrel Yates exit the stairs to the local radio station—the only radio station in town—that stood less than a hundred feet away. A flaming redhead not yet forty years old, Mr. Yates had arrived in East Texas from the Kansas-Missouri border just a few years earlier and bought KRBA, becoming the first outsider to challenge the longstanding dominance of the local newspaper that had been owned and operated by the local powers-that-be for decades. To us, he had his finger on the pulse of the world.

Or so it seemed.

That night, though, his finger had slipped. He looked around, his face flushed, his demeanor agitated. His gaze fell on me and he headed my way.

My first thoughts were to wonder what I had done wrong. Nothing makes a sixteen-year-old boy feel guilty like a grown-up bearing down on him. Mr. Yates spoke before he reached the corner where I stood.

"How would you like to be a radio announcer?"

Better words to hear than, "I'm going to tell your father what you did," but totally incomprehensible to me at the time.

"When I grow up, maybe," I thought, but I could see he had something more imminent in mind.

Just exactly how imminent became clear when he explained that he had just fired one of the only two announcers he had, and he had until the end of the long-playing disc covering his absence from the studio to find a replacement. In those few minutes, he convinced me that I would be a great broadcaster. I often wonder if Mr. Yates would have been nearly so convinced of my potential had he had the opportunity to conduct a proper search for experienced announcers. But, either way, next thing you know, I was a by-golly radio announcer.

It didn't take long for Mr. Yates to teach me how to operate the "board," which controlled everything that went out over the airwaves. My job consisted of spinning records, reading commercials, and periodically checking the Associated Press machine. Every hour on the hour we broadcast the news for five minutes, except for fifteen-minute newscasts at 7:00 A.M., noon, 6:00 and 10:00 P.M. Just like in the big cities.

But we were more than just a proud source of world and national news. We were also the exclusive source on the airwaves for local news, which we gathered from the courthouse, city hall, the sheriff's office, police station—even from the local funeral homes, the Chamber of Commerce, and telephone reports from listeners who thought they had news items of interest.

I matured rapidly in the position. From a scared, sixteen-year-old novice, I grew to insufferable confidence in a scant three weeks. My classmates thought I had it made, and who was I to say different? After all, I was making $22.50 a week, more money than I had ever seen. I never bothered to calculate it against the ten-hour days I was working, six days a week. Thirty-seven and a half cents an hour might have sounded depressing.

After turning eighteen a year and a half later, and at last eligible for military service, I left the world of radio broadcasting to pursue my original dream: to become an air ace. Alas, such was not to be. A seemingly harmless neck injury I had suffered in a fall some time earlier while working at a mom and pop grocery store cost me my chance at the Army Air Corps. I guess it's entirely possible that the Air Corps simply had its suspicions about someone who could actually fall at a mom and pop grocery store. What would such a person do if actually allowed to fly in the air? I had also flunked the physical for the regular army, as well, so "War Hero" was struck from my list of ambitions.

Kept out of military service, I next opted to pursue higher education, enrolling at North Texas State College in Denton, about an hour north of Dallas. I even received a part-time scholarship to play tenor saxophone in 'Fessor Floyd Graham's Aces of Collegeland band. Multi-talented, I was. On top of that, I wrote a sports column for *The Campus Chat* and rounded out my schedule working part-time in a department store.

Over the next two years, I managed to acquire a wife and a son, and quickly learned that pocket change from part-time work had its limitations for a family man. I confided my problem to Holford Russell, owner of the department store, who also owned a manufacturing company that bore his name.

"Murphy, how would you like to sell women's lingerie for me?" he asked.

Who could refuse an offer like that? The lure of a new car and a weekly salary guarantee didn't hurt, either. That, and the chance to see the world. My territory as a traveling salesman would be Kansas, Missouri, and Nebraska. So, I dropped out of North Texas College after my third year and we moved to Junction City, Kansas, fully believing that wealth lay in women's underthings.

That might have been true for those who could travel and sell and collect commissions. But not for those who got snowbound for weeks on end, and who couldn't travel and sell, and who couldn't collect their commissions. After a while, playing tenor sax, writing for *The Campus Chat*, and working for pocket change started to look good again.

And so did radio broadcasting back home in Lufkin, which is exactly where I found myself, again, in 1949. Progress reached the hinterlands of East Texas a little slower than it did in the big cities, but got there soon enough. In 1955, I became anchorman, news director, and sales manager at KTRE-TV, the first television station in that part of the state.

A few years later, I felt I was ready to move to the big-time. And what could be more big-time than New York City? While there checking on a possible job opportunity, I stopped by to see the folks at ABC-TV, ready to conquer the world. But apparently New York City wasn't ready for me just yet. Instead, they suggested I talk to Mike Shapiro, general manager at WFAA-TV, the ABC affiliate in Dallas.

A good lead, as it turned out, because Shapiro hired me to work at WFAA Radio. In June of 1961, I went on the air at WFAA-TV, Channel 8, as the lead news anchor in Dallas. Just two years later, I would be a network news anchor in New York City, covering the fourth assassination of a president in American history.

—◇◆◇—

"As we were about to enter the triple underpass, we heard gunfire."
—DALLAS COUNTY SHERIFF BILL DECKER

Now, here I was again, back in Dallas. Joyce had slept on the plane; I couldn't. Too many things still swirled in my mind, not the least of which were the words Wally Pfister, my producer, had spoken on the phone two days earlier. He hadn't said, "The president has been shot in Dallas." No, he had said, "The president has been shot in *your town.*"

My town! Had there been a hint of an accusation there? Perhaps it was just my imagination as far as Wally was concerned, but I would soon learn it wasn't where others were concerned.

Dallas had been such a sparkling city when I had moved from there just ten months earlier. Confident, progressive, competent— these were words that defined the Dallas I knew. But I was beginning to sense a boiling rage against *my* town in the minds of many in the country who held it responsible for gunning down their beloved president. A town that couldn't even keep his alleged assassin alive long enough to stand trial.

It was well after midnight when we arrived, and minutes later we checked in to the Marriott Inn just across Stemmons Freeway from the Apparel Mart, where President Kennedy had been en route when the fatal shots were fired. A short three hours of tossing and turning and I was on the move again, speaking to those I hoped could provide some answers.

My first stop was the County Courthouse to talk with Dallas County Sheriff Bill Decker, the nattily dressed lawman who had been deputy sheriff for fourteen years before being elected sheriff in 1948. Known as a straight-shooter, Decker was highly respected by everyone, including the criminal element, many of whom he had known while growing up on the streets of Dallas.

Sheriff Decker had been riding in the lead car of the motorcade, along with Dallas Police Chief Jesse Curry, Secret Service Agent Forrest Sorrels, and Winston G. Lawson of the Secret Service, primary planner of security arrangements for the Dallas trip. According to Sheriff Decker's account, "As we were about to enter the triple underpass, we heard gunfire. I heard two shots and, as I turned to see where they were coming from, I saw the last shot strike the president. It made a halo about Mr. Kennedy's head when it struck."

That's when everyone sprang into action. "I saw the Secret Service agent in the car behind the president's attempting to climb into the presidential limousine from behind. At about this time, Lawson gave the order to 'get out of here!'" Decker also saw another Secret Service agent raise his weapon in the direction of the Schoolbook Depository. He then radioed police headquarters and asked them to contact the Sheriff's Department, located near the scene, to secure the Schoolbook Depository, the building adjacent to it, and the park across the street. He ordered everyone in the department, off-duty or on, to report to the scene immediately. These were rapid-fire directions as his lead car showed the way to Parkland Hospital for the limousine carrying a dying president and a critically wounded governor.

When I redirected my questioning to Oswald's shooting, Sheriff Decker became a little defensive, but more disgusted than anything. In his mind, the real culprit was the media, whose thirst for information so bewildered Police Chief Jesse Curry that it impaired his judgment.

The Dallas Police Department had been catching heat long before Jack Ruby slipped down that ramp with a gun in his pocket. Never mind that the department had succeeded in capturing Oswald less than two hours after he had been seen by no fewer than three eyewitnesses in the window of the Schoolbook Depository and after the death of one police officer. As far as many in the media were concerned, the police weren't doing their job correctly because they weren't cooperating with the press.

One network news commentator showed a picture of Oswald on the air, then said, "This is what Oswald looks like. Make that, this is what he looked like before he was taken in by the Dallas Police Department. Who knows what he might look like now? The press has been unable to see him." As if the police had a duty to show the prisoner to the press.

In the gang-type journalism of that day, reporters ascended like a rising tide into the halls outside the interrogation room. The pressure became intense on Police Chief Curry to bring Oswald out to satisfy the media, as well as public curiosity. As reporters crowded hallways to the point that the police could barely move from place to place, Chief Curry decided to give in rather than fight.

That was when he made the fatal decision to tell the media the exact time Oswald was to be transferred to the County Jail, so they could file their stories, complete with photographs and rolling film.

"I pleaded with the chief to move Oswald in the dead of night, without any announcement about the transfer time, but he felt he had to appease the press," Sheriff Decker said. "His prisoner never made it to my jail."

Disappointed, he almost spat out his next words: "It didn't have to end this way!"

"We commit him unto the hands of an understanding God."
—REVEREND LOUIS SAUNDERS, PRESIDING OVER THE FUNERAL OF LEE HARVEY OSWALD

It seemed that Monday, November 25, 1963, was the day for funerals. On that day President John F. Kennedy was buried, with full pomp and circumstance, at Arlington National Cemetery, while in another service, Police Officer J.D. Tippit was remembered before an overflow crowd in Dallas.

And in yet another service, Lee Harvey Oswald was laid to rest in a plot bought long before by his mother, Marguerite, at Rose Hill Cemetery in Fort Worth under the watchful eyes of local, state, and federal law enforcement—less than twenty-four hours after Jack Ruby had put a bullet into his side. The speed and secretiveness with which Oswald was buried would later serve as grist for the conspiracy rumor mills. It was as if someone wanted to make sure Oswald's body would be interred before questions could arise. Why else such a rush?

Funeral director Paul Groody told me that the entire funeral had been orchestrated by the Secret Service. They had called him to pick up Oswald's body at Parkland Hospital, then instructed him to provide an "inexpensive funeral."

"I don't know who's paying for this," Groody said, "but I'm sending the bill to the Secret Service."

The service itself was a dreary affair. There were only two floral arrangements, one of red carnations, the other white. As I looked around the funeral tent, I saw nothing but newspeople and law enforcement. There were no friends or mourners other than Oswald's immediate family: his wife, Marina; two daughters, Junie and Rachel, one just a baby; his brother, Robert; and his mother, Marguerite. There weren't even enough from which to draw pallbearers, so six newsmen were drafted to carry the casket to the grave.

Reverend Louis Saunders, presiding only because no one else would, spoke briefly, admonishing that, "We are not here to judge." But I knew most of us were there for exactly that reason—and, perhaps, out of morbid curiosity.

Reverend Saunders finished his remarks at 4:16 P.M., and the casket was then opened for five minutes, satisfying some of that curiosity.

The Oswald family was allowed to see the body of Lee Harvey—husband, son, father, and brother—for the first time since he had been slain.

And it would be the last.

"I recall that evening we spent going over the Warren Commission Report. The first section that I went to was to look for what the Commission came up with as a motive, and it simply wasn't there. That has always been the big why . . . and it still is today."
—ROBERT OSWALD

Lee's funeral was the first time I ever saw Robert Oswald, Lee's brother, although we didn't speak to each other then. Later, I would be the first reporter Robert would choose to talk to after I met him through William McKenzie, an attorney advising him and Marina.

Robert assured me that he would not make any public statement about the assassination until he had made one with me.

That occurred on September 27, 1964, when the Warren Commission Report was issued at 6:30 P.M., EDT. Networks were given advance copies the day before and, with mine in hand, Robert and I locked ourselves in a Dallas motel room, where we studied the report together for almost thirty hours. The next day, as part of special ABC network programming, I interviewed Robert in a live feed from WFAA-TV in Dallas.

On the air, I wondered aloud why Robert had not made any public statement before but had chosen, instead, to keep his silence. "I felt there was too much speculation and rumor within a matter of days after the assassination," he said. "I felt in my own mind that perhaps I could best serve the investigation by dealing with the federal authorities involved in the investigation rather than dabbling into perhaps speculation and things of this nature through the news media."

When our discussion turned to the Warren Commission and the report that we had both studied exhaustively, I asked him whether he agreed with their conclusions. He said that it had satisfied a lot of his questions about time factors and whether all the shots fired had come from the Schoolbook Depository. Of particular interest to Robert had been what had transpired in the time from when Lee had left the Depository until his capture in the Texas Theater.

His conclusion? "I am satisfied that it has been very well covered entirely and leaves no doubt in my mind that Lee actually did assassinate the president of the United States and kill Officer Tippit."

What a lot of people forget is that Lee Harvey Oswald was more than just an assassin, more than just a communist sympathizer, more than just a patsy, more than just a (fill in the blank with all the rumors and theories that have surrounded his name for four decades). He was also, as I mentioned before, a father, a husband, a son, and a brother. Robert had great difficulty believing his brother could, or would, kill the president of the United States. I saw the gut-wrenching effect this had on a solid citizen like Robert Oswald. How could such opposites be brothers?

I had a chance to speak to Robert again, in February of 2003. After all these years, he still speaks fondly of his long-dead brother.

He remembered Lee showing him ten typed pages he had written about his visit to Russia. Lee had actually written fifty pages in long-hand but had only enough money to get ten of them typed. According to Robert, Lee envisioned himself becoming a writer, another Ernest Hemingway. But Lee shortchanged his writing career just as he shortchanged his life on November 22, 1963.

Even today, there is still a part of Robert that continues to search for the "why" of it.

"Has anything changed your mind in the past years about the Warren Report?" I asked.

"Not really," he said. "Through the years, I would ponder it, and think, and look for different answers, but nothing has really changed."

Then he recalled those hours in the motel room with me, scouring the advance copy of the Warren Commission Report. There had been nothing there to tell him why Lee had done what he had done—the very question that haunts him to this day. His face grows wistful, even sad.

"It is so repugnant to me that my brother Lee was even remotely involved," he said. "I would give my right arm—and my left—to know why he did it."

—◈◈◈—

"Damn it, Jack, why'd you kill him?"
—BILL ALEXANDER, ASSISTANT
DISTRICT ATTORNEY FOR DALLAS COUNTY
"The son of a bitch killed my president."
—JACK RUBY

After I filed my story on the Oswald funeral with ABC-TV, I looked up Assistant District Attorney Bill Alexander, right-hand man to legendary D.A. Henry Wade. The tall, lanky, sometimes arrogant, oftentimes brash prosecutor, who was known to pack a pistol into the courtroom, had been one of the first, along with Police Captain Will Fritz, to question Oswald after his arrest. Though his dry wit sometimes backfired on him, as it had that weekend, it didn't quell his drive for the truth.

By the time I caught up with Alexander, he had already found himself enmeshed in controversy. Joe Gouldon, a former Dallas reporter who was covering the story for a Philadelphia newspaper, asked how the charge against Oswald would read.

"Well," Alexander said, "we could say that, then and there, voluntarily and with malice aforethought, Lee Harvey Oswald killed John F. Kennedy, president of the United States in furtherance of a communist conspiracy." Gouldon, not recognizing the intended humor, ran with the story as an extra edition in Philadelphia. According to Alexander, the story quickly reached the ear of newly sworn-in President Lyndon Johnson. Things started rolling downhill—from President Johnson's lips to presidential adviser Clark Clifford's ear, and on to D.A. Wade, who bolted red-faced into Alexander's office.

"What's all this communist stuff?" Wade asked.

"The son of a bitch *is* a communist," Alexander said.

"Well, here's a message straight from the president of the United States. 'Knock all that stuff off. What the hell are you trying to do—start World War Three?'"

Of course there was no mention of the words "communist" or "conspiracy" in the indictment, Alexander told me. Nor did he ever mean for such a thought to reach the public. But I guess it's an open question whether Alexander's off-the-cuff joke may have been the genesis of some of the conspiracy theories that have since taken on lives of their own, fueling a cottage industry that thrives to this day.

Who said lawyers don't have senses of humor?

One of Alexander's more intriguing observations arose out of his first questioning, along with Captain Fritz, of Oswald. "Oswald answered most questions with a question," he said. "It was almost as if he had been programmed to participate in a deal like this.

"Let me say it another way," Alexander went on. "It was almost like he had rehearsed a confrontation with authorities."

Now, there's a big difference between being programmed, which implies an action by someone else, and merely rehearsing. I had a chance recently to talk to Bill Alexander again, probing his memory after forty years, looking for a little clarification. After he and Captain Fritz interviewed Oswald, were they satisfied that no one else had been involved? That, after all, is the linchpin to conspiracy theories past and present.

Alexander said he had his own questions at the time—questions that linger to this day. "There was no doubt in our minds that we had the right man," he clarified. "The real question was how deep did this thing go? How many were involved? Who was he? What was he? And why?"

Letting his mind roam back over four decades, Alexander continued, "There was no evidence that anybody else participated in the shooting here in Dallas. Now, frankly, we had no idea what motivated him or whether he was a *Manchurian Candidate* operating on pre-programmed or whether he was paid or what. Nobody knows. But there was nothing else to connect anybody else with the assassination in Dallas."

"What about Marina Oswald?" I asked. "Could she have shed any light in the immediate hours after the assassination?"

"Who knows? She wasn't handled properly that night but, hell, I couldn't talk Russian. We didn't have anybody that could talk Russian. How are you going to talk to somebody in pidgin English and find out anything?"

Well, what about Ruby? Was he part of a conspiracy to shut Oswald up? Alexander doesn't think so. According to him, Ruby had no reason to believe he could see Oswald that Sunday morning. Instead, he had been at the Western Union office sending a money order to one of his strippers in Fort Worth when the attempt to move Oswald began. The time stamp on the money order proved that.

Ruby had just left Western Union and walked the less than one block toward City Hall when, Alexander said, he "looked down the ramp and saw all the news people and activity going on there. While Officer E. R. Vaughn briefly chatted with Lieutenant Rio Pierce as he reached the top of the ramp, driving out of the Dallas Police Station, Jack just walked down the ramp. He had no idea Lee Harvey Oswald was about to be led out to an armored vehicle to be transported to Dallas County Jail."

When Ruby saw Oswald, according to Alexander, he was simply overcome with emotion and, without any advance planning, pulled his gun and shot him.

Never one to mince words, and with the benefit of hindsight, Alexander also has plenty of opinions on other matters. "How about Oliver Stone's *JFK*?" I asked.

"Oh, that was a bunch of crap. I think it was a disservice to the country. It'll have the conspiracy buffs running with lies and myths long after you and I are dead."

Okay, then, how about New Orleans District Attorney Jim Garrison and his attempts to weave the assassination conspiracy that served as the basis for *JFK*?

"The world is full of f——— idiots and a lot of idiots are paid to be idiots. Some politicians just naturally do things like that for whatever reason. I have found that in public life—politics—people do and say the most outlandish things.

"And, if they tell a lie big enough and often enough, somebody will believe it."

CHAPTER 2

Bizarre, Unbelievable, Unreal: The Trial of Jack Ruby

"This is a kangaroo railroad and every one of you know it, too. I hope the people of Dallas are proud of the jury that was shoved down our throats."
—MELVIN BELLI, JACK RUBY'S ATTORNEY

Little did I realize when I stepped off the plane in Dallas to report on the Oswald and Tippit funerals that my days as anchorman of *Murphy Martin with the News*, late night at ABC-TV, were numbered. Just five weeks later, I was summoned to a meeting with Elmer Lower, president of ABC News, and two company vice presidents, Jesse Zousmer and Steve Riddleberger. I thought it unusual for them all to be present, but I had no sense of impending doom. At least not at first. While the atmosphere was friendly enough for the unexpected get-together, it did not take long for them to get to the meat of the subject: It was time to make a change in anchormen on the late night news.

I wondered if I was hearing right. Had they really said they wanted to replace me with Bob Young, who had been doing the weekend news at the network? After all, just a few days earlier, Steve Riddleberger had written me a letter in which he said, "Elmer Lower, who is presently traveling abroad, has asked me to convey to you his personal thanks for your outstanding contribution to ABC News' coverage of the tragic events over the November 22-25 weekend. Because of your efforts and skill our department has received high critical and professional acclaim. You were called upon to report to the largest audiences any newsperson has ever faced. You did this well and gave of yourself unselfishly."

That's when I should have sensed something in the works. On more than one occasion, I had seen praise as the forerunner to something more ominous. The same hands that patted Julius Caesar on the back also held knives. And how many baseball managers have been fired after receiving a "vote of confidence" from ownership?

I reminded them that ratings had moved up appreciably since I moved into the anchor slot, and the number of stations carrying the program had increased. They listened politely—even said I had been doing a good job—but the decision had been made. January 10, 1964, would be my last night as anchor.

I wondered, as I sat there, what was really behind the change. After all, the ratings numbers belied what they were telling me. I thought back on the words my producer, Wally Pfister, had first spoken when he called me on November 22: "The president has been shot in your town."

In *my* town.

Could that really have anything to do with this? Mr. Lower never suggested that it did, and I preferred to think that, new to ABC from NBC, he simply wanted his own team in place. It wouldn't be the first, nor would it be the last, time that a change was made in television simply for the sake of change. But Jesse Zousmer later told me that ABC had been taking heat from a number of affiliates, most notably their affiliate in Philadelphia, for using a Dallas man to anchor a prime newscast.

Forty years later, I queried Mr. Lower about "affiliate pressures" in 1963. On the eve of his ninetieth birthday, he wrote me: "Forty years is a long time to draw on the memory. But my recollection today is that the ABC News 11 P.M. network news was doomed before I walked in the door of 7 W. 66th Street. Whether fair or unfair, you were doomed with the product. I learned much later, in the case of Bob Young, the person identified with a failed product gets tarred with the same brush. It is sad but true."

At the time, I don't remember anyone even hinting that the news program was "doomed" when Mr. Lower walked in the door.

If it was, why didn't he mention it to me then? Why not just shut it down? Why continue a program that was destined to fail? I felt as if my journalistic capabilities and integrity had been indicted. I wasn't feeling particularly charitable to the men who had issued that indictment, so I declined their offer to buy out the remaining portion of my contract, though that would have been the easier thing to do— to take their money and go on about my business. But I had no intention of leaving ABC until I had removed any questions that had been raised about my abilities.

A second option ABC offered was for me to become their chief roving correspondent. While there was some appeal to that, I didn't want to make a quick decision. "I'll think about it," I said, then headed for the Bahamas.

Over the next five days, and after several lengthy conversations with Nick Archer, the director of basic news at the network and my most trusted friend in the department, I considered my options. I figured I could do a variety of journalistic work as a roving correspondent, and Nick pointed out that I would be used to fill in for Ron Cochran, the prime ABC News anchor, and also for the weekend anchor from time to time. So I chewed on my pride enough that it could be swallowed and accepted the position.

My first assignment was not long in coming and, irony of ironies, it took me back to Dallas, to cover the Jack Ruby trial. Anxious to reprove my abilities, Joyce and I headed straight to Dallas, even though the change of venue hearing for Ruby was more than a week away. I took advantage of that week to travel to Birmingham, Tuskeegee, and Montgomery, Alabama, to cover civil rights stories, then on to Jackson, Mississippi, for a story on Byron de la Beckwith, who stood charged with killing civil rights worker Medgar Evers. I also interviewed Gen. Edwin A. Walker, the controversial Texas segregationist, who was in Jackson for the de la Beckwith trial.

With the Ruby hearing looming on Monday morning, February 10, 1964, I returned to Dallas the preceding Saturday for a brief interview with Marguerite Oswald, Lee Harvey's mother. She was preparing to leave for Washington, D.C., to testify before the Warren Commission when I spoke with her, and she spent most of the interview simply complaining that Jack Ruby had denied her son the right to clear his name.

Then, with Monday just around the corner, it was time to focus on my old acquaintance, Jack Ruby.

"When I was incarcerated, a lot of false accusations were made against me. The underworld thing, the communist association. Do you know how I felt, and how I loved my president, to be accused of all those things?"
—JACK RUBY

Newspeople from all over the world gathered for the Ruby trial, which got under way with a hearing on Ruby's motion to change venue. Ruby's lawyers, Melvin Belli and Joe Tonahill, asked the judge to transfer venue from Dallas to—well, to just about anywhere else. They claimed a fair and impartial jury could not be chosen in Dallas because of the incredible publicity surrounding the trial. Of course, that could have been said for just about any city in America. After all, Ruby had executed Oswald in front of a national television audience of countless millions. Judge Joe B. Brown denied the motion to transfer venue, and the trial began.

After a week of jury selection, which began on February 18, 1964, the jurors were ready to be sworn in. As Judge Brown later described the twelve who had been selected, "No juror had less than a high school education. There were four people with college degrees on the jury ... The defense eliminated 18 veniremen with peremptory challenges. The prosecution challenged another 11 and I excused 120. Of that number, one was ill, 58 admitted having fixed opinions and 62 were excused because they could not pass a sentence of death on another human being."

Television was still in its relative infancy as a major medium for news, but television was present in full force for the trial. The Jack Ruby trial, beginning less than three months after President John F. Kennedy had been assassinated, opened the doors for the world news spotlight to shine brilliantly on Dallas. Even gossip columnist Dorothy Kilgallen was a fixture in the courtroom each day, and she provided fodder for some of the more lighthearted in the group as a female deputy sheriff searched her handbag each day. Now, that was "heavy" stuff, according to some reporters.

The proceedings had been moved from Judge Brown's regular courtroom to one of the largest in what is now the Dallas County Records Building. But even the enlarged courtroom could not begin to accommodate the more than 300 news personnel from throughout the world who tried to cram inside its doors. It was a media frenzy of epic proportions, even producing some of the trial's lighter moments.

Throughout the trial, a lot of Ruby's "girls" from his strip club appeared at the courthouse. One morning, my wife, Joyce, and Ginger Stanford, the wife of one of my cameramen, entered the hallway outside the courtroom, which was filled with press people and camera crews. As Deputy Sheriff Rosemary Allen searched them before they entered the courtroom, a reporter asked, "Who are those ladies?"

"Oh, those are a couple of Jack Ruby's strippers," I said.

The lights immediately went on and cameras started grinding. That afternoon, as I edited the film of the day, the only sound that stood out over the usual hubbub in the hallway was Joyce's distinct voice screaming at me.

Both NBC and CBS had at least two television crews each in Dallas, but I was the only ABC reporter on the scene for the first two weeks. Although outnumbered, my prior contacts in Dallas nevertheless gave ABC a distinct advantage, and we provided our audience comparable, if not superior, coverage. It may have cost me an anchor job, but being from Dallas definitely proved to be a great help in my coverage of the Ruby trial.

Judge Joe B. Brown, whom I had known well during my Dallas days, presided over the trial. An overachiever, he never finished high school, but in those days a college degree wasn't required for a law license provided you could pass the Texas Bar exam. He attended night classes at the now defunct Jefferson Law School in Dallas, while working days as a rate clerk for the railroad. Then he sat for, and passed, the Bar exam in 1934. Within ten years, he was a sitting judge in Dallas and, for the next thirty years, never lost an election in fourteen campaigns.

Politics had long been Judge Brown's passion. As a judge, he developed a well-known love for the limelight. When the grand jury he impaneled returned eighty-two indictments on November 26, 1963, including one against Jack Rubenstein, alias Jack Ruby, for the murder of Lee Harvey Oswald, he wasted no time assigning the case to his own court.

No one in the Dallas County Courthouse was surprised.

Notable players on the prosecution team, with whom I was very familiar, included legendary District Attorney Henry Wade, a University of Texas classmate of Governor John Connally; Wade's chief prosecutor, Bill Alexander; and two assistant D.A.'s, Jim Bowie and Frank Watts. Wade, the former FBI agent, cigar-chomping, tractor-driving prosecutor, loved to spend time working his farm in the Dallas suburb of Rockwall. (As it turned out, politics ran in the Wade family. His younger son is now a criminal district judge in Dallas.)

On the other side of the trial table sat Ruby's defense team, led by the flamboyant San Francisco attorney Melvin Belli. A flashy dresser in custom-made suits and expensive boots, lover of gourmet foods and high profile, big-dollar lawsuits, Belli was truly the King of Torts. Jack Ruby's brother, Earl Ruby, had brought him in to replace local Dallas attorney Tom Howard. In retrospect, that move might have been Ruby's second biggest mistake, the first coming when he put a gun into Oswald's side and pulled the trigger in front of dozens of law enforcement officials and newspeople with cameras rolling. It is impossible to gauge exactly how big a mistake *that* was.

Not a high-profile lawyer, Howard was known as a "courthouse" lawyer—always around the courthouse. Perhaps his clients were less desirable than most, but they would all vouch for their attorney. Ralph Paul, a business partner of Ruby's, knew of Howard's reputation and asked him to make bond for Ruby less than three hours after Ruby's arrest. Howard quickly met with Ruby and told him what all good defense lawyers tell their clients: *You have a right to remain silent; exercise that right.*

Prosecutor Jim Bowie later told me that the Ruby family had misread Howard's legal abilities. They were convinced that, in such a high profile case, Ruby needed a high profile attorney. Criminal defendants and their supporters often confuse flamboyance with skill, with generally predictable consequences. Not to belittle Belli's skills, for surely he was an able attorney, but he lacked a working knowledge of Dallas County juries, Dallas County judges, Dallas County prosecutors, and Dallas County justice—skills that Tom Howard had in spades. As Prosecutor Bowie put it, "They [the Ruby family] forgot that, even though Tom Howard defends whores and pimps, he does it damn well!"

According to Howard, Earl Ruby hired Belli after first talking to a friend in Los Angeles, Mike Shore. Howard said Shore then contacted Frank Sinatra, who suggested they call Belli. Although that was the first and last time I ever heard Sinatra's name mentioned in connection with the trial, Howard remained positive that that is indeed what Earl Ruby told him. If nothing else, it offers an interesting footnote to the whole affair.

Belli agreed to take on the case for a fee that might range from $40,000 to $75,000. Sounds awfully cheap by O.J. standards, but remember that these were 1964 dollars.

"I might be able to raise twenty-five," Earl Ruby said.

"No problem," Belli said. "I'll get the rest by writing a book."

The man was ahead of his time. His book, by the way, which was published in 1964, was called *Dallas Justice*, one of those things in which he got educated the hard way.

Assisting Belli in the trial was attorney Joe Tonahill, who hailed from Jasper, Texas, about sixty miles from my hometown of Lufkin. Tonahill was well known throughout Texas, particularly in Dallas, Houston, Austin, and East Texas. He was a good choice, and would have been even better had Belli listened to him more.

Perhaps the busiest man around the courthouse during the trial was Sheriff Bill Decker, who was determined to learn from the mistakes Police Chief Jesse Curry had made with Oswald. As far as Sheriff Decker was concerned, Jack Ruby was *his* prisoner, not Dallas County's. He hand-picked twenty-one men to serve as the detail to guard Ruby before, during, and after the trial, and to transfer him to and from the courtroom. Each man was specially schooled for this duty and, during the trial, many of them often worked sixteen to eighteen hours a day.

Each day of the trial, five deputies would escort Ruby from the jail elevator to the holding cell for Judge Brown's courtroom. They would stay in the room with Ruby until Judge Brown gaveled his court to order, at which time they would escort him into the courtroom to his seat at the defense table. Four of the deputies would then sit to provide a shield around Ruby, while the fifth assumed a seat facing the spectators.

And quite a sight it made: five fully armed deputies in business suits surrounding the little strip club owner at every move. There weren't going to be any lynchings on Sheriff Bill Decker's watch.

The tight security provides some parallels to present-day airport security following the September 11 attacks, both in terms of its strictness and its occasional absurdity. One routine handbag search at the courthouse turned up a child's water pistol, which the embarrassed mother explained she had taken away from her son in Sunday school the previous weekend. Unsmiling deputies then held the "weapon" outside the courtroom while the woman was allowed to observe that day's proceedings. Fingernail clippers were also victims to tightened security.

The trial ran for thirty-four days, during which 117 witnesses testified, running the gamut of status in Dallas, from former boxing champion Barney Ross, who testified about knowing Ruby as a boy, to Stanley Marcus, founder of the Neiman-Marcus department store, right down to former Ruby employees and strippers. In my days at WFAA-TV in Dallas, Ruby had been desperate for publicity. Well, he finally got it.

During the trial, I was also able to collect a number of leads in the JFK assassination. I say "leads" because we certainly didn't have time to separate fact from fiction while the trial was still ongoing, but I filed them away to check later. These leads came from various sources, including some well-known acquaintances, but also from perfect strangers determined to get their information into the hands of a reporter.

Throughout the trial, we did feature stories outside the courtroom, interviewing witnesses as they entered or exited. We even staged a reenactment of the shooting by utilizing the same two detectives who had been escorting Oswald at the time, J. R. Leavelle and L. C. Graves. I posed between them as Oswald while they talked about the shooting. Despite the clutter of newspeople crammed into the basement, both said they had been relaxed as they escorted Oswald, who said nothing. Their relaxation turned to total shock when Ruby lunged from their left and fired. They tried to turn to place themselves between Oswald and Ruby in case he shot again, but the damage had already been done.

My cameramen, Wes Marks and Steve Stanford, performed superbly throughout the trial, but, as the sole ABC reporter, I simply couldn't be everywhere at the same time. I spent my weeks in Dallas but spent weekends flying to New York City each Saturday morning to write and deliver ten newscasts on the ABC Radio Network (four on Saturdays and six on Sundays), then I returned to Dallas on Sunday evenings to be in place when the trial resumed on Monday morning. Feeling stretched too thin, I asked the network for added reporter help after the second week. ABC responded by sending Ed Silverman, who had also lived in Dallas at one time and was a welcome relief to me for the rest of the trial.

Near the end of the first week, I began lobbying Sheriff Decker to allow me to interview Ruby. He finally agreed, provided Ruby's defense team approved. All necessary parties gave their approval, and several reporters, including Tom Pettit of NBC, joined me in that interview, which was for radio and TV only. Also present were Ruby's lawyers and several sheriff's deputies.

Ruby was anxious to do the interview. He looked healthy and seemed somewhat at ease—at least when we started. I began with a rather mundane question: "Anything special on your mind you want to say, Jack?"

"Well, first I want to know if you are going to be honest with me about eliminating anything I state, Murphy ... Martin?"

Interesting. He was on trial for his life and yet he seemed more concerned about being misquoted or taken out of context. I explained to him how we couldn't use long, rambling statements and that the producers of each news program controlled their program's content.

"I'm a little disillusioned about print reporting," he said. "I wonder if I can have more faith in the radio and television as to what you are going to delete out of the tape, or whether it is going to be authentic."

I was curious about his concern, but he quickly cleared it up for me. "A writer in this particular courtroom, just to gain readers, falsely stated that I was nervous and frightened—as though someone was coming into this courtroom and was going to disintegrate me right here in this room."

"Are you nervous and frightened?" I asked.

"No. On the contrary, but ... who would be calm and collected unless you've had the experience of running for public office? ... I'm not scared, Mr. Martin, about anything."

Strange. I would have thought he had more important things to worry about than whether the press had depicted him as nervous and frightened. But, as I learned, he was terribly concerned about how he was being depicted to the world. On the verge of tears several times, he said, "When I was incarcerated, a lot of false accusations were made against me. The underworld thing, the communist association. Do you know how I felt, and how I loved my president, to be accused of all those things?"

I reminded Ruby that there had been a few witnesses who testified that he had brought shame to the city of Dallas. "Do you think you did?" I asked.

That seemed to touch a raw nerve. "Now that the thing has happened, I didn't know what would react in people's minds. I love this city; maybe that was part of it. Great civic-minded people, they are helpless. I know they will be prejudiced towards me now."

Then he began to cry, as if he felt great shame at bringing disrepute to a city he loved. "But getting back to our great people who try to do so much for this city, who are caught so much off guard. The people in the police department who were my friends. I never felt so much at ease in a city. I left Chicago and came here because there is so much culture here, so much civic-mindedness. They accepted you for what you were. No prejudice, I thought. I never tried to do one illegal thing in my life."

Then his voice trailed off in sobs, halting his rambling dissertation.

—◆◆◆—

"We find the defendant guilty of murder with malice as charged in the indictment and assess his punishment at death."
—DALLAS COUNTY JURY IN THE JACK RUBY TRIAL

You have to give Melvin Belli his due—he was certainly creative in his defense strategy. Of course, when your client commits perhaps the most public murder in American history, a little creativity is probably called for. Relying on an insanity defense, not nearly so popular in those days, he spent his time trying to convince the jury that Ruby suffered from psychomotor epilepsy and didn't know what he was doing when he killed Lee Harvey Oswald.

Bill Alexander, Henry Wade's lead prosecutor, said that Belli "was guessing that we wouldn't be prepared, we just wouldn't know anything about that sort of thing . . . He steered it over into the neurology side on mental conditions rather than the psychiatric side. It might have worked except for the fact that Belli let the words 'psychomotor epilepsy' drop during a hearing and I wrote it down. We contacted the Menninger Clinic up in Kansas, got all the briefing and materials, and we were ready for him when trial came and he was caught totally unaware."

Dueling experts—psychiatrists—debating whether Ruby was responsible for his actions on November 24, 1963, consumed pretty much the entirety of the last two weeks of trial. The prosecution's experts testified that brain wave tests on Ruby did not show any serious abnormalities. Bottom line: No way, they said, was Ruby suffering from psychomotor epilepsy causing blackouts.

Then came closing arguments. Prosecutor Bill Alexander started, but quickly aroused Belli's ire with these remarks: "Now, I am not going to defend Oswald to you. But Oswald was entitled to protection of the law . . . Oswald was a living, breathing, American citizen, whatever he may have done. Jack Ruby killed a man who was in handcuffs. Now don't tell me it takes guts to shoot a man that is manacled. It doesn't. Lee Harvey Oswald didn't get justice. Lee Harvey Oswald cannot be recalled. He is dead, he is silent, and the Lord knows what secret went to the grave with him."

Belli sprang to his feet. "Wait a minute!" Not a proper legal objection, but his words, nonetheless. "There is no issue here whatsoever that Lee Harvey took any secrets to the grave with him."

Alexander continued. "I tell you that Jack Ruby misjudged public temperament. He thought that he could kill Oswald, that perhaps he would be a hero by doing it. He thought he could get away with it because of the condition of the public temperament at that time ... I tell you that warrants the death penalty."

In rebuttal, Melvin Belli offered this: "Let us think who we are trying for the crime. Who would do a thing like this? The village clown? The village idiot? The man who is always around the police station bringing coffee, donuts, sandwiches? Publicity he wants, publicity he seeks. Ladies and gentlemen, I suppose we would all like to engrave our initials on some oak tree, or be in some column or be sculpted into Mount Rushmore. I think it is part of our craving to seek after some bit of immortality.

"But this poor sick fellow—and sick he is. And you know he is sick in your hearts."

After arguments had ended, the jury retired to deliberate.

Joyce and I had had dinner with Judge Brown several evenings during the trial. Most of those evenings, I had tried to pitch him on the idea of permitting cameras in the courtroom for the reading of the final verdict. This was before the days of Court TV and was practically unheard of.

On the night before the jury returned its verdict, we took Judge Brown and his girlfriend, who later became his wife, to dinner at Vesuvio's Restaurant in Dallas, where I again spent most of the evening pleading with him to allow cameras in the courtroom for the verdict. I even talked him into going down to the courtroom after dinner so I could show him where a "pool" camera could be set up unobtrusively. I assured him he would become a part of courtroom history, and the American public would have a chance to see justice in action!

I could see the look of resignation on his face as he said, "Okay, we'll do it." Then he added, "One camera—only one."

Following my suggestion, the three networks drew straws to see whose camera crew would serve all the networks. Nelson Benton of CBS won the draw. When the jury announced, after only two hours of deliberation, that it had reached a verdict, the CBS crew set up inside the courtroom.

A deathly hush fell over the packed courtroom as the twelve jurors filed into the courtroom and took their places in the jury box. In a scene that would now be commonplace, from the O. J. Simpson trial to the Clara Harris case, at 12:23 P.M., Central Standard Time, Saturday, March 14, 1964, with cameras rolling live to millions of Americans, Judge Brown unfolded the verdict slip. He looked at it for a brief moment, then read aloud: "We, the jury, find the defendant guilty of murder with malice as charged in the indictment and assess his punishment at death."

An explosion of voices filled the courtroom, the television camera taking it all in. Over the bedlam of confusion, Melvin Belli shouted, "This is a kangaroo railroad and every one of you know it, too. I hope the people of Dallas are proud of the jury that was shoved down our throats."

Through it all, Jack Ruby sat impassively at the defense table. Worried about his image, I guess.

"I'm about to throw up."
—RUBY DEFENSE ATTORNEY JOE TONAHILL

In addition to railing about the jury that had been shoved down his throat, Belli had a few choice words about the presiding judge as well: "He [Judge Brown] went down the line for every motion that the District Attorney made and they led him into thirty errors. Every Texas jurist knows this thing was the greatest railroading court disgrace in the history of American law."

Ever flamboyant, Belli wasn't above hyperbole. Greatest court disgrace in the history of American law? That covers quite a lot of territory. I don't suppose it ever occurred to him that his client's public execution of Oswald had anything to do with the jury's decision.

Texas attorney Joe Tonahill had his own, somewhat scaled-down view, although certainly in the same rhetorical ballpark as Belli's. He told ABC's Ed Silverman that the verdict was "a violent miscarriage of justice." He paused for a moment, then added, "I'm about to throw up."

Not surprisingly, the prosecution team's stomachs weren't nearly so queasy. District Attorney Henry Wade said, "I am very well satisfied with the verdict and I think it was a proper one. I think it signified that the jury was convinced by the evidence that he was sane, and it didn't take them long to deliberate and arrive at the verdict."

"What testimony do you think most affected the jury?" I asked.

"By far the most damaging evidence was the officer's testimony showing premeditation, the assassination as seen on television, and then the statements Ruby made, such as, 'I hope I killed the SOB,' and 'I meant to shoot him three times but you all stopped me.'"

I suppose that certainly could have made a difference to the jury. In fact, those statements by Ruby served as a point on appeal by the defense team, which had tried to have them excluded.

I don't expect Belli to ever see eye-to-eye on this with Henry

Wade because to do so would be to admit weakness in the case he presented. Wade sure didn't think much of that case.

"They pitched their whole case on insanity," he said. "And made a weak case on it rather than asking for mercy or leniency. The jury probably subconsciously got the idea it was either insanity or death."

In 2002, I asked Bill Alexander if he thought things might have gone differently had Dallas lawyer Tom Howard remained Ruby's lawyer instead of being replaced by Melvin Belli.

"He probably would have had a murder without malice verdict and gotten Ruby off with a suspended sentence," Alexander said.

That struck me as a bit odd. I could see "murder without malice," but a suspended sentence?

"Tom Howard would have put Jack Ruby on the stand," Alexander said, "and, in a very low key way, would have asked Ruby how he got into the basement of the Police Department. Ruby would have said he just saw all of the activity going on and just walked down the ramp.

"Tom Howard would have then asked Ruby, 'Did you shoot Oswald?' Jack would have said, 'Yes, sir.'

"'Why did you shoot him?'

"'When I saw him in the basement, something came over me. I thought here is the man that killed *my* president.'

"Then Howard would have asked Ruby if he *planned* to shoot Oswald. Jack would have said, 'No, sir.'

"Then Howard would have asked, 'Are you sorry you killed Oswald?' and Ruby would have answered, 'Yes, sir.'"

And that would have done it, Alexander said. Instead, in their haste to get a "name" defense attorney, Ruby's family let Belli "parlay a pretty good murder case into a death sentence."

> "I don't think Dallas was on trial. I don't think
> I was on trial. I don't think Belli was on trial. I
> think Jack Ruby was on trial, period."
> —DALLAS COUNTY DISTRICT ATTORNEY HENRY WADE

Besides the defense team, there were others in Dallas who weren't happy about the outcome—or at least about the death sentence, including some of the most unlikely folks.

When it became apparent the verdict would be forthcoming that Saturday morning, I had Oswald's mother, Marguerite, waiting in the WFAA-TV studios so we could get her reaction first. When the verdict was announced, she told our ABC audience, "I wanted him alive because I believe Jack Ruby was a paid killer who deprived my son of his trial. I do not believe in capital punishment."

Oswald's wife, Marina, echoed that sentiment and seemed to buy in to the defense's insanity theory. "Frankly, I do not believe in capital punishment," she told me in her halting English. "I don't want Jack Ruby to be executed. He's just a sick man and I think better if he would be in a hospital. I think it is hard punishment for him to live. He executed himself. By living, he executes himself. He has now a very hard time. Maybe he seldom wants to live, but I don't want him to be executed."

After all the interviews had been completed both inside and outside the courtroom, ABC asked Ed Silverman to wrap up with a short spot on Jack Ruby, the man. The man who used to hang out in the newsroom at WFAA-TV, looking for free publicity. The man who tried to convince me our viewers would want to see a stripper who used snakes in her act. The man who might have five grand in his pocket and not a dime in the bank.

Ed reported the following: "The electric chair will never claim Jack Ruby. Oh, maybe a physical shell but not the man, because somewhere along the line in the past four weeks, Jack Ruby, the man, or what was left of him, died. We all saw him die a little each day. The man who was described by one doctor as having a Messiah complex became, instead, a pitiful insignificant creature. A minor actor almost forgotten throughout the trial as flamboyant, arrogant Melvin Belli strolled across the stage seeking his moment in history.

"He was not alone. The other principal actors were District Attorney Wade, his assistant Bill Alexander, Belli's assistant Joe Tonahill, the doctors and strip teasers.

"As the play came to a close last night, Ruby sat and heard himself compared to the village idiot by his counsel. He barely reacted; there was nothing left. He might have had his moment if he were permitted to testify. He wanted to but was denied even this. No one can deny the enormity of his pride and so, perhaps, in this case justice should not be tempered with mercy, but certainly with pity. Ed Silverman, ABC News, Dallas."

It then fell to me to wrap up the trial for our viewers. But how could I summarize, in one minute, all that had transpired in the past six weeks? How could I capture all the insanity—both that urged on the jury by Melvin Belli and that which surrounded the events, both inside and outside the courtroom? Here is what I said:

"It has been called bizarre, unbelievable, unreal. Whatever name you placed on the tragic chain of events that began with the death of John F. Kennedy, another chapter has now been completed. With the verdict of guilty and sentence of death in the electric chair, the Dallas portion of the assassination of Mr. Kennedy and the subsequent murder of his alleged killer, Lee Harvey Oswald, may be closed.

"Jack Ruby's trial ran thirty-four days. Five thousand pages of testimony were taken from one hundred seventeen witnesses by two alternating court reporters. Judge Joe B. Brown, in his charge to the jury, received one hundred thirty-nine objections from defense attorneys. One hundred thirty-seven of those were overruled.

"Perhaps never in the annals of American trials have so many expert witnesses appeared. And there are those who say Jack Ruby's attorneys spent too much time on evidence from the field of psychiatry and not enough in pleading leniency for the man who killed the killer of the president of the United States as millions watched.

"But as you sat in the courtroom, it was easy to see Melvin Belli was building a record for the appellate courts. Chances are above average appeals will keep the case tied up for several years. All the while, Jack Ruby, a Chicago native who told us during the early days of the trial that he moved to Dallas because there was so much culture here, must sit in the Dallas County Jail facing death in the electric chair.

"It's hard to find culture in a jail cell. Murphy Martin, ABC, Dallas."

"I wish I were adept at words. I wish I could speak . . . I wish I was as full of bullshit as Belli."
—Judge Joe B. Brown

So was the jury right or wrong? Jack Ruby—murderer? Or Jack Ruby—insane? No question Jack Ruby killed Lee Harvey Oswald;

the question that lingers in many minds is "Why?" Was it as he said, that he simply acted on the spur of the moment and killed the "son of a bitch" who killed his president? Was he in the grip of an epileptic seizure, unable to distinguish right from wrong or to control his conduct? Or was he, as Marguerite Oswald speculated, a paid killer silencing her son?

About a year after the trial, I again interviewed Judge Joe B. Brown. Hard on the heels of Melvin Belli, he, too, had plans to publish a book about the trial, to be entitled *Ruby, Dallas, and the Law*. Gonna set the record straight, he said.

"There have been so many periodicals and pamphlets, magazine articles and books that do not convey the truth in any manner, that I feel something should be written based upon the record of the case. That's what I intend to do and have done."

So what kinds of untruths was he interested in correcting? An interesting array, as it turns out.

"Well, a great deal of comment was made about my reading a comic book during the trial. Can you imagine a judge trying a man for his life reading a comic book? Of course, on its face it is ridiculous, but I want to refute it.

"There was another statement made that I sat up there while chewing tobacco. Well, I tried chewing tobacco when I was ten years old and never found it successful for me, so I quit. They even commented about the fact that I used aqua *Kleenex*. Of course, I asked one of the court personnel to get me a box of *Kleenex*, and it just happened to be aqua."

Shades of Jack Ruby. He seemed more concerned about his image than the actual trial. Which is not to say that Judge Brown didn't have strong opinions on other things, of course. The press? Sure, he had an opinion there.

"The newspeople, as a whole, were courteous, but the ordinary run of the press didn't print the truth. I remember reading about one newspaper reporter from up in Ohio who caught a plane and came to Dallas and wrote his story on the way down to Texas. Had it written with the exception of names and dates, and he contacted one of our local news reporters to get those names and dates. When the local reporter found out about it, he refused to give the information to the reporter from Ohio."

Judge Brown also had strong feelings about his decision,

at my suggestion, to allow cameras in the courtroom for the reading of the verdict. He felt betrayed by the CBS cameraman who failed to turn off the camera after the verdict had been read and ended up capturing the bedlam that ensued in the courtroom.

After Brown had announced that court was adjourned, he returned to his chambers. He was there only a few minutes before receiving a phone call from his girlfriend, Joy Corliss. "You better get back down there," she said. "They're making you look like a fool."

"The televising of the courtroom after the trial is what irritates me so much," Judge Brown said. "Actually, the person who was operating the pool camera in the courtroom told me that he had no orders as to when to turn his camera off—and I hold CBS responsible. It was our agreement that no television would be shown after I said, 'Court is adjourned.' It sets television back with me. It makes me awfully disappointed because, if they don't keep their agreements with the courts, we cannot have it done."

Of course, it's hard to blame the television camera for what happened in the courtroom. That would have happened whether CBS had been rolling or not. Americans act the way Americans act, and sometimes it isn't very pretty. Often the cameras capture it, but more often they don't. In this case, they did. Viewers saw cameramen and reporters climbing atop counsel tables, chairs, anything to get a clean shot among the post-verdict actions.

But what about the real issues in the case? Judge Brown told me he received more than 4,000 pieces of mail regarding the Ruby trial in just one year. And everybody had an opinion on Ruby's guilt or innocence.

"Many people thought Jack Ruby should have gotten the Medal of Honor because he killed a man who was alleged to have killed the president. And many people thought he got exactly what he deserved," Judge Brown said.

As for the judge's own opinion? Well, he wasn't saying. "The jury's duty was to find guilt or innocence and set the punishment, and I find no fault with its finding. And had they found him not guilty and acquitted him, I still would find no fault. That's their duty, not mine."

After all was said, Judge Brown moved forward with his plans for a book. His publisher, Holt Rinehart, offered an advance and even went so far as to arrange for Paul Crume, noted columnist for the

Dallas Morning News, to help with the project. Judge Brown then began dictating his story to court reporter Jimmy Muleady. It all went downhill from there.

One of Ruby's appellate attorneys, Phil Burleson, filed a motion to recuse Judge Brown from any further proceedings on the basis that he had an economic interest in the outcome of the appeal. Burleson said that, because Judge Brown was writing a book about the trial, he had a vested interest in seeing the appeal fail. If it succeeded, and a new trial was ordered, his book about the original trial would be worthless, according to Burleson.

A recusal hearing was held, and at the hearing Ruby's lawyers showed that Brown had been paid an advance to write the book. Concerned about the appearance of impropriety, the judge voluntarily stepped down.

But the damage had already been done. Judge Brown had delayed completing the book because of the recusal hearing to the point that the publisher decided not to go forward with publication and returned all rights to him. Judge Brown then started a quest to find another publisher.

Despite his efforts, Judge Brown was never able to interest another publisher before he died in February of 1968. Subsequent efforts by his wife, Joy, were also unsuccessful prior to her death. However, as an example of never-give-up, Judge Brown's son, Joe B. Brown, Jr., paid to have his father's original manuscript professionally edited in 2001 by Dr. Diane Holloway, the author of *The Mind of Lee Harvey Oswald*. Himself now a Dallas County district judge, Brown then published the book under the title *Dallas and the Jack Ruby Trial: The Memoir of Judge Joe B. Brown*.

Subsequent history to the recusal hearing showed that Holt Rinehart's decision not to publish was probably a good one at the time. On October 5, 1966, the Texas Court of Criminal Appeals granted Jack Ruby a new trial on the grounds that statements he had made immediately following the murder of Oswald should have been excluded from evidence. The court also held that the motion to change venue, which was heard prior to the start of the trial, should have been granted.

The court then ordered a new trial to be held in Wichita Falls, Texas. When authorities from Wichita Falls went to pick up their new, celebrated prisoner in Dallas, Ruby complained of an upset stomach, so they returned to Wichita Falls without him. Ruby's upset stomach turned out to be something much worse, and he was subsequently moved to Parkland Hospital, where he was diagnosed with cancer.

Seemingly content to spread conspiracy theories until the day he died, Ruby later told his family that he had been injected with cancer cells. His latter days were spent ranting about a plot to kill Jews, often telling anyone who would listen that Jews were being killed by the thousands. The cancer finally claimed him on January 3, 1967.

CHAPTER 3

The Kennedy Assassination: Fact or Fiction

*"Kennedy had turned the CIA loose to over-
throw Castro and they were in touch with one of
Castro's Cabinet officers. They were trying to
pull an inside coup as opposed to a Bay of Pigs
type operation. Castro found out about it and
threatened Kennedy. Five days later, Oswald
goes to Mexico City and tells the Cubans, 'I'll kill
Kennedy.'"*
—Retired FBI Agent James P. Hosty, Jr.

In the forty years since John F. Kennedy was murdered on the
streets of Dallas, theories have abounded about who fired the fatal
shots. Conspiracy theorists have created a cottage industry, target-
ing everybody from the Mafia and the Cubans right down to Vice
President Lyndon Johnson. More than 2,000 books have been published on the subject, which collectively list nearly fifty gunmen *by
name*. As with most high-profile stories, people come out of the
woodwork for their fifteen minutes of fame. The more sensational,
the more shocking, the more books they hope they'll sell.

I don't intend to take on all these theories and their suspects. To
me, the far simpler and more logical suspect remains Lee Harvey
Oswald. But the one thing that has continued to trouble me down
through the years is, if Oswald, then why? Or, as Robert Oswald
once told me, "It is so repugnant to me that my brother Lee was

even remotely involved. I would give my right arm—and my left—to know why he did it."

I recently spoke with retired FBI Agent James P. Hosty, Jr., who offers a most intriguing, if not convincing, answer to that question. Agent Hosty had been assigned to the Dallas FBI office in the early 1950s, and his involvement with the Kennedy assassination predates the actual event. Learning that Lee Harvey Oswald apparently had both communist and Cuban ties, the FBI assigned his file to Hosty when Oswald first moved to Dallas from New Orleans. On at least two occasions, Hosty sought to interview Oswald but was never able to locate him.

He was successful, however, in upsetting Oswald's wife, Marina, by talking to her at the home of Ruth Paine in the Dallas suburb of Irving. Shortly before November 22, 1963, an agitated man, later determined to have been Oswald, went to the Dallas FBI office in search of Hosty. Told that Hosty was unavailable, the man gave the receptionist, Nannie Fenner, an unsealed envelope that contained a note to Hosty which said something to the effect of "If you want to talk to me, you should talk to me to my face. Stop harassing my wife and stop trying to ask her about me. You have no right to harass her."

In my recent conversation with him, Hosty said that, after reading the note, which he said was unsigned, "I tossed it in my file drawer and didn't give it another thought until November 22, 1963, at approximately 3:18 P.M."

What was it that resurrected the note? "I went back to the FBI office," Hosty said, "and was told I was wanted in [Special Agent-in-Charge J. Gordon] Shanklin's office, pronto. When I arrived at Shanklin's office, I found my supervisor Ken Howe with him. They told me to shut the door.

"'What the hell is this?' Shanklin asked, holding what appeared to be a letter. I took it and immediately recognized the anonymous note I had received ten days before."

The note was subsequently destroyed before investigators could see it, and controversy rages to this day as to how, when, and why. Hosty said the decision to destroy the note was not his. Rather, the order came from higher up, from Gordon Shanklin. But, Hosty said, Shanklin was "very clever" in his discussions of the note.

"If you don't ask him exactly the right question then he will deny it. Now, for instance, I'll say, 'Did you order Hosty to destroy the note,' and he'll say, 'Absolutely not.' Then you ask him, 'Did you hand the note back to Hosty and say I never want to see this again?' and he'll say, 'I can't remember that.'" Hosty does find it strange, though, that Shanklin resigned from the FBI in 1975 "very suddenly, right before [FBI Director] Clarence Kelley found out about the note."

Over the years, Hosty has taken a lot of heat for his failure to track Oswald down and question him prior to the assassination. There is even speculation that, had he done so, the assassination could have been prevented. In fact, a number of FBI agents were later reprimanded for the way they handled the whole matter—for failing to "connect the dots," as it were. But, Hosty said, his own actions held up to scrutiny. "One year later, everything was clear. [J. Edgar] Hoover told me that I had done everything correctly, and he went before the Warren Commission and swore under oath that I had done everything correctly."

In fact, Hosty went on, the initial draft of the Warren Commission Report contained no criticisms of the FBI. It was only in subsequent drafts that the Commission took aim at the FBI. "You see, Earl Warren had it in for Hoover, for when Hoover tried to prevent Warren's appointment to the Supreme Court in 1953. So he and John McCloy, who also had a beef with Hoover, told the staff to rewrite the report and criticize the FBI."

And this is where Hosty first fell under criticism for his failure to locate and interview Oswald. But, Hosty pointed out, "Under the regulations, I was forbidden to interview Oswald."

Why? That's where the story gets interesting. And that's where Hosty postulates the answer to another "why" question—why Oswald did it.

Earlier that year, Oswald, a known Cuban sympathizer, had gone to Mexico City and visited the Cuban Embassy there. According to Hosty, Kennedy had "turned the CIA loose to overthrow Castro and they were in touch with one of Castro's Cabinet officers. They were trying to pull an inside coup as opposed to a Bay of Pigs operation. Castro found out about it and threatened Kennedy."

That was when Oswald made his trip to the embassy in Mexico City "and tells the Cubans 'I'll kill Kennedy for you.'"

From there, Oswald then met with Valery Kostikov, the second secretary of the Russian Embassy in Mexico City—and, according to Hosty, "a chief Russian assassin for the Western Hemisphere." The

CIA sent the information on the meeting via cablegram, but the cablegram got routed to the wrong supervisor at the FBI, one who didn't know who Kostikov was. Had it been routed to Burt Turner, as it should have been, he would have known Kostikov for the assassin he was, and "that would have put it in a different light."

But Hosty claimed he was in the dark at the time. "Now if I had known that this was going on—you see all this was available but it didn't get through. Left hand didn't tell the right hand." He said he only learned this later, after the assassination, and that the information came from "our top undercover agents." And that's why Hosty was forbidden to talk to Oswald. The CIA feared that if anyone did interview Oswald, it would tip him off that the United States had coverage on the Russian Embassy.

If that was true, I asked Hosty, then why was he trying to track down Oswald in Irving, Texas? "I was interviewing Marina," he said. "Marina was who we were interviewing, not Lee. You see, Marina was a suspect, too. Don't forget, Marina was raised by her uncle in Russia who was a ranking officer in a division of the KGB."

Which brings us back to the big question: Why?

"Simple, simple, simple," Hosty said. "If they had told the truth, they were afraid of starting World War III. If they had said that Oswald killed Kennedy because Kennedy was trying to kill Castro, they had the answer. Castro threatens Kennedy, Oswald goes to Mexico City and says, 'I'll do it,' and they say, 'Okay, get out of here—we don't know who you are.' Then he goes back and does it."

Hosty, who joined Dallas Police Captain Will Fritz to interrogate Oswald after his arrest, said that the only time Oswald lost his cool during questioning was when Hosty asked him about Mexico City. "Oswald denied being there, but he was definitely shook."

It certainly makes one wonder why none of this was pursued as part of the assassination investigation. Hosty said he told the House Assassination Committee about it during a preliminary information session, but "they had their mind made up that it was the Mafia, so they never called me to testify. The Warren Commission never asked me about this either. The Warren Commission knew about Oswald's threat to kill Kennedy. We gave it to them in writing in March or April of 1964."

I found Hosty to be a wealth of information when I talked to him in 2003, much of which he said could be found in his book

Assignment: Oswald, which he published in 1995. I couldn't help but ask another question that has also preyed on my mind for a lot of years. Some months before the Kennedy assassination, Oswald had taken a shot at the extremely right-wing Gen. Edwin Walker. Politically, Walker and Kennedy stood at opposite poles on the spectrum. Did it really make sense that the man who tried to kill Walker had also killed Kennedy?

"What did they have in common?" Hosty asked. "They both wanted to get Castro. Walker was calling for the demise of Castro and so was Kennedy."

But the ultimate question still remains: Was it really Oswald? Was he the lone gunman who killed John Fitzgerald Kennedy?

"Without a doubt," Hosty said.

—◇◇◇—

"Let this be a warning. I will blow up the FBI and the Dallas Police Department if you don't stop bothering my wife. Lee Harvey Oswald."
—TESTIMONY OF FBI RECEPTIONIST
NANNIE LEE FENNER

The mysterious note left for FBI Agent Hosty by Lee Harvey Oswald has been the topic of some controversy for years. After having gotten Hosty's version of events surrounding the note, I recently spoke with Retired FBI Special Agent Robert P. Gemberling, who had been named, on November 24, 1963, by Special Agent-in-Charge J. Gordon Shanklin to coordinate the assassination investigation, including a comprehensive look into Oswald's background. Not surprisingly, Gemberling has a little different view of the circumstances surrounding the note than does Hosty. Gemberling has no doubt that Hosty has been motivated by an agenda to clear his name, perhaps willing to sacrifice accuracy in the process.

"I readily recognize Hosty's reasons for writing his book and his right to do so," Gemberling said. "He feels that he was unjustly publicly criticized for his actions, and he is seeking vindication. I take exception, however, to his characterizations of other people, including some of our fellow agents. I question his judgment in describing, in some detail, certain sensitive investigative techniques and FBI policies and procedures, which appear to border on a violation of his FBI employment agreement. He has erroneously reported certain information and suggests another speculative theory. As a result of extensive criticism of others throughout his book, its goal appears to be self-serving."

So what about that mysterious note? What did it say and what happened to it? Here, too, Gemberling's version diverges from Hosty's. For instance, Hosty said that the note was unsigned and that he didn't make any connection between it and Oswald until *after* the assassination. But, according to Gemberling, that doesn't jibe with the testimony of FBI receptionist Nannie Lee Fenner, who was called before the House Judiciary Committee in 1975 looking into the assassination, where she testified that the note said, "Let this be a warning. I will blow up the FBI and the Dallas Police Department if you don't stop bothering my wife." She further testified that it was signed "Lee Harvey Oswald."

But Gemberling said that Hosty, appearing before the same committee, testified that the note was unsigned and simply said "If you have anything you want to learn about me, come talk to me directly. If you don't cease bothering my wife, I will take appropriate action and report this to proper authorities."

Gemberling also said that on Sunday evening, November 24, 1963, Hosty was called in to a meeting with his supervisor, Ken Howe, and Special Agent-in-Charge Shanklin, who showed Hosty the note along with a memorandum Hosty had prepared explaining the circumstances of the note. According to Hosty, Shanklin said, "I don't ever want to see them again." Whether Shanklin actually said that or not, Gemberling can't confirm. But what he can confirm is that "Hosty then tore the note and the memorandum into small pieces and flushed them down the toilet."

Lamenting the fact that the exact contents of the note will never be known, Gemberling said, "The destruction of the note, however, with no proof of what it said was a mistake of considerable magnitude and was extremely damaging to the credibility of the FBI's investigation. I have difficulty believing the note was not signed by Oswald. Oswald obviously wanted Hosty to know that he was upset about his visit to the Paine residence where he spoke briefly with Marina on November 1, 1963. Why would he fail to sign the note?"

Gemberling also noted that Hosty was reprimanded for the way he handled the Oswald investigation. On October 5, 1964, Hosty received a letter of censure that suspended him for thirty days without pay, placed him on probation, and transferred him to Kansas City. Although Hosty passed the censure off as an "Aw, shucks" letter which he said was sent to "practically everyone involved in any degree with the assassination," Gemberling said, "During my more than thirty-three years in the FBI, I never heard this term used to describe a letter of censure. As coordinator of the assassination/Oswald investigation from November 24, 1963, until my retirement in December 1976, I was not censured or given an 'Aw, shucks' letter."

And so, Gemberling believes, Hosty's words have to be taken with a grain of salt. After all, said Gemberling, Hosty seems embittered by his experiences with the FBI surrounding the assassination investigation. As he states in his book, "Bureau policy had screwed me far too many times. Someday I would find a way to set the record straight."

"His book is his attempt to do that," Gemberling said. "But he joins the multitude of conspiracy buffs when he alleges there was involvement of the Cubans and Soviets in encouraging Oswald to commit the assassination." And any justification for Hosty's bitterness has to be "weighed against the admitted fact he destroyed a note from Oswald delivered to him at the FBI office in Dallas ten days to two weeks before the assassination. He maintained no record of what the note said, and his claim that the note was not signed is subject to question."

After plowing through Hosty and the note with Gemberling, I finally got around to asking him what I really wanted to know: Does he believe that Oswald acted alone in the murders of John F. Kennedy and Officer J. D. Tippit?

And here, his views merge with those of James P. Hosty. Gemberling's answer is yes.

Why? Because Oswald "just wanted recognition."

"They [Kennedy and Oswald] are waiting there in Purgatory or somewhere to see whether they are going to get into heaven. He would be asking Oswald, 'Why did you do it?'"
—PRISCILLA JOHNSON MCMILLAN,
AUTHOR OF *Marina and Lee*

Priscilla Johnson McMillan first met Lee Harvey Oswald in Russia in 1959. She was working as a correspondent and Oswald was living as a defector. It was ironic that only a short time before, she had worked on the staff of Massachusetts senator John Kennedy. How could she have known then that just a few years hence, the man she described in Russia as "a kind of boy who was lost—hardly knew where he was, alone and kind of sad," would be accused of killing the man who, as senator, had made countless sexual advances to her.

That's right. Count Priscilla Johnson McMillan among those who caught Kennedy's eye during his political career. And he caught hers, as well.

Her position on his staff began as a temporary one, but permanent enough for a relationship to develop. "He said he was sorry he didn't have a permanent job for me … I had another job lined up in New York City and I wrote him a note and said I enjoyed working for him very much, but he forgot to pay me. Then he wrote me a most apologetic letter and asked me out for a drink. I went to my job the next day all dressed up to meet him that evening, and he stood me up. The next day I went to this place with another man and they seated us, and then the Senator and Jackie came in and were seated at the table immediately next to us.

"At some point when Jackie went off to the ladies room, he leaned over and shook my hand … he had perfect aplomb. And then for about the next four years, he would call me when he was in New York and ask me out."

As Priscilla and I talked recently, I pressed her for more details about her relationship with Kennedy, wondering if it had anything to do with her writing of the book *Marina and Lee*. "I had this kind of bantering relationship with him," she told me when we spoke in May of 2003. "But he was married and we had many funny conversations about the whole thing. But how he managed to spend that much time on some girl who was not going to sleep with him— that's what I wondered."

What conclusions did she draw?

"Maybe it was just the game was what he enjoyed," she said. "If you gave in to him, that would be the last you saw of him. I saw him until 1957 or 1958. Then I went to Russia and he probably had better things to do."

Which was not to say it was totally nonsexual. "Although he was married, I have a lot of strength in my arms. I used to think that most of that strength I had in my arms came from pushing him away. But I enjoyed the whole thing very much."

She said she even once posed as one of Kennedy's sisters—at his suggestion— to gain admission to his hospital room following one of his back surgeries.

Given her affection for Kennedy, and her having met Oswald in Russia, I wondered if those events combined to drive her to pursue writing Marina's story in *Marina and Lee*. "Sure, that was why I did it," Priscilla told me. "I knew Kennedy would want to know why some guy would take the time and trouble to kill a man he didn't even know. Kennedy was always just full of questions, and he always peppered you with questions. About all kinds of things, not necessarily the sort of things you would know about. They were just random questions about every kind of thing on earth. So I figured he would do the same thing to Oswald—if he met him."

She and Marina even joked about that, according to Priscilla. "Marina and I talked about this—that they are waiting in Purgatory or somewhere to see whether they are going to get into heaven. He would be asking Oswald, 'Why did you do it?' That's why I wanted to answer it, because I felt a little guilty toward [Kennedy] for stringing him along for such a long time."

I first met Priscilla in Texas in 1964 when she was pursuing Marina's story, hoping that Marina might be able to answer that burning question of why. When she and I spoke recently, I asked whether she had ever found an answer to that question.

"Lee wanted to be somebody," she said. "To be known and to be somebody."

And if she could ask Oswald just one question today, what would it be?

"Why Kennedy?"

—◆◆◆—

"Lee is guilty. I saw it in his eyes."
—MARINA OSWALD, 1964
"Lee is innocent. He was a patsy."
—MARINA OSWALD PORTER, 2003

Lee Harvey Oswald's Russian wife, Marina, spoke very little

English when she first came to the United States in the early 1960s. When I first spoke with her in March or April of 1964, her English had improved a little, at least enough to carry on a conversation. I was still with ABC-TV then as my wife, Joyce, accompanied me to Marina's home to talk with her about her husband. We talked for three hours without cameras or tape recorders rolling—just pen and notepad. She told me then of her belief that Lee had indeed killed President Kennedy.

"Lee is guilty," she said. "I saw it in his eyes."

During much of that conversation, Marina sipped crème de cacao with beer and, at the conclusion, showed Joyce a closet filled with clothes that had been sent by unknown Americans who wanted to express their condolences. She invited Joyce to pick out a dress or two, but Joyce declined. Later that year, Joyce and I stood with Marina as she baptized her youngest daughter, Rachel, at St. Seraphim Eastern Orthodox Church in Dallas. Father Dmitri Royster presided, and Mrs. Declan Ford stood as godmother. Because I was the only man present other than Father Royster and the photographers, I became Rachel Oswald's godfather. I have not seen Rachel since that day.

Joyce and I recently saw Marina again, in June of 2003, after many years. We had stopped at an Army/Navy store on McKinney Avenue in Dallas and, as we were checking out, noticed that the cashier looked familiar. "Are you Marina?" Joyce asked.

The cashier looked suspiciously at her before answering in the affirmative. When Joyce told her who we were, Marina rushed around the counter to give us a warm welcome. Before long, she was telling me as rapidly as she could a far different story from the one she had told me in 1964.

"It was a set-up," she said. "Lee is innocent. He was a patsy."

I couldn't believe what I was hearing. This was a woman who nearly forty years earlier had accepted the findings of the Warren Commission. She had told me then, "The Commission has more information about what happened on November 22 and this is the business of the Warren Commission. Yes, my intuition tells me it was Lee."

Now, in 2003, she denied her husband had been on the sixth floor of the Schoolbook Depository on that day. "Yes, he was in the building," she said, "but he was on one of the lower floors. He was not upstairs."

I didn't ask for, nor did she offer any explanation about how Lee's fingerprints could be on the murder weapon if he hadn't fired it—the same weapon he had carried to the Depository that morning disguised as curtain rods.

We talked for a bit longer, and then Joyce and I left. We could see that the years had not been kind to Marina. I couldn't help but wonder how life would have turned out for Marina, who obtained American citizenship in 1980, had Lee made different choices. Maybe she would have been the wife of a famous writer. Maybe she wouldn't have had to work as a cashier in an Army/Navy store at the age of sixty-two.

—◆◆◆—

"That would have been an insult to my father and grandfather. I would have dishonored them if I had changed my name."
—ROBERT OSWALD

I first saw Robert Oswald at his brother's funeral at Rose Hill Cemetery in Fort Worth on November 25, 1963, but I didn't actually meet him until the spring of 1964. Since then, I have spent a lot of time with him, beginning with those long hours sequestered in a hotel room going over the Warren Commission Report—a report that left Robert convinced his brother had indeed been the gunman who killed President Kennedy. He could have run from the truth, but that just wasn't in Robert's make-up. When asked whether he ever considered changing his name, he said, "That would have been an insult to my father and my grandfather. I would have dishonored them if I had changed my name."

In fact, rather than distancing himself from his brother with the infamous last name, Robert actually wrote a book, *Lee: A Portrait of Lee Harvey Oswald*, to set the record straight about Lee Harvey Oswald, the brother, not Lee Harvey Oswald, the assassin. With proceeds from the book's sales, he was able to quit his job as a sales manager for a brick firm, enroll in Midwestern State University at Wichita Falls, and graduate at the top of his class three and a half years later.

Over the years, he's seen the conspiracy buffs come and go. And he's seen the rewriting of history on the big screen, emphasizing more fiction than fact. I asked him recently if it ever got him down.

How did he handle the constant trotting out of the Oswald name with sometimes highly imaginative spins?

"I sit there and listen to these individuals," he said. "I have read their material and I have not shut the door on anything. But when they find a 't' that has not been crossed and then take it and twist it to make a conspiracy out of it, it's asinine and ridiculous. And the classic example is Oliver Stone."

Ah, I said, but what about the paragon of accuracy, Jim Garrison?

Robert could not disguise the contempt in his voice. "Abuse of power. You might recall I had a short conversation with Garrison that you arranged and he said, 'I'm going to get back with you, Robert.' But I never heard another word from him. Wonder why? He was just there for Garrison."

When I talked with Robert in May of 2003, I asked him if, thinking back, there was anything in Lee's childhood or upbringing that might have led him to that fateful day in Dallas. Robert thought for a moment, then said, "I believe his scarred childhood, without exception, played a big role. If I have any advantage in trying to understand, it's that I know from whence he came and all the details that go in there. And this is by reflecting back—not that I was conscious of it at the time, but I have put in the time. I did the evaluation. I looked at it hard and I understand it.

"To say he was not a sick person, in my judgment, is wrong. But he could still function at a certain level and so can a lot of other people. But the bottom line is—the childhood, the constant moving from place to place, the constant changing of schools—all this contributed to his actions later in life."

I asked him about something else I had been wondering ever since 1963. Paul Groody, the funeral director for Lee Harvey Oswald's funeral, had told me then that he was sending the bill for the funeral to the Secret Service, but I had recently obtained a copy of the statement which reflected payment by check by Robert Oswald. "Who paid for it?" I asked.

Robert told me that, following the assassination, the Secret Service had been keeping him and the rest of the family at a hotel near Six Flags Over Texas in Arlington. About a week after the funeral, Groody called the hotel looking for payment. Robert asked the Secret Service to drive him to his bank in Denton, Texas, where he obtained a cashier's check for $710. The Secret Service then delivered that check directly to Miller Funeral Home at Robert's request.

According to the statement from the funeral home, there was a $25 charge for a casket spray; $48.50 for clothing, including a suit, socks, and underwear; $300 for a #31 Pine Bluff casket; $200 for a Wilbert vault; and a $135 fee to Rose Hill Cemetery.

One mystery still remains: That totals $708.50, not the $710 paid. What was the other $1.50 for?

—◆◆◆—

"Somewhere amongst all those dollars from conspiracy books, the truth got lost."
—ASSISTANT DISTRICT ATTORNEY BILL ALEXANDER

One of those closest to the assassination scene and its aftermath was Bill Alexander, for many years Dallas County District Attorney Henry Wade's chief prosecutor. It was Alexander who once said, "If everyone who claims they questioned Oswald at some point that weekend got together, it would take a convention center to hold them."

And Bill Alexander would know because he was one of those who actually did question Oswald, along with Police Captain Will Fritz early that Friday evening after the shooting. It was also Alexander who, perhaps inadvertently, started one of the rumors that later blossomed into a full-blown conspiracy theory. You will recall from the first chapter of this book his joke to *Philadelphia Inquirer* columnist Joe Gouldon that the indictment of Oswald should include the phrase "in furtherance of a communist conspiracy." How could he have known then that his ill-advised joke, along with a later story given credence by a member of the press corps in Dallas that Oswald had been a paid informant for the FBI, would become the focus of a special meeting of the Warren Commission in January 1964?

The Commission summoned Alexander, Wade, and Texas Attorney General Waggoner Carr to Washington to testify about some of the disturbing stories that were starting to make the rounds purportedly as fact. According to Henry Wade, the Commission reprimanded Alexander, who subsequently became far more serious about assassination matters; however, at least as relates to the communist conspiracy theory, the damage had likely already been done. For many, that fiction spoken in jest had become fact.

The second part of the subject of that Warren Commission meeting—the rumor that Oswald had been assigned payroll number S-172 as an informant for the FBI—was not of Alexander's making, nor even that of Lonnie Hudkins, the *Houston* news reporter who first gave life to the rumor. That bit of fiction was the creation of yet another reporter, Hugh Aynesworth, but its chief distributor had been Allen Sweatt, chief deputy for Sheriff Bill Decker. Apparently, Sweatt enjoyed being the source of information no one else had, even if the information was somewhat questionable. Aynesworth made the statement to get Hudkins off his back while he was trying to finish a story to meet a deadline.

I caught up with Bill Alexander in June of 2003, still practicing law in Dallas. To this day, Alexander is not a big fan of federal officials. (Perhaps that Warren Commission reprimand still leaves a bad taste even almost forty years later.) And whether it was that reprimand or Alexander's having a little fun with reporters, or perhaps his handling of the Ruby trial, his relationship with his old boss, Henry Wade, was never the same after that. I could sense some hard feelings by virtue of Alexander's harsh criticisms of the way Wade handled matters back then. Alexander wouldn't say much but did admit that he and Wade "had a falling out." Wade, who died in March of 2001, never mentioned any problems with Alexander other than his penchant for having fun at the expense of reporters or federal officials.

So what does Alexander think of the thriving conspiracy industry that still perpetuates fiction even today?

"Somewhere amongst all those dollars from conspiracy books, the truth got lost," he said.

"We have solved the murder of John Kennedy."
—NEW ORLEANS DISTRICT ATTORNEY JIM GARRISON

In December of 1967, I conducted an exclusive interview with flamboyant New Orleans District Attorney Jim Garrison. In that interview, which aired on WFAA-TV in Dallas, Garrison claimed that "we have solved the murder of John Kennedy." He went on to say that the federal government was concealing the identity of the assassin. And just like that, this former FBI agent from the Pacific Northwest who had ended up in the Big Easy grabbed center stage in the Kennedy assassination investigations.

For the next several months he spent a lot of time spreading his conspiracy gospel, and I spent a lot of time trying, unsuccessfully, to verify what he said. He called me often with "new information," and on more than one occasion played cloak-and-dagger. I remember once that he called and asked me to meet him at 2:00 A.M. at Dallas Love Field, near the statue of the Texas Ranger. "I have some very sensitive developments I want to tell you, and only you, about," he said.

When I met him at the Ranger statue early that morning, I discovered that the secretiveness of our meeting was nothing more than the result of his having just caught the red-eye out of Las Vegas back to New Orleans after a weekend of "high visibility relaxing." And the information he shared with me was no more than speculation and conjecture, as was so much of the information he had shared over many months. I soon learned that Jim Garrison had mastered the art of sophistry, which *The American Heritage Dictionary* defines as "plausible but faulty or misleading argumentation." That's apparently the same art he applied in the courtroom when he tried to convict Clay Shaw in the assassination. The jury took less than one hour to find Shaw "not guilty."

One of the most troubling marriages of ideas in the conspiracy world connected those of Jim Garrison with those of Oliver Stone, resulting in a gross misstatement of history, the film *JFK*. Far too many viewers walked away from theaters thinking they had just seen historical fact played out on the silver screen when in reality most of it was pure fiction, relying extensively upon Garrison's notoriously unproven theories.

Only Oliver Stone can answer the question whether he consciously set out to rewrite history, but former FBI Agent James Hosty offers an interesting take on the origins of the movie. He claims that the idea originated with Fidel Castro, who suggested it to Stone while Stone was in Havana to receive an award from Castro for his movie *Salvador*.

The truth behind that idea is unknown. But we do know that

Stone recently made a documentary on Castro for HBO called *Commandante*, which was subsequently postponed indefinitely by HBO due to Castro's crackdown on Cuban dissidents. According to HBO, Stone's portrayal of Castro was undercut by those crackdowns and, as HBO spokeswoman Lana Iny said, "In light of recent events in the country, the film seems somewhat dated or incomplete."

And what does Stone think of Castro? He issued a statement in February 2003 at the Berlin Film Festival, where *Commandante* was screened, saying that his three-day encounter with Castro left a deep impression on him: "We should look to him as one of the earth's wisest people, one of the people we should consult."

Beginning in the mid-1970s, congressional committees convened new hearings on the Kennedy assassination, dredging up names of people and organizations that many thought were new suspects behind the shooting but which were in reality merely repeats of those heard countless times before: The Mafia (Carlos Marcello, Santos Trafficante, Sam Giancana, and Meyer Lansky), Teamsters Boss Jimmy Hoffa, the CIA, the FBI, the Secret Service, the KGB, Fidel Castro, Lyndon Johnson, Charles Harrelson, and the list goes on.

And just as the names remained the same, so, too, did the strategy: Pick a name or group or country, manufacture a motive, write a book, and spread the story. Never mind fact; just use fiction. Credit Jim Garrison's follies for at least slowing down the conspiracy buffs for a number of years, but the hearings of the '70s breathed new life. Still, the bottom line remains that, though thousands have tried, no one has yet disproved the findings of the Warren Commission.

For me, the most likely scenario is that Lee Harvey Oswald—that "lonely little lost boy" in Moscow, the brother with enough childhood scars to create a sick mind, the man who told the Cubans in Mexico City that he would kill Kennedy for them—did, in fact, assassinate President Kennedy and gun down Officer J. D. Tippit.

One shooter, one gun, one dead president.

It hasn't changed in forty years.

CHAPTER 4

The Violence of the Times

"Should we kill him now or wait 'til morning?"
—Unknown Ku Klux Klansman

The 1960s in America was a period seared by disquieting civil rights struggles—struggles which scorched many cities with unrest and contributed to the biggest continuing story of what would become one of this nation's most trying decades. As a roving correspondent for ABC-TV, I was constantly confronted by ever-changing developments that were totally new, even for someone whose roots were in the Deep South.

For decades, many black Americans had often been treated as second-class citizens. Although it had been almost one hundred years since the institution of slavery had been abolished, for many it must have seemed like only yesterday. Separate-but-equal labeled the lie that divided America into two distinct classes—white and black. But, by the advent of the 1960s, black Americans had become decidedly more involved in trying to change that thinking.

A number of civil rights leaders emerged during the early to mid-'60s, none more universally accepted than Dr. Martin Luther King, Jr.—the man who had a dream, and who dedicated himself to fulfilling that dream. His voice rose above a cacophony of voices as he called for a "just and peaceful world" and preached nonviolent action against individuals and institutions who stood in the way of his dream.

Other notable leaders of the movement who also preached Dr.

King's message of nonviolence included Whitney Young of the National Urban League; James Farmer, a native of Marshall, Texas, who headed the Congress of Racial Equality (CORE); Roy Wilkins, director of the NAACP; and Dr. Ralph Abernathy, Dr. King's number-one assistant in the Southern Christian Leadership Conference. Dr. Abernathy was not the only aide to Dr. King to assume a prominent role, as Dr. King also served as mentor to future leaders such as Andrew Young, Jesse Jackson, Hosea Williams, John Lewis, James Bevel, James Orange, and the Reverend C.T. Vivian.

But not all voices advocated nonviolence; not all voices preached peace. There were those for whom the ends justified the means, even if those means were violent—no matter how destructive both to property and to humanity. Evangelists for this message included Stokely Carmichael, H. Rap Brown, Eldridge Cleaver, James Forman, and Malcolm X.

Change in social institutions comes hard, and the line-up on the other side of the race issue was just as formidable. Names like Governor George Wallace of Alabama, Sheriff Jim Clark of Selma, the Ku Klux Klan's Robert Shelton, and Governor Lester Maddox of Georgia headed a roster that also included many other politicians who opposed civil rights legislation. Is it any wonder, then, that when the two extremes clashed, violence and unrest often followed?

I spent the majority of my time in 1964 and 1965 covering those civil rights stories that rocked the nation: the Selma-to-Montgomery march; the integration of public schools in Alabama, Mississippi, and other southern states; the integration of previously all-white beaches in St. Augustine, Florida; riots in Newark, Harlem, and Birmingham; Dr. King's March on Boston; and the funeral of Malcolm X in New York City. Each story had its own stars, its own poignancy, and its own tragedy. But out of those stories came radical changes in American life and in Americans' ways of thinking.

One of the problems with news coverage, particularly television news, is that publicity attracts publicity-seekers. When the cameras arrive, simple stories can, and often do, become bigger, more complex stories. There have always been those who have mastered the art of manipulating news coverage to advance agendas. Television simply offered a new, and far more influential, medium. We see it today, dozens of times each day, on every network and on a hundred cable channels. But in the '60s, America was still just learning the power of television.

Even then, as now, there were those who tried to color the stories for their own purposes, using every device within their grasp. Almost as a matter of course, groups would call television newsrooms to announce a planned demonstration. "What time will it begin?" the newsroom would ask so that the station could schedule coverage.

"Whenever you get here," seemed to be the stock response.

We learned the hard way to steer away from "staged" outbreaks, peaceful or otherwise.

An early innovator in manipulating the news media was the Ku Klux Klan; the device they used was intimidation. I learned this firsthand in St. Augustine, Florida.

Dr. Martin Luther King, Jr. arrived in St. Augustine the week of June 22, 1964, seeking to integrate the previously all-white beaches in that historic city. He brought with him well-known men and women from Eastern cities to help open up food and hotel service on the beaches to black Americans. As a focal point, he staged daily "wade-ins," in which groups of civil rights protesters, both black and white, filtered to the ocean through the crowds of white sunbathers and, ultimately, obstacles of state and local law enforcement officers. Some days they stopped short of the water; on other days they tried to force their way past the line of police.

It made for good television, a fact not lost on the Klan. ABC had assigned me to relieve reporter Paul Good, who had been on the story in St. Augustine for a couple of weeks already when I arrived. As I checked into my motel, Paul took me aside and said, "The Klan will try to intimidate you. Just be careful and watch your backside."

Well, that was a little dramatic, I thought. Besides, I was from Texas, and we Texans don't intimidate easily. So I brushed it off and went on about my business. On the first day, my cameraman, Larry Smith, and I went to the beach area that had become the focal point of Dr. King's efforts. Our plan, well executed that first day, was simply to cover the story and not to allow the demonstrators to play to our camera. That evening, after dinner, I went to bed early.

I was awakened about 2:00 A.M. by voices outside my motel room door. The voices were loud enough for me to hear and understand clearly—and deliberately so, for the express purpose that I be able to hear and understand. One said, "Should we kill him now or wait 'til morning?"

Not what you want to hear outside your door in the middle of the night. A man with a keen sense of comedy might have said, "Don't I have a say in the matter?" or "Look, fellas, you're disturbing my sleep." But, as I lay there alone in my room, avoiding flippancy seemed the better part of valor. Needless to say, the faceless men on the other side of that thin door had my undivided attention—Texan or not. And, boy, did that door seem thin at that moment. Even though the latch-bolt was secure, I knew that if they really wanted to kill me, no lock on earth could protect me.

I picked up the phone and called the ABC news desk in New York. It seemed like hours instead of seconds before the man at the assignment desk picked up. Much as I thought Paul Good had been overly dramatic when he had issued his warning to me, I'm sure that anonymous fellow at the assignment desk must have thought the same of me as I said, speaking in a low voice, "Listen carefully. Nothing will probably happen, but there are some men outside my room. I think they're just trying to scare me—and they did—but if you don't hear from me every two to four hours during the next twelve hours, alert the FBI to check on my whereabouts."

By the time I hung up, the voices had gone. I tried to go back to sleep but found that I couldn't. Who could? I thought that they were simply trying to scare me, but I couldn't be sure. Believe me, I have never been so glad to see daylight as I was that next morning when the sun's rays peeked through my window and no one was waiting outside. Fortunately, I heard no more from the Klan that day or the next, but I sure looked over my shoulder a lot during those forty-eight hours.

I should have kept looking.

On the third day, Larry Smith and I were covering the daily confrontation between demonstrators and law enforcement officers on the beach when I suddenly found myself shoved to the ground. I was more shocked than hurt, trying to figure out what had happened. But before I could recover, I felt something hard connect with my ribs. I sensed a crowd of people standing around Larry and me, encircling us. My brain couldn't quite register what was happening as I searched for their identities. It was hard to see faces, though, when everywhere I looked all I saw were shoes and boots, kicking at me.

Larry sprawled in the sand next to me, trying to protect himself, just as I was trying to protect myself from the flurry of feet. As we ducked and covered, our assailants showered us with racist epithets, as if we, the media, were responsible for what was happening on the beach.

Fortunately, the attack ended in just seconds, although it seemed longer, as Florida State Troopers came to our aid. We were left with only bumps and bruises, which healed soon enough, and injured pride, which took a little longer. Although we didn't know, specifically, who our assailants had been, it wasn't hard to guess their sponsorship.

I later called Hoss Manucy, the self-proclaimed Klan leader in the St. Augustine area, and told him that abusing and intimidating reporters would never help his cause. I have seen more than one media-hog turn thespian when it suited him, and Manucy was no different. He feigned shock that I would think Klansmen had any part in the attack. It reminded me of Claude Rains's famous line from *Casablanca*: "I'm shocked—shocked—to find gambling in this institution."

Manucy later agreed to an on-camera interview with me, but the American public was never aware of his novel way of carrying a loaded .38-caliber pistol: on top of his head, under the wide-brimmed black western hat he always wore. Manucy usually started his news conferences with what almost became his mantra: "Y'all ain't got nuttin' on, have you? Just remember, I know every one of you when I see you."

After the scare tactic at the motel and the pride-scarring on the beach, my boss in New York, Nick Archer, decided I needed company and suggested that Joyce join me in St. Augustine. He and I both thought the Klan stalkers were more talk than stalk, and he knew Joyce and I could enjoy a little beach time together. And we did, as we proceeded to get the worst sunburns ever, sitting on the seawall to watch the demonstrations. We were becoming quite familiar with a brand new product called Solarcaine.

But we witnessed another hard-won victory for Dr. King.

—◆◆◆—

"Just keep singing until CBS gets set up."
—Dr. Martin Luther King, Jr.

While the Klan had one tactic for manipulating the media, they paled next to the master, Dr. Martin Luther King, Jr. Articulate, knowledgeable, and never at a loss for words, he had a built-in clock in his brain that told him how much he could say to make a network sound bite. And he knew which reporters and cameramen were with which network. Never underestimate the power of knowing who's who.

Case in point:

Twenty-six-year-old civil rights worker Jimmie Lee Jackson was murdered during a voters' rights registration in Marion, Alabama, on February 26, 1965. Following his death, and prior to his funeral on March 3, 1965, an emotional rally was held in a small church in Selma, where approximately 300 people crammed into a sanctuary built for 200, and another 250 folks gathered outside. It took me twenty minutes to make my way through the shoulder-to-shoulder crowd to place my ABC microphone on the lectern, then I sat on the floor along with dozens of other newspeople, my trusty tape recorder ready and a clear line of sight to my cameraman.

Dr. King and Dr. Ralph Abernathy sat just behind the speaker's stand, while a young man led the congregation in singing the civil rights anthem, "We Shall Overcome." Voices filled the tiny church, very moving in their earnestness. After several verses, Dr. King leaned over to the songleader and said, "We'll start after you sing one more chorus."

Just then, a cameraman pushed his way past the throng of people, fighting down the aisle to the front, camera in tow. Never missing a beat, Dr. King leaned forward to the young songleader again. "Just keep singing until CBS gets set up."

They did, and Dr. King ultimately spoke to a much larger audience with all networks once again covering his eloquent remarks.

And eloquent he was, every time he took out his pen to write or opened his mouth to speak. Setting the stage for his leadership in the civil rights movement, he wrote from the Birmingham jail in April of 1963: "The Negro's great stumbling block is not the White Citizen's Councilor or the Ku Klux Klanner, but the white moderate who is more devoted to 'order' than to justice . . . who paternalistically believes he can set the timetable for another man's freedom."

In Detroit, on June 23, 1963, he said, "If a man hasn't discovered something that he will die for, he isn't fit to live."

Upon accepting the Nobel Peace Prize in 1964, these words: "The torturous road which has led from Montgomery to Oslo is a road over which millions of Negroes are traveling to find a new sense of dignity. It will, I am convinced, be widened into a superhighway of justice."

And who can forget his "I Have a Dream" speech on August 28, 1963, which concluded the 200,000-person March on Washington. Perhaps no more powerful line was ever spoken in the civil rights movement than his concluding words, quoting from the old Negro spiritual, "Free at last! Free at last! Thank God Almighty, we are free at last."

Or who can understand the depth of the irony of his words the night of April 3, 1968, speaking to striking sanitation workers in Tennessee: "Like anybody, I would like to live a long life. Longevity has its place. But I'm not concerned about that now. I just want to do God's will." Less than twenty-four hours later, he would lie in a pool of blood at a Memphis hotel, struck down by an assassin's bullet.

America lost one of its great leaders with his death, but his legacy still lives on today.

—◆◆◆—

"Murphy, they're peeing in the streets."
—Alabama Governor George Wallace

There will always be those who insist that Dr. King's speeches fueled the very violence that ultimately claimed his life. I submit that those who say that refuse to let facts get in the way of a good polemic. They have shut their ears to his words in Oslo: "Nonviolence is the answer to the crucial political and moral questions of our time; the need for man to overcome oppression and violence without resorting to oppression and violence. Man must evolve for all human conflict a method which rejects revenge, aggression, and retaliation. The foundation of such a method is love."

Their claims are further belied by the facts, including Dr. King's actions and remarks that concluded the Selma-to-

Montgomery march in 1965. I personally witnessed those events and took from them a deep respect for this Baptist preacher who had devoted his life to making this country a better place for everyone.

Beginning at midday March 24, 1965, the day before the marchers reached Montgomery, demonstrators had already started filling the street in front of the Alabama state capitol in anticipation of the marchers' arrival. They served as sort of an advance contingent for the next day's big finale. Mostly young and decidedly intense, their decibel level rose throughout the afternoon and early evening, and, along with it, the tension level in the streets—to the point that an order went out from state officials in Montgomery for additional law enforcement help from all available agencies at city, county, and state levels.

By nightfall, Alabama State Troopers had totally surrounded the capitol, cutting it off from the demonstrators, who were themselves encircled by local and state law enforcement officers. Alabama Governor George Wallace—target of liberals, stump-speaker-made-good, political opportunist—had devised a novel strategy for dealing with the crowd: The demonstrators would be allowed to remain inside the area surrounded by law enforcement, but if they left the area for any reason, they would not be allowed to rejoin.

The strategy was simple—and transparent. If nature called and demonstrators left to find restroom facilities, they would effectively exclude themselves from the demonstration. But, although it might have seemed brilliant on paper, in actual practice it didn't hold water. Nor did the demonstrators, who took to urinating in the streets rather than leave their designated area.

Two truck trailers had been moved in to serve as a stage in front of the Alabama capitol. I was to anchor ABC's live coverage of the event from a card table on the capitol steps behind the stage, with an elevated view of the goings-on. As I observed the demonstration from my vantage point the evening before the finale, one of Governor Wallace's bodyguards tapped me on the shoulder.

"The governor wants to see you."

Being summoned to the governor's office is not unlike being summoned to the principal's office. Though the reason might ultimately be innocuous, one's mind roils with the possible scenarios before arriving, and such was the case as I followed the bodyguard to Governor Wallace's office.

As I entered, I saw Governor Wallace standing at the window, chewing on an ever-present, but unlit, cigar. He parted the slats of the blinds and looked down to the street below.

"Murphy," he said, his tone wreathed in indignation, "they're peeing in the streets. Why don't you have your camera crews take a picture of that and show your network bigwigs in New York? See what they think then."

I replied as evenly as I could. "Governor, my crew has already filmed the demonstrators relieving themselves. But you know as well as I do that there's not a snowball's chance in hell of this being shown during the dinner hour in millions of American homes."

With that, I left an even more frustrated governor peering in disbelief at the indignities being inflicted upon his capitol. And so, in the darkness lessened only by street lamps and an occasional light from a television crew, an uneasy night passed.

The film was not shown on ABC.

That same night, at St. Jude's Field just outside Montgomery, the thousands of marchers who had made the fifty-mile trek from Selma settled in for an evening of rousing entertainment by some of America's best known performers. Among them: Harry Belafonte; Sammy Davis, Jr.; Peter, Paul and Mary; Alan King; James Baldwin; Shelley Winters; Nipsey Russell; Ossie Davis; George Kirby; Billy Eckstein; Mike Nichols; Elaine May; Pete Seeger; Tony Perkins; and Tony Bennett.

The next day, the marchers arrived in Montgomery. I watched as a veritable Who's Who in civil rights spoke to the assembled throng that numbered from 35,000 to 50,000. Among those who spoke were Andrew Young, Dr. Ralph David Abernathy, Hosea Williams, Dr. Fred Shuttlesworth, Dr. Ralph Bunche, Dr. A. Philip Randolph, Roy Wilkins, John Lewis, and Whitney Young.

Then came the crown jewel of the movement: Dr. King, who slowly and methodically moved the crowd to a fevered pitch. You could almost feel the tension ratchet up with each carefully chosen word. The crowd shouted its "amens" to the message he preached. I sensed the potential for violence, merely awaiting its invitation. I am convinced to this day that, had Dr. King wanted them to storm the capitol, all he would have had to say was "Take it!" and the battle would have been joined with the Alabama police.

Instead, just as intently as he had built the crowd to crescendo levels, he used soft and deliberate tones to moderate the crowd from its high emotional state. As the throng hushed, leaning forward to catch every word, he challenged them to reach new heights, but through nonviolent means. He called for constructive, not destructive, efforts as they moved forward in their quest for justice and equality.

Again, leadership at its best.

"More violence in New Jersey. A policeman in Plainfield, New Jersey, has just been beaten to death with a grocery cart, reportedly by ABC's Murphy Martin."
—ABC RADIO NEWS ANNOUNCER

Despite Dr. King's best efforts, not all of civil rights history can be written with a happy and peaceful ending. In a nation founded on revolution and violence, it shouldn't surprise anyone that the riots of the '60s occupy such a prominent place in so many memories. And it shouldn't be any surprise that they even occurred, or that they received wall-to-wall coverage on television. Beginning in the Watts area of Los Angeles, they soon spread their death, fear, and destruction across the country.

Name any city in the country during that time, and you would have found racial tension. In many cities—no, make that in most cities—leaders both black and white, acting in good faith, worked out peaceful compromises to those tensions. But those peaceful resolutions weren't news. Not to television, anyway. Adapting a famous slogan of the Texas Rangers, "One riot, one Ranger," television's watchword seemed to be "No riot, no story."

News reporters are not, thank God, expected to give their lives for their craft, even though some have. I don't know whether I could ever muster the courage I have seen displayed by police and firefighters in times of unreasoned madness. Never will enough credit be given to those courageous people as I discovered firsthand when I found myself, unbelievably, in harm's way as I covered the civil unrest that swept across our nation.

My unexpected brush with death occurred in Newark, New Jersey, in mid-July 1967. The Newark riots first hit the news bigtime when word got out that snipers had occupied several downtown buildings. Taking pot shots at passing traffic and people, they succeeded in paralyzing the city for six days.

My second night on the scene, my cameraman and I were moving from vantage point to protected vantage point as an occasional crack of rifle fire pierced the night air. Moving across an open area, someone, I don't know who, yelled for us to find cover quickly. Almost immediately, a shot rang out. A bullet skipped off the pavement within ten feet of where I stood, and I suddenly found myself, like everyone else, scurrying for safety. We settled on a huge fire truck parked in the middle of an intersection and clambered underneath.

For the next thirty minutes, which seemed like thirty days, we hugged the pavement under that truck, praying that no bullets would ricochet with our names on them. Other fire trucks and ambulances came and went nearby, their sirens blaring, but all I could hear was the occasional crack of a rifle and the zing of skipping bullets.

As we waited and prayed for help, we tried to determine which building provided the sniper's nest. But, with echoes playing tricks among the many tall buildings and concrete streets, sirens in the distance, and a loud heartbeat in my chest, I must admit I had some difficulty locating the culprit. I think my companions under that truck shared my dilemma, but we finally agreed on which building. We got word to the Newark police, who sent up another team to capture the sniper.

When the shooting stopped and we finally—gratefully—crawled out from under that truck, no doubt all of us emerged with new appreciation for bulletproof vests and steel helmets. There is nothing quite like the sound of a near-miss from a rifle to add a flavor to one's reporting that you can't get just anywhere.

The day after the sniper incident, I was having lunch with New Jersey Governor Robert Hughes at a country club outside Newark—never happier to not be under a fire truck getting shot at. While we were eating, his driver, clad in a New Jersey patrolman's uniform, approached and whispered something in the governor's ear. I could see by both their faces that the news wasn't good.

And it wasn't. Violence had spread to the suburbs, and a police officer had been killed in nearby Plainfield, New Jersey. A group of rioters had held him down then beaten him to death by repeatedly bashing him in the head with a shopping cart.

I always get a sinking feeling in the pit of my stomach upon hearing news like that, knowing that a life has been taken and, perhaps, loved ones left behind. One of the more unsatisfying things about being a news reporter is knowing that even a personal tragedy such as that is still news and, as a reporter, it is my job to report it.

I glanced at my watch—ten minutes before the hour, just five minutes before the ABC Radio Network's hourly newscast. Time to make the air if I moved quickly. With the governor's blessing, I found a nearby telephone and called the news desk to report the killing.

Although we got the story on the air, it also earned me a spot of immortality in the albums of "Radio Bloopers," when the announcer read the hastily prepared copy that had just been handed him: "More violence in New Jersey. A policeman in Plainfield, New Jersey, has just been beaten to death with a grocery cart, reportedly by ABC's Murphy Martin."

"It is not what one says; it's not how loud one can curse. It is to what extent one can improve the life situation for his people."
—WHITNEY YOUNG, EXECUTIVE DIRECTOR OF THE
NATIONAL URBAN LEAGUE

As violent as those years in the '60s were, they might have been worse—devastating to the point of irrevocable damage to the nation—had it not been for the controlled voices of many black leaders such as Dr. King. In the search for answers to complex civil rights questions, two others I encountered, and for whom I developed the deepest respect, were Whitney Young and Gen. Daniel "Chappie" James, Jr. They were two of the most rational and clear-thinking men I have ever met in my life.

At a time when the ghettos of America seethed with unrest and frustrated young blacks threatened revolution, Whitney Young remained a calm voice amid the chaos. Truly remarkable, considering that he served as a target for criticism from both white and black America.

As executive director of the National Urban League, this native of Lincolnbridge, Kentucky, had earned the damnable title of "moderate" because he spent most of his time calling on corporate

America to create more opportunities for black Americans. Branded an "Uncle Tom" and an "Oreo" (black on the outside, white on the inside), on the one hand, by the militant arm of the civil rights movement, he was equally distrusted by even some of the main-stream element of white America, on the other. Some newspaper editorial writers consistently viewed his visits to speak before pre-dominantly white groups, such as the American Bar Association, as potential flashpoints for trouble. After all, they reasoned, he was black, wasn't he?

Wrongheaded thinking if ever there was. Then, as now, labels and stereotypes have a way of creating barriers to understanding. If we could find a substitute for such outworn words as "ultra-liberal" or "ultra-conservative" or "right" or "left," or even "moderate," I believe we would make progress toward finally understanding the enormous complexities of social and political shadings.

Whitney Young was only one great man in our country's history whose potential effectiveness was lessened by a too-easy character-ization at a time when this nation needed all the greatness it could muster. But, somehow, he rose above the labels to do what he did best: to work for understanding and progress in race relations. Throughout the 1960s, successive presidents called upon him for his opinions. And, despite criticism from his own people, the Urban League continued to keep white corporate leaders on its executive board. While the streets of America teemed with unrest, with many whipped into frenzy by black militants, the League provided coun-seling and service to more than 600,000 black Americans and found jobs for almost 100,000.

In my conversations with Young, it became obvious that he had once considered taking the same road the black militants had taken. But, rather than give in to his baser instincts, he reached a more rea-soned conclusion as to the path he should follow.

"I rode the train through Harlem and New Rochelle, where I live with my family," he said. "I thought to myself, 'Should I get off the train this morning and stand on 125th Street cursing "whitey" to show I'm tough—or should I go downtown and talk to an executive of General Motors about 2,000 jobs for unemployed blacks?' Of course, my choice has always been for going downtown to get the jobs.

"This is the important thing: It is not what one says; it's not how loud one can curse. It is to what extent one can improve the life situation for his people—and I think we are doing that."

Imminently reasonable, in my estimation. I found it hard then, and still do today, to understand how any thinking person could disagree with that approach—particularly those of his own race whom he was trying to help. But there were those who did, and did so violently. I asked Young for his thoughts on this and found him astutely philosophical.

"I think, historically, black people have been afraid of taking on white people. They feel more comfortable damning other black people.... They spend their time entertaining white people by engaging in all kinds of conflict among themselves. There is nothing new about black people attacking black people. We've been doing this on Saturday nights for generations."

But he admonished, "The new thing today is to recognize that we are in a war against racism, against poverty."

That was the war he fought. While militants rioted and cities burned, Whitney Young's Urban League increased its budget from $3 million a year to almost $40 million, and its number of branch offices increased from 60 to 100. But he never achieved the "folk hero" status of so many of his peers who would rather tear down than build up. In my opinion, the media must share some of the blame for this because that "folk hero" status was typically conferred only as a result of the high profiles raised by media attention—those about whom the print media chose to write, and those whose faces television chose to put on screens. And, more often than not, militants like "Rap" Brown, Stokely Carmichael, Eldridge Cleaver, and organizations like SNCC (Student Nonviolent Coordinating Committee) and the Black Panthers made for more exciting copy.

Even Young had to admit that they were effective, at least when it came to garnering media attention. He dreamed, though, of a world in which those tactics would never be needed.

In his own way, Young served as the conscience for not only black America but for white America as well. While whites bemoaned violence in the inner cities, clucking their tongues and shaking their heads in disbelief as they watched young black people riot in the streets, Young reminded them that "the far more violent people in our society are white people." He thought it was a "neat trick" for whites to paint blacks with the brush of violence while ignoring their own history.

"After all," he said, "the black people didn't kill Abraham Lincoln and John Kennedy and Robert Kennedy and Martin Luther King. Black people haven't lynched people. White people have done those things."

Ultimately, Young's reasoned approach achieved far more success in the long run than did looting and burning, although he was far too diplomatic to boast. But there's no denying history. Congress didn't pass the sweeping civil rights legislation that hallmarked Lyndon Johnson's administration because of fires in Watts, looting in Harlem, and snipers' bullets in Newark. No, it passed the legislation because people like Whitney Young worked within the system, played the political game, and helped make Johnson's Great Society a success.

"How would history judge Lyndon Johnson?" I asked Young.

"I think he deserves to be judged well. He was a victim of circumstances over which he had little control—the Vietnam War, in which he depended on others. There have been few presidents who have done as much for little people and who cared as much, and had all the heart and the feeling toward them, and had the skills besides.

"Lyndon Johnson believed deeply in the Great Society. He was the best example I know of my favorite saying: 'The truly best liberal is a reconstructed southerner.' I think Lyndon Johnson didn't just like black people; he liked America. He really wanted to make this a country in which there was truly equality of opportunity.

"I learned to love him."

> *"If someone calls me an 'Uncle Tom,' I place the insult in the same category as being called a 'nigger.' But I don't have time to stop and take issue with everybody who throws a label my way. I'm too busy progressing, moving ahead to more important things."*
>
> —GEN. DANIEL "CHAPPIE" JAMES, JR.

Whitney Young died tragically in March 1971, when he suffered a heart attack and drowned in Lagos, Nigeria, while swimming with friends. It was only fitting that President Johnson sent another great man of reason to accompany his body back to the United States: Air Force Gen. Daniel "Chappie" James, Jr.

I had the good fortune to spend many pleasant hours with General James, whose greatness as a decent man and dedicated American exceeded even his imposing physical size: a muscular 240 pounds carried ramrod straight on a six-foot-four frame.

As a pilot, General James flew 101 combat missions in Korea and another 78 in Vietnam. Yet taps sounded for him all too soon in 1978, when a heart attack claimed him while he was still in his mid-fifties, just weeks after he had retired as commander of NORAD. I had had the privilege of being his guest in Colorado Springs when he became the first black man to receive a fourth star on his shoulder. The day General James died unexpectedly, I thought back on all those wonderful conversations I had with him over the years. Whether at the Pentagon, in my home in Dallas, at NORAD headquarters, on the golf course, or in his quarters at Peterson Air Force Base in Colorado Springs, Chappie James always unabashedly expressed a deep love for his country—a country he served well.

I first visited with Chappie in 1973, a still turbulent time in our nation's history. Despite the signing of the Paris Peace Accords in 1973, America would remain involved in Vietnam until Saigon fell in 1975. Anti-war militants had turned their attention from the war, in particular, to the military, in general. On the racial front, many black leaders, frustrated at the seeming slowness of the integration process, suggested a return to separate-but-equal status. Opinions had polarized between white and black, young and old, liberal and conservative, and, notwithstanding huge gains in communications technology, there seemed to be a breakdown at the human level.

It was against this backdrop that I first talked with Chappie at the Pentagon, where he served as deputy public affairs officer. What struck me almost immediately was his sense of history, coupled with a confidence that the country would weather the current storms just as it had weathered countless others in years gone by.

"We tried for so long to get away from polarization and separation," he said. "We made great strides. Those people who are crawling back under that separate-but-equal blanket are going to find it very separate but never equal. I feel that both I and my children can seek our own level, and I feel it's going to be near the top. I want them at least to have that chance."

Born and raised in Pensacola, Florida, Chappie was the youngest of seventeen children. Strongly influenced by the parents who raised him, his mother, in particular, had great influence on him. A schoolteacher, she dedicated her life to teaching neighborhood children at a time when public education for blacks was substandard at best.

"That movie *Hans Christian Andersen* could have been plagiarized," Chappie said, "because it looked like some scenes from my mother's school. We would sing the addition tables, the multiplication tables in little jazzy routines. We'd start each day by saying The Lord's Prayer and singing 'The Star-Spangled Banner,' and from then on it was strictly business, teaching and learning."

But in addition to his addition and multiplication tables, Chappie's mother taught him his values, as well.

"My mother gave me my blueprint for living. She said, 'Don't get so busy practicing your right to dissent that you forget your responsibility to contribute. You are no African; you are an American. African descent, yes—but you are American and your heritage is here and you owe your devotion to this country.'"

His mother also offered sage advice on how to deal with racism. "She told me if the bigot says you are dirty, make yourself clean; if he says you are dumb, make sure you learn; if he says you lie, make sure you speak the truth; if he says you are scared, make sure you are brave. Don't ever turn your back on your God, your country, or your flag."

After graduating from Washington High School in Pensacola, Chappie attended Tuskegee Institute, where he developed a deep appreciation for black history. He longed to fly fighter planes in World War II, but, at that time, blacks were not accepted for pilot training. Then one day Eleanor Roosevelt visited Tuskegee, and Chappie was assigned as one of her guides. When he mentioned his ambition and its obstacle to her, she said she'd talk to her husband, the president, and see what she could do.

Whether that conversation at Tuskegee had anything to do with it is another discussion, but things did change after that. Chappie entered and completed pilot training under the government-sponsored Civilian Pilot Training Program, and in 1943 he received a commission as a second lieutenant in the U.S. Army Air Corps. He was one of the first black men to earn his wings, and quickly he started his trek to four stars.

Through three wars, Chappie followed his mother's advice and maintained his respect not only for his country but also for its military. He credits the latter for providing a home for young blacks seeking acceptance in this country.

"When we have a young man or a young woman come to us with an armful of hurt and a fistful of hate, fresh from the ghetto, we've got to change their attitudes first of all. They don't trust us. Some try to handle situations in the violent fashion no longer necessary in the military because the military is listening. You don't have to burn it down to get anybody's attention."

In retrospect, I can see how Chappie was a kind of military Jackie Robinson, breaking color barriers. But, just like others who followed the constructive, rather than destructive, course, he received his share of unjust criticism. And he would always suffer his share of unfair disadvantages because of his color. Yet he never joined protest marches, or urged violence, or turned his back on his country. He had his own agenda.

"If someone calls me an 'Uncle Tom,' I place the insult in the same category as being called a 'nigger.' But I don't have time to stop and take issue with everybody who throws a label my way. I'm too busy progressing, moving ahead to more important things."

Chappie also found that heroes come in all colors. Among black Americans, he counted Whitney Young, the man whose body he accompanied home from Europe, at the top of the list. Roy Wilkins was another. "When it was unpopular and dangerous to really get out and fight for change, they did it—and they did it within the framework of existing laws. They went about it by using the system and making the system responsive to us, and this was what they were preaching."

At the other end of the color spectrum, Chappie found a hero in a white southerner. "Claude R. Taylor was a fighter pilot I met when I was sent to the Philippines as a member of the 18th Tactical Wing. This white man from Texas befriended me and my family. We were close as brothers and I felt I had lost a brother when he was killed in Korea. One of my sons is named Claude R. James, and he is known by everybody as 'Spud,' just as my friend Taylor was."

Through it all, one of Chappie's most outstanding characteristics was his abiding faith in people of every hue. I never saw him bitter or strident. As he said of Governor George Wallace and Senator George McGovern, whose politics staked out positions on opposite ends of the political spectrum, but both of which he opposed, "They have a right to their opinions; I have a right to mine."

What about the militants in his own race? Those who called him an Uncle Tom, who advocated and practiced violence as a way of life and a means to change? For them, he offers this wonderful piece of advice, which still rings true down through the years: "There are many hands reaching out in friendship and down to pull you up. Many of those hands are white, and I say that they find it hard to grasp a hand to hold in friendship, or to help pull you along, if your fist is pulled tightly together in a fist of hate."

In the next breath, he offered this admonition to white America: "Don't make me a liar. Because in this country, we don't have time for bigotry and the ills caused by racism of any sort."

Chappie James never stopped working to make America a better place. As he said, "This is my country and I love her. And if she's got ills as some people claim, let us hold her hand, as we would our mother, until, working together, she is well again. I am going to continue to work on this problem until we get it solved."

He did that as long as he lived, and his tradition lives on. One of his sons, Chappie James, III, is now a three-star general, brought to Washington from overseeing the Texas Air National Guard by President George W. Bush. If Chappie Three should get a fourth star, he would round out the first four-star father-son team. I suspect Gen. Daniel (Chappie) James, Jr. would like that very much.

I miss him. And America misses him.

"If we don't show in the United States that we can live together with respect, with dignity, and with love, I think we're going to have problems we can't even begin to think about handling."
—FORMER U.S. ATTORNEY GENERAL RAMSEY CLARK

Perhaps one of the greatest rewards I enjoyed during my television career was to gain a better understanding of civil rights. My education was helped along by many people, black and white, militant and passive, all of whom had something to say about man's injustice to man. Although great strides have been made in the civil rights struggle in America, we're not finished yet. Unfortunately, it's not as simple as passing legislation because, until hearts and minds are changed, the problems will remain.

The stereotype in America is that racism is more prevalent in the South, but I learned through my travels that no geographic spot had a monopoly on it. The sad truth is that wherever two or more races exist, one is almost certain to think itself superior. They don't realize that it is the very variety that adds richness to life and to culture.

Racism is a subject many people would just as soon not discuss. And for good reason—it is a subject that can and does, as it did in the '60s, divide nations, states, cities, and even families and friends. But if we can follow the examples that have been set by great men and women of all races who have come before—like Whitney Young and Chappie James—maybe there is hope.

Murphy Martin (front row extreme right) playing in Aces of Collegeland at North Texas State in 1945. Singers later became the Moon Maids, who toured for several years with the Vaughn Monroe Orchestra.

Martin reads about the death of President Roosevelt while on a USO tour with North Texas Aces of Collegeland in 1945. The girls were violinists in the band.

Murphy Martin in the very first television appearance of his career. Hosting the signing-on of the first television station in East Texas, KTRE-TV in Lufkin, 1955. The show originated in the Lufkin High School Auditorium.

On the set of his nightly news program, Murphy Martin with the News.

Murphy
Martin news
logo (1963).

First official Murphy Martin promotion picture for ABC-TV News, 1963.

Martin (right) with Jim Hagerty, vice president of ABC-TV News, who hired Martin to
anchor only late night news on network television in January 1963. Hagerty was press
secretary to President Dwight Eisenhower before moving to ABC News.

Murphy Martin working a story from his network news office at ABC.

Murphy Martin (standing) with Ron Cochran (seated) in 1963. Cochran anchored the early news and Martin the late news at ABC-TV.

At work preparing news at ABC-TV in 1963.

With Walter Pfister (right) at ABC-TV in 1963. Pfister was producer brought over from the Huntley-Brinkley show at NBC-TV to produce Murphy Martin with the News at ABC-TV. It was Pfister who called Martin at his New York apartment and told him: "The president has been shot in your town."

Murphy Martin (left) with Elmer Lower, vice president of ABC-TV News. Lower removed Martin from his anchor position following the assassination of President Kennedy in Dallas.

Murphy Martin (seated left) with Don Gardner (seated center) and Pierre Salinger (seated right) at Democratic National Convention in 1964. Martin and Gardiner co-anchored both the Democratic and GOP conventions in 1964.

Murphy Martin, with cigarette, with co-anchorman Bill Beutel (left) at promotional party for WABC-TV in New York. Also in picture (third from left) is Ed Silverman, news director of Channel 7, and Sy Siegel, vice president of ABC-TV (fourth from left).

Martin (extreme left) with Mayor John Lindsay of New York and Martin's co-anchor from WABC-TV, Bill Beutel, on extreme right.

79

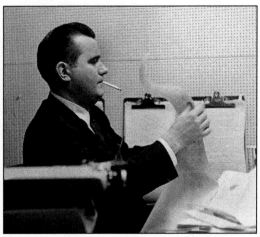

Murphy Martin (left) and co-anchor Bill Beutel (right) with weatherman Tex Antoine in center at WABC-TV in New York City.

Checking wire copy, ABC-TV, 1963.

With co-anchor Bill Beutel at WABC-TV.

Murphy Martin, with wife Joyce, honored at Fort Worth Press Club in 1963 with ten-gallon Stetson before returning to New York.

Martin pointing to his former hometown of Dallas on map in ABC-TV newsroom in New York City.

PHOTOGRAPHS OF LEE HARVEY
OSWALD TAKEN IN MINSK

COMMISSION EXHIBIT 2891

COMMISSION EXHIBIT 2892

PHOTOGRAPH OF LEE HARVEY OSWALD
PROBABLY TAKEN IN LATE SEPTEMBER, 1963
(COMMISSION EXHIBIT 2788)

OSWALD IN FRONT OF
TEXAS THEATER
(HILL EXHIBIT B)

OSWALD AT DALLAS POLICE DEPARTMENT

(FRANK PIZZO EXHIBIT 453-C)

COMMISSION EXHIBIT NO. 1797

Murphy Martin about to interview Dallas Police Chief Jesse Curry as Channel 8 newsman Bert Shipp explains camera angle to the chief.

Martin interviews Judge Joe B. Brown during the trial of Jack Ruby. Martin convinced Judge Brown to allow cameras in the court-room for the final ver-dict in the trial.

Martin is among reporters interviewing District Attorney Henry Wade fol-lowing the death sentence verdict for Jack Ruby in Dallas.

Jack Ruby is escorted back to jail in 1964 following his being sentenced to death for the murder of Lee Harvey Oswald.

Martin is partially hidden behind Melvin Belli's right shoulder following the verdict in the Jack Ruby trial where Belli defended Ruby. Belli ranted and raved about what he called a miscarriage of justice.

85

Marina Oswald with youngest daughter Rachel in Richardson, Texas, home during first in-depth interview with Murphy Martin, 1964.

First in-depth interview of Marina Oswald in 1964 in her Richardson, Texas, home.

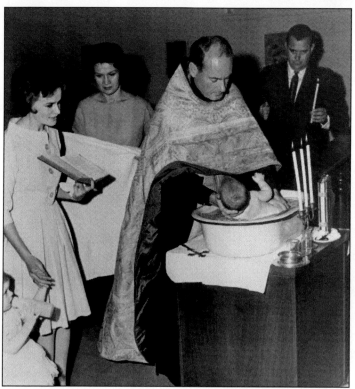

Murphy Martin, at extreme right, holding candle while serving as godfather for the baptism of Rachel Oswald by Father Dimitri Royster in 1964. Mrs. Declan Ford was godmother.

American Broadcasting Company

7 WEST 66TH STREET · NEW YORK 23. N. Y.

SUSQUEHANNA 7-5000

December 11, 1963

Mr. Murphy Martin
116 Central Park South
New York, New York

Dear Murphy:

Elmer Lower, who is presently travelling abroad, has asked me to convey to you his personal thanks for your outstanding contribution to ABC News' coverage of the tragic events over the November 22-25 weekend. Because of your efforts and skill our Department has received high critical and professional acclaim. You were called upon to report to the largest audiences any news person has ever faced. You did this well and gave of yourself unselfishly.

The management of ABC News is proud of you and the part you played in helping to perform this very necessary public service. Enclosed with this letter is a token of the appreciation which we feel. While we recognize that you gave of yourself during those trying hours without requesting any specific recompense, we feel you are fully entitled to this sum for the services you rendered.

Again, our sincerest thanks for a difficult job well done.

Sincerely,

Stephen C. Riddleberger
Vice President and General Manager
ABC News

Letter of thanks from ABC-TV for work as anchor during assassination coverage, November 1963.

Jim Garrison, who claimed he had solved the murder of John F. Kennedy, makes initial claim in exclusive interview in New Orleans with Murphy Martin. Garrison later used his unfounded claims to write a book, which became the basis for Oliver Stone's movie JFK, *criticized by many as a vast disservice to American history.*

Interviewing Gen. Daniel "Chappie" James in the Pentagon in 1972. General James became the first black American to receive four stars in the U.S. military. His son is now a three-star general handling the National Guard for President George W. Bush.

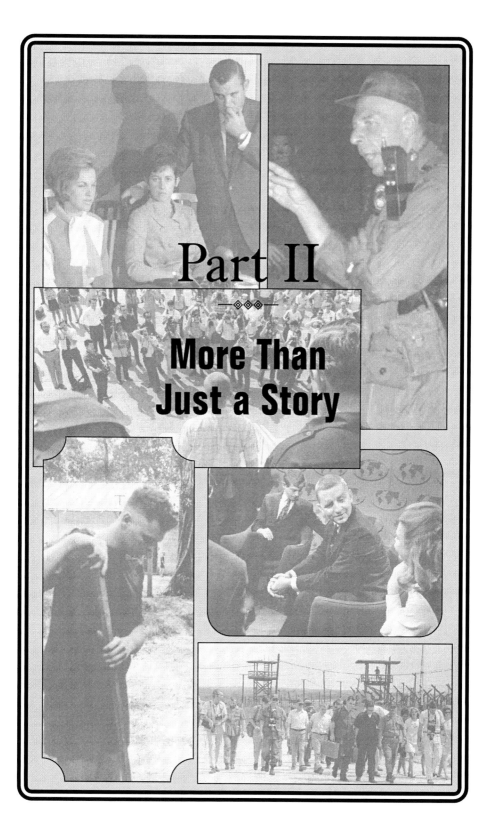

Part II

More Than Just a Story

CHAPTER 5

The Most Rewarding Moment

"My dream, always, in the early years when I had business success was that my biggest riches would be if my children turned out to be really outstanding citizens who cared for other people and did something about their society."
—H. ROSS PEROT

In 1969, *Fortune Magazine* dubbed H. Ross Perot "The Fastest, Richest Texan Ever." Now, when you're talking about Texas and its history of rags-to-riches oil men and land and cattle barons, that's quite an accomplishment. Even more remarkable was the fact that few people even knew who he was in 1969. He had reached the top so fast and so dramatically, no one had even noticed. But the "Fastest, Richest Texan Ever"—well, people started to take notice after that. I know I did.

Gearing up for my first interview with Perot, I dug into his background and quickly discovered there was never a more unlikely Fastest, Richest Texan. Born the son of a local cotton broker in Texarkana, Texas—where they pronounced his name with a Cajun accent, *Pea*-row, rather than emphasizing the second syllable—he had not yet reached his thirty-ninth birthday, but, by my reckoning, was already a legitimate billionaire on paper. And that's 1969 dollars, to give it a bit of perspective.

A genuine Boy Scout, he had grown up dedicated to duty, honor, and country. Upon graduating from high school, and seemingly unable to obtain an appointment to the Naval Academy, it was time to consider Plan B. He set his sights on the University of Texas in Austin, with his ultimate goal being law school. But a funny thing happened on the way to becoming a lawyer.

Texas Senator W. Lee O'Daniel, recently defeated for reelection, was cleaning out his desk in Washington, D.C., to return to Dallas, when he discovered he had one remaining appointment he could make to a service academy. "Who can we give it to?" he asked an aide.

"There's a young man in Texarkana who's been writing to us for an appointment to the Naval Academy," the aide said.

"Give it to him." And so the world was deprived of an attorney named Perot.

A natural leader, Perot served as chairman of the Brigade Executive Committee and as class president while at the Academy. And it was during his days at the Academy that Perot went on a blind date with Margot Birmingham, who would later become his wife and mother of his five children.

In 1957, following four years of active duty as a naval lieutenant aboard the USS *Sigourney* and the aircraft carrier USS *Leyte*, Perot entered corporate America as a salesman for IBM, earning $500 a month (less than four dollars an hour). But Perot saw beyond the salary to the financial potential of the computer business and used his free time to educate himself on all the things a properly programmed computer could do. He spent the rest of his time selling IBM products. And sell he did, busting IBM's compensation structure.

In late 1961, concerned about morale among its lesser-compensated salesmen, IBM management developed a program designed to close the earnings gap between the top and bottom. "They thought that was the only way to keep my salary under control," Perot said.

Under the new program, each salesman was allotted a quota that he was permitted to sell for the calendar year. Can you imagine that? Nothing like striving for mediocrity. In 1962, the first year IBM implemented the program, Perot sold out his quota by January 19.

"I had a backlog of prospects," Perot said, "so if I was only going to get twenty cents on the dollar, I may was well get them sold."

That left Perot with plenty of free time—time he used wisely. "I didn't have anything to keep me busy, and I had this idea that became EDS. I was sitting in the barbershop one day, reading an old *Reader's Digest*, and there was a quote from Thoreau: 'The mass of men lead lives of quiet desperation.' That's when I decided to try it."

From the end of January until his scheduled vacation period in April, Perot devoted himself to learn everything he could about IBM, analyzing the things it did right, the things it did wrong, and the things it didn't do. Then, while vacationing in Hawaii, he spent his days studying the state of the computer business as a whole. As others around him baked on sun-drenched beaches, he recorded the pluses and minuses of each major company's approach to the business. Surely the other tourists must have wondered at this strange little man filling yellow legal pad after yellow legal pad. Perhaps they thought he was writing a thriller or a hard-boiled mystery set in paradise. If they only knew that, by the time he returned to the mainland, those pages would be filled with the outline of what he considered the ideal company—one that could offer turnkey computer services, a revolutionary idea in the early 1960s.

As Perot explained the idea that sparked the creation of his company: "Our business is the intelligent use of computers. The computer is virtually a universal tool. It's the bulldozer of the information business. Just as a bulldozer moves large quantities of dirt, a computer has the ability to move large quantities of information. The intelligent use of a computer within an insurance company, a bank, or manufacturing company, or distribution company, determines its value to that company. Acquiring the tool only increases the expenses of the company; the intelligent use of the tool makes it valuable. Our business is the designing and building and operating of complete business information systems for major corporations."

Once back in Dallas, Perot took $1,000 from his schoolteacher wife's savings account and used it to form Electronic Data Systems, now better known as EDS. By the time I interviewed him in February of 1969, Perot had taken EDS public, but still owned eighty percent of its stock. Those nine million shares were selling, at that time, for upwards of $140 a share on the New York Stock Exchange— well over the billion-dollar mark.

As you can imagine, I had a lot of questions about a young man with that kind of wealth. After all, money can do things to even the most well-grounded of people. So, as I approached that first interview in February of 1969, I wasn't sure what to expect. What I found was a clean-cut, well-dressed young man with an incredibly refreshing attitude. He quickly pointed out that acquiring wealth had never been his goal. Rather, his goal had been to build a great company; wealth was merely a by-product of that success.

"I hope that thirty years from now," he said, "if someone should take the time to think about me, I hope he would think about a lot of things before he thought about my net worth."

Thirty-four years later, I again asked Perot about acquiring great wealth. And, thirty-four years later, his response was virtually the same: "Money doesn't bring happiness—the two are unrelated. As a young man, I had the opportunity to meet some very wealthy people, and one of the patterns I saw was that most of them were unhappy. So that has never been my goal. My goal has been to build great companies, and financial success comes as a by-product of that."

During that first interview, I found myself enamored with Perot and his seemingly uncluttered mind. At times he came across as somewhat naive, but always as a man of action. I quickly learned that that action included an almost publicity-free generosity. Among other things, I discovered that he had:

- given $2.5 million to the Dallas public schools to finance an experimental school for 1,000 mostly minority students;
- contributed $1 million to the Boy Scouts of America, with the stipulation that BSA investigate ways to take scouting into ghetto areas;
- purchased 1,000 acres in Texas for the Girl Scouts, with a suggestion that the summer camp, later named for his sister, Bette Perot, be used during the remainder of the year as a boarding school for poor children; and
- committed $50,000 a year to Catholic Jesuit High School in Dallas, despite being a Presbyterian.

Over the years since then, I have observed Ross Perot through many peaks in his life—and very few valleys. Whether I have watched him from a distance, or from days of up-close work with him on POW-MIA activities or his presidential campaign in 1992, I have seen very little change in him.

—◇◆◇—
"We're going to have to get those men home!"
—H. Ross Perot

From that first interview, Perot and I forged a friendship that was to build and last for the next thirty-plus years. It was also to yield what I consider the most rewarding moment in my life.

The Vietnam War was at its most intense in those later years of the 1960s and, in fact, fueled much, if not most, of the turmoil that swept the nation during that decade. Somehow lost in all of that was the fact that, by 1969, more than 1,400 American servicemen were unaccounted for in Southeast Asia, assumed to be prisoners of war.

I first became acquainted with the problem when I received a letter from Mrs. Charles Powell of Gatesville, Texas, telling me that her son was a missing pilot in Vietnam. Following up, I interviewed her and the wives of three other missing pilots, along with U.S. Rep. Olin Teague, on an interview program in Dallas. The women had no idea whether their loved ones were alive or dead, and neither our government nor the one in North Vietnam was doing much to answer their questions.

So, I decided to lead a group to the Paris Peace Talks in hopes of raising attention to the problem. In September 1969, my wife, Joyce, and I, along with WFAA-TV cameraman Mal Couch, accompanied four wives from the Dallas area whose Air Force husbands were missing in Southeast Asia, to Paris. Those women—Bonnie Singleton, wife of Capt. Jerry Singleton; Joy Jeffrey, wife of Capt. Robert Jeffrey; Paula Hartness, wife of Capt. Gregg Hartness; and Sandy McElhanon, wife of Maj. Michael McElhanon—with letters to their husbands in hand, became the first such group seen by the North Vietnamese since the war had begun. They hoped to learn, as Bonnie Singleton put it, "Are we wives or widows?"

Through dogged determination, and with the help of a French interpreter named Anick Montagu who had been located for me by the ABC News Bureau in Paris, we finally got an appointment with the North Vietnamese. With our driver, Robert Herve, at the wheel of our minivan, we drove from the tiny Alexander Hotel, where we stayed in the heart of Paris, to the North Vietnamese compound in the suburb of Choisy-le-Roi.

The wives were met by Xuan Oanh, a Mr. Bai, and a third man

who was never identified, who made up the North Vietnamese delegation, and were ushered inside a meeting room. The North Vietnamese were cordial enough, offering the women red tea and cookies but little in the way of assurances. They accepted the personal letters the wives had brought for their husbands and promised to deliver them as soon as possible—if, in fact, they could actually find their husbands. The North Vietnamese also assured them that if their husbands were prisoners of war, they were being treated well despite the fact that "they are murderers who dropped bombs on innocent children."

Those "ifs" were hardly comforting. As Bonnie Singleton described it, the North Vietnamese told them to tell their children "that the prisoners in Vietnam are receiving—if their daddies are there—are receiving humane treatment."

Joy Jeffrey said, "I got the opinion that they didn't know where our husbands were."

The delegation asked the wives to write down complete descriptions of their husbands, including name, rank, and when they were shot down, and to leave pictures behind. Using that information, they promised to locate the women's husbands and let them know their fates.

But I guess cordiality had its limits in the big propaganda machine. For the next two hours, the communist delegation harangued the distraught women about the evils their husbands and others like them had inflicted upon the North Vietnamese people, telling them repeatedly of the great suffering their people had endured for twenty-five years, going back to the days of the French occupation.

They also tried to enlist the wives in their propaganda campaign. Bonnie Singleton said the delegation asked them to go back and make people understand "that Washington wants to pursue the war ... they don't believe Washington wants to end the war."

"And that Washington is profiting from the war," Joy Jeffrey added.

The meeting ended with a promise that the North Vietnamese would see any other groups of wives who came. "They said that their doors would be open," Joy Jeffrey reported. But it was a promise we would later learn was as empty as the others they had made.

After we returned to the States from Paris, we looked at the film Mal Couch had shot of the trip and knew immediately we had the makings of a solid documentary. We quickly settled on the title *Red Tea and Promises*, which is all the North Vietnamese had offered the wives in Paris, and set about looking for money to sponsor the project. I thought immediately of the young billionaire I had interviewed earlier that year.

A few days later, Perot came to the WFAA-TV studio at my invitation along with a trusted employee, Tom Marquez, the first person he had hired at EDS. We showed him a rough-cut of the film in a darkened screening room, with very little light other than that which was put out by the three-foot screen. Throughout the screening, I studied Perot in the flickering light. His attention was riveted to the screen, his mind taking in every nuance.

Near the end of the film, when the wives were arriving back at Love Field, little four-year-old Ricky Singleton raced to the waiting arms of his mother, Bonnie.

"Ross," I said, "that little boy has never seen his father. He was born after his father first went to Southeast Asia."

When the lights went up, I looked at Perot. His eyes met mine, tears glistening. "We're going to have to get those men home," he said.

I nodded. He got it!

And having gotten it, from that moment on, Ross Perot never let go of the POW-MIA problem, tackling it with the same single-minded devotion he showed as a young IBM salesman planning the perfect company. Once committed, Perot dove in with abandon. He immediately orchestrated and underwrote a nationwide media campaign under the slogan "United We Stand" to win support for President Nixon's Vietnam policies. The movement ultimately became a formal organization of the same name and, even later, a political party.

In January of 1970, I left my position as special projects director of WFAA-TV in Dallas to accept a position as president of United We Stand.

"I hope through the meeting, the four ladies will understand better why their husbands have been captured . . . and will know the crimes which the American pilots have committed in our country."
—LE PHU HOU, NORTH VIETNAM NEWS AGENCY OFFICIAL

A few weeks after our trip to Paris, I returned alone to check on progress. And there wasn't much. None of the four wives had received any mail from their husbands, nor had they heard anything from the North Vietnamese about their husbands' status.

Once in Paris, I sought another face-to-face with the North Vietnamese delegation, but I found that the doors that were supposedly open had been closed. I then checked with my contacts, hoping for some news of progress either on the Peace Talks or on the status of the POW-MIAs. Unfortunately, I found little of either—news or progress.

One to whom I spoke was Wilfred Burchett, a communist news reporter who traveled frequently in and out of North Vietnam. I explained the dilemma of hundreds of wives in America who had no concrete evidence that their husbands were being held captive or were even alive, for that matter. Burchett expressed interest in filming some of the Americans being held, an offer I was ready to jump on. What better proof for the wives than actual film footage of their husbands, alive?

"Let me think about it," Burchett said, "and see if it's something I can do." Then the communist showed his grasp of capitalism as he added, "And let me think about what it might be worth if I were successful."

He ultimately failed to follow through. Whether he decided he couldn't, wouldn't, or it just wasn't worth it, I don't know.

Others with whom I spoke were equally unhelpful. Jean Sainteny, the former French commissioner of North Vietnam who was still close to Le Duc Tho, North Vietnam's premier, repeatedly promised help, but consistently failed to follow through. Jean Lacoutre, a ranking French official, also extended hollow promises.

One bit of help I did get was from Madeleine Riffaud, a reporter for the French communist publication *L'Humanite*. She had interviewed at least one American pilot after he was shot down, and she sent pictures to me without her paper knowing. Unlike that good communist Wilfred Burchett, she never asked for payment.

Just before leaving Paris, I called on Peter Tarnoff, an aide in the U.S. Embassy to Ambassador Henry Cabot Lodge. "What if we bring the wives back over here to talk to the North Vietnamese again?" I asked.

"It's a long shot," he said. "But might as well try." After all, he explained, the previous trip had opened the world's eyes to a problem that had been buried—to the delight of Ambassador Lodge and the consternation of the North Vietnamese. "No one knew the lock was open on the POW issue until you opened the door," he said.

In mid-November, I spoke with Dick Capen at the Pentagon about a return trip to Paris. He was all for it, but it had to be conducted as a private enterprise and not as an official government endeavor. WFAA-TV had covered the expense of the first two trips, but Perot offered to pay for the third. This would be his first, but certainly not his last, financial expenditure on the POW problem.

Perot also suggested we take with us Lt. Robert Frishman, who had recently been released by Hanoi as a supposed sign of good faith. The Pentagon nixed this idea, afraid it would look like our trip was a sanctioned government trip if we had military personnel with us.

Nevertheless, my wife and I, accompanied by Bert Shipp and Chuck Butt, both of WFAA-TV, and wives Bonnie Singleton and Paula Hartness, left Dallas the Monday before Thanksgiving of 1969 and returned to Paris to the Peace Talks. Our first step was to call the North Vietnamese delegation for a meeting.

"We're very busy," they told us. "It would be very difficult to find time for another meeting. Besides, we have no news for you about the missing pilots." Ah, those open doors. Then again, who could blame them for not wanting to meet with us, given their empty promises from before?

Then they added what would become a constant refrain: "You should be telling President Nixon to end the war. Then you could find out about your husbands."

I later found that this line had almost become a mantra for the North Vietnamese when I interviewed Le Phu Hou, head of the North Vietnam News Agency. I asked him how we could bring the North Vietnamese to the table to discuss the release of POWs. "The best thing to do, in my opinion," he said, "is to try to ask Mr. Nixon to fix a date for withdrawal of American forces from Vietnam." How about getting more mail delivery from the families to the POWs? "The best thing to do for the wives is just to ask Nixon to fix a date . . ." And on it went.

After two fruitless days in Paris, we next appealed to Premier Olaf Palme of Sweden, who reportedly had some influence with the North Vietnamese and an interest in seeing an end to the war. When

I called the prime minister's office, he agreed to meet with Bonnie and Paula in Stockholm. Elated, we flew to Sweden and met with him for about two hours, during which time he was very gracious, obviously concerned about the welfare of their husbands. However, politics is politics, and he was hesitant to take any strong positions on their behalf lest he offend his contacts in Hanoi.

The meeting was successful in one respect, though, in that it attracted still further world attention to the plight of the POWs, as had the original meeting with the North Vietnamese delegation in Paris a couple of months before. Determined to capitalize on that, I accompanied Bonnie and Paula to the North Vietnamese Embassy in Stockholm. Bitterly cold, snowing as it can only in Sweden during winter, we were forced to stand outside the Embassy as the *charges d'affairs* refused to allow us inside. With cameras and microphones rolling, he spoke from the warmth of just inside the door.

"Your husbands are war criminals," he told Bonnie and Paula. "Still, our government treats them well, better than they deserve. In due time, you might hear from them."

Then he repeated the mantra: *Go back to America and spend your efforts persuading President Nixon to end the war.*

Disappointed, but not disheartened, our next stop on what seemed like a whirlwind tour of Europe was Rome. Surely the Pope could offer comfort and encouragement, and exercise influence, to aid the women in their quest. We made an appointment to see the Pope's secretary of state at the Vatican, but were disappointed again. Although he offered concern and sympathy, as had Premier Palme, he wouldn't promise anything more. By then, we had received concern, sympathy, and promises up to our eyeballs; at this point we preferred unconcerned, uncaring action.

When we returned to Dallas, I briefed Perot on the fruits of the trip he had underwritten. There were no fruits. But while the rebuffs had taken their toll on the wives' morale, they had the opposite effect on Perot. Every rejection, every failure to act simply strengthened his resolve. With United We Stand at the center of the battle, he took out full-page ads in newspapers across the country and financed a half-hour documentary narrated by astronaut Frank Borman, all designed to bring world attention to bear on the plight of those 1,400+ servicemen unaccounted for in the jungles of Southeast Asia.

The fight was just beginning.

"Tell Braniff if we lose their plane, we'll buy 'em another one."
—H. ROSS PEROT

For all our publicity efforts, by mid-December we had still received nothing in response from those who had made promises. With Christmas fast approaching, I met with Perot in his Exchange Park office in Dallas for a strategy session. Our purpose? To figure out something we could do for the POWs for the holidays.

"It's a shame we can't just take 1,420 turkey dinners and fly them to Hanoi for Christmas," I said.

You could almost see the light bulb go on over Perot's head. He sat up in his chair, leaned across his desk, and said, "Let's do it!"

And, as simply as that, a decision was made. As I said, Perot is a man of action.

Over the next few days, you can't imagine the activity and the numbers of people involved in this project to bring Christmas to Hanoi—not just to take turkey dinners, but anything and everything the POWs might need. We conducted careful research as to what we should take, from interviewing doctors at Walter Reed Hospital, who filled us in on the medical supplies needed, to consulting those few freed POWs, who told us firsthand what the physical necessities were.

Armed with that information, we set about collecting those items. It seemed as if the entire country pitched in, and, in short order, we had received more than thirty tons of supplies at gathering points in Dallas and Los Angeles. The variety of items was unbelievable: food, clothing, medicine, mattresses, Bibles. The generosity of the American people can be overwhelming at times.

Chartering a plane to carry those supplies to Hanoi turned into a little bit of an adventure after a fairly uneventful start. I talked with a number of airlines, explaining our need and our mission. I even talked with Russia's Aeroflot Airlines. But, ultimately, Braniff Airlines in Dallas had the fewest questions and a helluva lot more "want to" than any of the other carriers. So we finalized a deal, and we had our airplane.

Three days later, I received a call from Braniff with a last minute concern. My guess is that the lawyers had finally gotten involved, because the last minute item had to do with insurance. Who but a lawyer would think of insurance at a time like that? Still, it was a valid concern. After all, we would be flying into a war zone, and we weren't flying the colors of the country into which we would be entering.

"Ross, we've got a problem," I told Perot as I explained about the insurance concern.

He thought for a minute, then asked, "How much does one of those planes cost?"

"About six or seven million dollars." Planes were a lot cheaper in 1969.

"Tell Braniff if we lose their plane, we'll buy 'em another one."

And with that guarantee, lack of insurance became a moot issue. The mission was on.

Because our thirty-plus tons of cargo would mostly go in the passenger compartment, we had room for very few passengers. A handful of reporters, plenty of Red Cross personnel, the Rabbi Saul Besser and Protestant minister Sidney Roberts, and United We Stand and Braniff personnel crammed in among the cargo and took off for Hanoi. As we lifted off from Love Field, we knew we had at least 12,000 miles to go on our great Christmas airlift adventure.

Our first stop was Los Angeles, where the remainder of our cargo was loaded while Perot met with a group of POW wives in a nearby hotel meeting room. That meeting was presided over by Sybil Stockdale, whose husband James was one of two POWs who would ultimately be awarded the Congressional Medal of Honor after his return—and later would emerge as Perot's vice presidential running mate in his 1992 third-party campaign.

With the rest of the supplies on board, we took off again, loaded with more than 1,400 Red Cross food kits containing cheese and crackers, chicken and rice, chicken and vegetables, tuna, salmon, chicken stew, beef stew, spaghetti and meatballs, macaroni, fruit cocktail, crackers, Life Savers, gum, instant coffee, tea, water purification pills, salt, jam, plastic spoons, and can openers.

In addition to the food kits, we carried everything the well-supplied POW could need:

- bottles of aspirin, vitamins, and painkillers
- quinine and aralen for treatment of malaria
- tetracycline
- 1,400 blankets
- 1,400 towels
- 1,400 pairs of socks
- 116 cartons of cigarettes
- 1,400 Gideon Bibles
- 6,000 razor blades
- 80 boxes of candy
- 1,400 air mattresses
- 1,400 pairs of BVDs
- 1,400 pairs of thermal underwear
- 1,400 T-shirts
- 1,400 sweatshirts
- 1,400 decks of playing cards
- 1,400 writing pens
- 2,000 envelopes
- 5,000 sheets of writing paper
- 140 medical kits

From Los Angeles, we hopped to Honolulu, then to Bangkok, Thailand. While most of the exhausted passengers headed to the Rama Hilton for some shuteye, Tom Marquez and I boarded a twin-engine aircraft for Vientiane, Laos, as advance men for Perot.

I thought my life was over a couple of times on that flight. Not ordinarily a white-knuckle flier, the short hop tested my resolve. Since it was after dark and the Pathet Lao guerrillas were known to move closer to the small Laotian airport near the capital after dark, landing at night could be a little dicey. For two first-timers in the area, though, almost everything was dicey.

I remember looking out the window at pitch-blackness just as the pilot said, "Tighten your seatbelts. We're going in."

Going in where? I wondered, my face pressed to the glass as I looked desperately for a landing strip below. All of a sudden, the plane dropped almost straight down just as I saw a few lights appear below. *Fat lot of good that's going to do us*, I thought, *when we impale the ground with the nose of this plane.*

Just as I was mumbling what I thought would be my last prayer, the pilot suddenly pulled out for the shortest landing I've ever experienced. And we were all alive.

Once in Vientiane, and happy to be on the ground, Tom Marquez and I met up with Tom Meurer, an EDS systems engineer and former Air Force officer. He had been there for a few days already, along with two POW wives who were seeking information about their missing husbands.

I had a fitful sleep that night, mulling over all the developments on our mission. The responsibility to the men being held captive and their families weighed heavily on my mind. We had come a long way—too far to fail now. At last I was finally able to drift off to sleep with the faces of people like Bonnie Singleton and her son Ricky haunting me.

I was awakened after about ten minutes by a noise in my room. I bolted up and strained to listen. Was someone there? I turned on the light only to be greeted by an iguana staring at me from the draperies in the window. Welcome to Laos!

Fortunately, I was able to go back to sleep, only to be again awakened about an hour later by another noise, this one a little farther away. Looking out the window, I saw the dry riverbed of the Mekong River in the moonlight. In the middle, two water buffalo were butting heads. Kind of made me homesick for Texas and some real bulls.

The next morning, the two Toms and I headed for the North Vietnamese Embassy, and by early afternoon we had made a firm appointment for the North Vietnamese to meet with Perot. He arrived the next day on the Braniff 707, ready for a face-to-face meeting, which turned into multiple meetings, and which dragged on unsuccessfully for days. Hopes for delivering the supplies to the POWs waned as Christmas arrived, and we were still at loggerheads.

I suspect that our Christmas in Vientiane was probably different from that experienced by virtually anyone else in the world that year. An impromptu Christmas service was set up at the Lang Xang Hotel, presided over by a regular coalition of clergy: Rabbi Besser; Reverend Roberts; and Father Matt Menger, who had headed up Catholic Charities in Laos for the previous eighteen years. We sang carols, listened to a solo sung by *Dallas Times Herald* reporter Bill McAda, and felt it was as good a Christmas as one could hope for, 12,000 miles from home.

I do know it was a particularly different Christmas for Perot in one respect, which reinforced the level of his commitment to this mission: It was the first, and only, Christmas he ever spent apart from his family.

At last, after those days of meetings, the North Vietnamese relented—sort of. Maybe we simply wore them down, but they agreed that, *provided* we would get the supplies to Moscow before December 31, and *provided* each package weighed no more than three kilos, and *provided* each package was addressed to a specific POW, the Russians could then deliver the packages to the men.

An awful lot of "provideds." I'm sure the North Vietnamese believed we would fail to meet their conditions by the appointed deadline, and they could then justify sending us back.

We immediately sprang into action, preparing to fly to Russia via Alaska. Just as we were about to take off, we got word that the North Vietnamese wanted to see us again. Hopeful that we would at last be allowed to carry out our mission, we delayed takeoff while Tom Marquez called the Embassy. It took some time to finally make contact and, when he did, he was simply told that Hanoi had now officially rejected our request to deliver Christmas packages to the POWs.

Later, the American ambassador in Laos, McMurtry Godley, reported to Secretary of State William Rogers: "North Vietnam's call to Perot may have been designed to delay Perot's departure ... and prevent his arrival in Moscow before the December 31 deadline."

With time to make up, we took off for Anchorage, Alaska, where we landed in a driving snowstorm. In Anchorage we put out a call for volunteers on local radio and television and were pleasantly surprised when hundreds of people from all walks of life showed up at a vacant hangar at the airport. For the next seven hours we repackaged more than thirty tons of food and supplies into individual packages for the POWs as the North Vietnamese had dictated.

Again, the generosity of the American people can be overwhelming.

From there, we flew over the North Pole to Copenhagen, Denmark, where Perot and I headed for the Russian Embassy—as close as we could get to Moscow under the geopolitical situation of the day. The folks at the Embassy knew nothing about our instructions from the North Vietnamese for our planeload of supplies. Not surprising, but frustrating nevertheless.

Still, we had come too far to give up now. I got on the phone, trying to make personal contact with Premier Alexei Kosygin in Russia. With the help of a hard-working Copenhagen operator, I finally got through to the premier's home. The person who answered seemed shocked that an American was on the other end, and even more shocked that I insisted on speaking to the sleeping premier. He refused to wake him. I really hadn't expected any other result, but it had been worth a shot.

We spent a long night in Copenhagen, still trying to figure out how to take our case directly to the Russians. The next morning we heard from Moscow, through Washington, that they knew nothing of the North Vietnamese plan for them to deliver the packages. Furthermore, they would have nothing to do with it. Even if we unloaded the Braniff charter and chartered a Russian Aeroflot jet to fly the packages to Hanoi, without official sanction from Moscow the plan was dead.

Case closed.

My spirits were dragging as we flew back to the United States. It seemed that all our hard work, all our good intentions, had gone for naught. Our boys were still in dirty North Vietnamese prisons, unaware whether, or if, anyone even knew they existed.

We stopped off in New York just long enough for Perot to appear with Joe Garagiola and Hugh Downs on *The Today Show* to report on the trip, which had riveted world attention for the first time on the POW situation, then arrived back in Dallas on New Year's Day of 1970.

Although we never did deliver those packages, they didn't go to waste. In May 1970, when a devastating tornado plowed through Lubbock, Texas, the supplies originally gathered for American servicemen imprisoned in North Vietnam provided relief to the tornado's victims.

I'm sure that, in the days ahead, the North Vietnamese wished they had allowed us in and out of Hanoi as quickly as possible. To borrow a cliché, they found they had a tiger by the tail and didn't know how to turn him loose.

His name was Ross Perot.

—◇◇◇—

"We are here because you cared. We came home because of your actions."
— FORMER POW COL. GEORGE (BUD) DAY

"I have screamed all night. When they torture you enough, you scream. You holler. Things changed because of your efforts."
— FORMER POW BRIG. GEN. ROBINSON RISNER

On our trip from Laos to Anchorage, Perot asked me to head up his United We Stand organization on a full-time basis. I was honored by the offer, but it wasn't something I could decide on the spur of the minute. I had already made several moves in my career, including leaving a network position in New York to return to my native Texas and the anchor desk at WFAA-TV. We were making big strides in a vicious ratings battle in the North Texas region, and I feared that if I left the anchor desk I might never regain my audience should I return in the years ahead. My head told me it could be a career-limiting move.

On the other hand, my heart was fully committed to the POW-MIA effort.

Over the next two weeks, I thought about Perot's request almost constantly. I leaned on Joyce for her advice, which was, "Do whatever you feel you want to do." It was a comfort to know I had her support, no matter what I decided. But that didn't make the decision any easier.

I also discussed my dilemma with Mike Shapiro, vice president of Belo Broadcasting, WFAA's parent, and Jack Hauser, WFAA-TV station manager. It may have been a little unconventional to talk about a possible job move with one's current employers, but I felt a sense of loyalty to them. They had been good to me, and I owed it to them to be forthcoming. Besides, I valued their counsel. You can just imagine how gratified I was to hear them say, "Go help a great cause. Your desk will be waiting for you here when you're ready to return."

So, in January of 1970, I assumed the position of president of United We Stand and never looked back until I knew those men in Southeast Asia were coming home. Little did I know then that the move would lead me to the most rewarding moment in my career.

Our mission at United We Stand was to keep the pressure on the

North Vietnamese to open up about the POWs they held. We traveled from city to city, state to state, igniting grassroots efforts all across the country. We taught folks how to organize massive letter-writing campaigns to Hanoi and gave them details on organizing visitations to the North Vietnamese delegation to the Paris Peace Talks. I wonder if those three delegates who first met with the four POW wives ever looked back and cursed the day they opened their doors to them.

We even got offers of help from some unlikely sources, such as Cora Weiss's anti-war organization. Of course, Ms. Weiss had an agenda of her own that became apparent soon enough. She and her group were allowed to come and go as they pleased from North Vietnam because they were so visible in demonstrating against United States policies in Southeast Asia. On occasion, she would approach us with so-called "new" names of POWs, but in reality, it seemed as if she merely wanted access to the wives so she could convince them to join her efforts. Fortunately, very few of the wives succumbed to her siren call, which was gratifying to me. Most of the POW families were extremely loyal to United We Stand; they truly understood and appreciated our efforts on behalf of their loved ones.

We also had to keep a sharp eye out for the opportunists who were eager to appear helpful, but only in order to get close enough to crawl into Perot's deep pockets. An example of this was a group of gold smugglers we met in Singapore who told us they could get our men out of North Vietnam. We were naturally skeptical but felt we had to hear them out. After all, help sometimes comes from the unlikeliest of places.

This smarmy group of characters assured us that, for the low, low price of $50,000 per man (combined cash and commodities—it seems everyone is a true capitalist at heart), they could deliver more than 400 men. If they could deliver, it would have been worth every dollar spent.

But Perot didn't get where he was in business by being stupid. When the smugglers demanded payment up front, we didn't have to go to the Better Business Bureau to smell a scam. Time to call their bluff and see what cards they held.

"We need some assurances," we told them. "First, we want proof that not a single dollar we pay will end up in North Vietnam."

That one didn't bother them too much. I suppose it was a bit far-fetched on our part to think, in the first place, that men who made their livings smuggling would be political or ideological enough to support a war effort. On the other hand, we didn't want dollars they might spend paying bribes to end up in the hands of the more ideological. It was ironic, of course, to think of the more ideological as willing to accept bribes.

Our next request was more problematic for them: We demanded proof that they could deliver. Who are your contacts? What are your plans? Where are the POWs located, and how are you going to lead them out? I guess the bright side was that their waffling was proof that none of the money would end up in North Vietnam; instead, they were just going to pocket it and run.

In April of 1970 we undertook one of our largest and most successful campaigns. As groups of Americans continued to descend on the North Vietnamese delegation in Paris, where they were continually rebuffed, we decided to try a bit of reverse psychology. The North Vietnamese weren't letting the world see the condition of the prisoners they were holding, so how about letting the world see the condition of those being held in South Vietnam?

With the help of my old friends at the ABC News Bureau in Saigon, through Bureau Chief Charles P. Arnot, we got approval from United States and South Vietnamese leaders to tour prisoner camps in the South holding North Vietnamese and Viet Cong POWs. We invited more than one hundred newspeople, mostly from the United States, to join us on the tour, and set up headquarters at the Caravelle Hotel, adjacent to TuDo Street, the black market center of Saigon.

When we arrived, the manager of the Caravelle came out to greet the American billionaire. Perot, dressed in khaki slacks and a short-sleeved sports shirt, introduced himself to the manager, whose first words were, "Nice to meet you. Where is your father?" Apparently, he thought Perot was far too young to be a billionaire. Who could blame him?

We divided the newspeople into four groups, then set off on our tour of the POW camps in the South. The media representatives were encouraged to film the prisoners and their surroundings, which depicted a group of men in good health, living in good conditions, obviously being treated well. We then took that film to the North Vietnamese Embassy in Laos and offered it to them.

"You can see for yourselves how your men are being treated," we told them. "All we ask is that you allow us into your camps to film the American POWs."

Not surprisingly, they refused to accept the film or to give us access to the camps in Hanoi. Fairness was not high on their priority list. Then, in a remarkable bit of denial, obviously meant for public consumption, they disavowed even having any men in the South. It didn't seem to bother them that the proof of their lie resided within the very film canisters they refused to accept.

Next stop: Paris, again. Armed with the film, and with cameras rolling, Perot and I went to the North Vietnamese delegation with the same offer we had made at the Embassy in Laos. They were polite but firm: "No, thank you."

When all was said and done, we had not succeeded in gaining any concessions from the North Vietnamese but had succeeded in the public relations war. Massive worldwide television coverage of our trip had turned up the heat, which had a positive effect on the American POWs. The changes implemented by the North Vietnamese were small, such as allowing the POWs to write letters to their families back home, but they were still changes. And this was a battle we were determined to win, small change by small change if necessary.

And we finally won that battle in February of 1973.

When I first became involved with the POWs and their families, I had no idea how deeply this effort would take root in my heart. I initially thought it was just another news story—a very worthwhile story, but a story nonetheless. Boy, was I ever wrong.

Meeting young women who didn't know if they were wives or widows. Meeting mothers who didn't know if they would see their sons again. Seeing children who couldn't remember their fathers or, like Ricky Singleton, had never seen their fathers. It was all about people. Real people.

The story played out against the backdrop of an enemy that denied the brutality and torture they dealt to young American servicemen around the clock and a government in Washington, D.C., that couldn't even tell the families whether their loved ones were dead or alive. Add to the mix the dedication of a local television station in Dallas, Texas, and the commitment of a dyed-in-the-red-white-and-blue, self-made billionaire, and it became much more than a story.

After pulling up my stakes and moving from behind an anchor desk to devote myself full-time to it, and traveling the world several times, things all fell into place when Hanoi finally released the American POWs in February of 1973. After their return, the POWs wasted no time telling us how our efforts had helped improve their conditions. You have no idea how good that made all of us at United We Stand feel.

I still remember, vividly, standing on the tarmac at Sheppard Air Force Base in Wichita Falls, Texas, waiting for a plane to land. Watching an attractive young woman standing less than ten feet away with her three children—two daughters and a son—anxiously waiting for the same plane. Nervous. Anticipating.

Then the plane touched down, the stairs dropped, and out stepped Col. Samuel Robert Johnson. Gaunt, long-suffering—but home at last!

Tears came to my eyes as I watched Shirley Johnson, daughters Gini and Beverly, and son Bobby race to a loving husband she hadn't seen in years. He put his arms around her and around his children as they reached him. And they hugged. Oh, how they hugged.

Without a doubt, more than just a story.

It was the most rewarding moment in my professional life.

CHAPTER 6

Perot's Plan B in Iran

*"You are the man in real life I am always playing
in the movies. It is an honor to meet you."*
—JOHN WAYNE TO COL. ARTHUR "BULL" SIMONS

The return of the POWs and the end of America's involvement in the Vietnam War seemed to breathe new life into America's spirit. It was almost as if the nation had just taken a deep breath and exhaled—suddenly expelling the bad taste that more than a decade of mouthwash had failed to erase. The nation had heroes again. Real live heroes, not just silver screen heroes. At the White House and throughout the country, parties were thrown saluting the POWs and their families as Americans welcomed home men who had given so much for their country. San Francisco, Las Vegas, and Dallas hosted parties, and Ross Perot and his people were involved in each of these.

Not content just to see the POWs return, Perot also wanted to honor them for their service. He, perhaps above all others, and certainly above all private citizens, had done more to try to bring them home. The extent of his efforts would only later become fully known.

One of those parties, in San Francisco the weekend of April 27, 1973, reunited a group of POWs with the Son Tay Raiders, a force that had unsuccessfully attempted a daring rescue effort to free them. A group of fifty-three highly trained Green Berets, under the leadership of Col. Arthur "Bull" Simons, had arrived at Son Tay in North Vietnam, just thirty miles from Hanoi, in December 1970, to rescue a group of POWs held nearby. Somehow the North Vietnamese had gotten wind of the rescue effort under way and had moved the POWs just in time.

With the war over, Perot determined that Colonel Simons and his Green Berets should meet the men they had been denied the opportunity to rescue. With that in mind, he asked several former POWs where such a meeting should be held, and when they told him San Francisco, he dispatched trusted employee Tom Meurer to make the arrangements.

The weekend started with a ticker-tape parade featuring San Francisco's fabled cable cars loaded down with former POWs and the Son Tay Raiders. Perot, the man who spent a quarter of a million dollars of his own money to make the weekend happen, observed the festivities from the background, remaining inconspicuous among thousands who lined the parade route, showering the men with confetti.

Following the parade, a luncheon was held at the Hilton Hotel, highlighted by Red Skelton's antics and John Wayne's salute. Next, cruises on chartered boats around Alcatraz Island, with the guests entertained by strolling violinists. At noon on Saturday, in an emotional meeting, the Son Tay Raiders finally had the chance to talk with the POWs they had tried to rescue. The weekend concluded with a star-filled evening at the Fairmont Hotel's Venetian Room. And star-filled it was, as the guests of honor mingled with the likes of John Wayne, Clint Eastwood, Red Skelton, Ernest Borgnine, The Andrews Sisters, and Nancy Reagan. It seemed as if the stars were as "star-struck" meeting the Green Berets as were the Green Berets meeting the stars.

"You are the man in real life I am always playing in the movies," John Wayne said upon being introduced to Bull Simons. "It is an honor to meet you." And it was just as big an honor for those Green Berets, who had traveled halfway around the world for the weekend, to sit up all night with The Duke in his hotel suite, swapping stories.

Bull Simons later recalled what he saw as striking differences between Perot's attitude toward the POWs and the Son Tay Raiders and that of official Washington. About a year after the Son Tay Raid, Chairman of the Joint Chiefs Admiral Moorer had invited Simons and other officers who were involved in Son Tay to lunch at the

Pentagon with Defense Secretary Melvin Laird, Gen. William C. Westmoreland, and other top brass. Simons thought it seemed like a bunch of "nonsense" to fly all day just to have lunch. As he put it, "The Pentagon trip was just a drill. A kind of calculated drill, as a matter of fact. What they were doing was taking you out of circulation on the anniversary of the Son Tay raid so the newspaper can't get anybody, not that I think they were interested in getting at them, anyway."

But the celebration in San Francisco? "It's authentic; it's real," Simons said. "I've been to a million damn receptions where the same people look at other people and say the same damn stupid things to them. The thing in San Francisco was entirely different."

Less than two months later, on June 2, 1973, Perot opened his Dallas estate for a lavish private party in the POWs' honor. That evening, despite threatening weather, more than 35,000 people descended on the Cotton Bowl in Dallas for another star-studded tribute, headlined by that great ambassador to our military, Bob Hope. High in the upper deck sat Ross Perot, again away from the limelight. Only a prodding by Hope got him to even take a bow.

Patriotism was never more prevalent on the grounds of the State Fair of Texas than on that glorious June night when Dallas said "Thanks!" to a very special group of heroes. I had the thrill of personally introducing each of the 415 former POWs and their spouses as they entered the stadium to take their places in the special section in front of the giant stage. Unfortunately, my exhilaration ended abruptly when I was called away from my emceeing chores to a Dallas hospital, where my wonderful mother-in-law, Mrs. J. I. Royal, finally lost her long battle with cancer.

Perot's involvement with the former POWs continued for years thereafter. It was as if he felt a personal obligation to those men long after their return. I believe he did, in fact, feel such an obligation because of the sacrifices they had made for him and the rest of the nation as we lived in comfort while they had suffered for our honor.

Two years after the homecoming parties, Perot used the retirement of Brig. Gen. Robbie Risner at Nellis Air Force Base in Las Vegas as the focal point for yet another POW reunion. Joyce and I went to Vegas a week early to make the arrangements. The cooperation we received in putting the weekend together was mind-boggling. Jack Binion and his father, Benny Binion, owners of the downtown Horseshoe Casino, put us in contact with the people who could make things happen in a hurry—and happen in a hurry they did. It seemed as if Vegas itself suddenly wanted to help honor the POWs in any way possible, from special dispensation from unions to cooperation from Vegas Strip hotels and entertainers.

Perot then flew in nearly 500 former POWs and their spouses from around the country for an unforgettable weekend at Caesar's Palace. The retirement of Brigadier General Risner, who had been a ranking POW brutalized by the North Vietnamese, occurred Saturday morning; Saturday evening, in the gigantic Caesar's Palace ballroom, a galaxy of stars, including Robert Goulet, Nipsy Russell, Phyllis McGuire, and a host of other Las Vegas regulars, entertained General Risner and his many friends.

Perot had arrived on that Friday with his wife and two older children, Ross, Jr., and Nancy. In the midst of all the hoopla, we made special arrangements for the kids to enjoy the weekend, too. Those arrangements included an escorted visit to the observation walkways above the casino used by security to observe the activities below. Just as the weekend proved memorable for the former POWs, Perot made sure it proved memorable for his family as well. And no one enjoyed the occasion more than the man paying the tab.

—◈◈◈—

"Hell, yes! When do we start?"
—COL. ARTHUR "BULL" SIMONS

Little did Ross Perot know that from all his activities on behalf of the POWs he would make a contact that would help him solve a crucial business problem later in his career. In fact, it led to one of those amazing moments that, if you had written it as a novel, people would have dismissed as being too fantastic.

By late 1978, Perot's company, EDS, had become involved in a number of computer projects in Iran, but the revolution that had displaced the Shah of Iran threatened the security of its employees there. Additionally, Iran had fallen behind on payments due for completed work under its contracts. So EDS delivered an ultimatum: Unless Iran immediately paid its delinquent bills, the company would withdraw all its employees from the country and shut down all the computer systems.

The ultimatum didn't sit well with the Iranians.

With his mother critically ill back in Dallas, Perot had reluctantly gone to Vail, Colorado, with his family for their traditional post-Christmas ski trip. On December 28 he received a phone call at his villa from Bill Gayden, president of EDS World, telling him that Iran had arrested EDS employees Paul Chiapparone and Bill Gaylord and thrown them into an Iranian jail.

With the same single-mindeness of purpose he had shown in his efforts to free the POWs, Perot immediately drove through a snowstorm from Vail to the Denver airport and caught a flight to Dallas. He initially focused on diplomatic channels to free his employees, working through contacts in Washington, D.C., such as Henry Kissinger and Adm. Thomas Moorer. They tried to placate Perot, telling him that the American government was already pursuing avenues to secure the release of Chiapparone and Gaylord. But as hours became days and his men remained in jail, it became clear to Perot that they were being held as hostages, not mere prisoners.

"The objective in holding these men as hostages was to assure that we would come back in and start up the computer systems when Iran went back to work," Perot said. "They felt that their best assurance was to hold our employees as hostages and later propose bail of twelve-million-seven-hundred-fifty-thousand dollars."

Perot put together a negotiating team to fly to Tehran to negotiate the release of the men through the Iranian legal system, but to no avail. He immediately swung into Plan B.

And what was Plan B?

Bull Simons.

Things had not gone so well for Simons since Perot's last contact with him. Now a pig farmer in Red Bay, Florida, he had fallen into a deep depression after losing his wife, Lucille, to cancer in March of 1978. The once-proud military man of thirty-five years seemed to have lost his will for life, giving darker thoughts free reign in his mind, at least temporarily. He had even let his hair grow a bit longer than usual—long by Bull Simons standards but still short by military standards.

He tried to keep busy by resuming gunsmith work he had done before in the Red Bay area. He also hoped to utilize a small sawmill he had purchased to mill timber from his forty-acre farm and was occasionally called back to Fort Bragg as a weapons consultant. But through it all, Lucille remained ever-present on his mind, even keeping him from sleep. He spent most nights in a recliner, not a bed, since sleep wouldn't come anyway.

"I thought about burning the house down," he said, "but then I said 'no, I'll give it a year and try to pull myself back together.'"

This was a far different Bull Simons from the one I had spent a day with in June of 1976 on the back screened porch of that same Red Bay farm. During that interview, Simons first told me his impressions of Ross Perot, who, unknown to either of us then, was soon to reenter Simons's life in dramatic fashion.

"So I say to myself," Simons said, "this is just a little different kind of human being here. Here is a guy who has decided something is worthwhile and he does something about it. There are a million people who sit down and say, 'my, isn't that terrible,' or 'isn't that too bad,' or 'isn't it too bad that somebody isn't helping these people.' But I find out through all these years he has been in contact with these POW wives, trying to solve small problems for them. And this is all un-public, un-political, un-anything. And he is spending, in fact, hundreds of thousands of dollars. And I see other people who donate something to somebody and, you know, there is umpteen damn inches in the newspaper, every itty-bitty thing. He does it because he wants to, and the fact that he wants to makes him a different guy."

When Tom Marquez called Bull Simons on Perot's behalf at almost 2:00 early one January morning in 1979, he caught Simons sitting in that recliner. Marquez explained the situation in Iran to Simons, then asked if he'd be interested in helping rescue the imprisoned EDS employees. Perhaps the request raised Simons's recently lost sense of purpose. Or maybe it just took him back, in his mind, to the raid at Son Tay. Either way, his response was curt and direct.

"Hell, yes! When do we start?"

The next day, as it turned out. Simons left his pigs behind and flew to Dallas. By the time he arrived, he had gotten a shorter haircut and again showed that familiar spark of leadership that was so deeply embedded in his career. If there was any doubt that this was the Simons of old, Bull quickly put that to rest when Merv Stauffer and Tom Marquez picked him up at the airport.

"Merv had a brand new car," Marquez remembers. "No one had

ever smoked in it. Simons, if he was awake, usually had a small cigar in his mouth. He was awake and had the cigar going full blast. Stauffer rolled down a window to get some air. Temperatures were sub-freezing outside the car and Colonel Simons asked if the window could be raised. It was too cold with it open. The window was closed, the cigar smoke filled Stauffer's new car—the Bull had prevailed again."

The Iranian rescue came together in Stauffer's EDS office. There, in what was to become the nerve center for the operation, Perot brought Simons up to speed. As Marquez had been tracking down Simons and bringing him to Dallas, Perot had been putting together his team for the mission. As Perot described it, "We identified all EDS personnel that had lived in Tehran and who had prior records as Marine officers, Rangers, Special Forces officers, Army officers, and others with specialized training that would be necessary for such an extraction. I met privately with each individual on January first. I told each man, privately, that I was about to discuss something with him that could cost him his life and if, for any reason, he should not be involved, our discussion would go no further. Every man I talked to volunteered."

But the key would be Bull Simons.

> "These guys are Americans and it doesn't make any difference whether they have blue suits on, or brown or green suits, or what the hell. They are entitled to feel that their own goddamn countrymen will make an effort at getting them out. And, by God, that's why we are going to get them out!"
>
> —COL. ARTHUR "BULL" SIMONS

Simons had been one of the toughest leaders in the United States Army, a motion that would have been seconded by everyone who had served under him in three wars and would, no doubt, be doubly seconded by the fifty-three men that he molded into the Son Tay Raiders. The Raiders had not known what their mission would be until weeks into their training when Simons announced it to them using, in part, the words quoted above. When he finished and started to walk away from his men, "These guys all stood up and started to applaud," Simons said. "I never saw anything like that in my life in the Army."

Simons found that same kind of attitude prevailing with the EDS team Ross Perot had put together—a team which included men like Ralph Boulware, Joe Poche, Ron Davis, Pat Sculley, Jim Schwebach, Glenn Jackson, and Jay Coburn. The team trained under Simons at Perot's weekend retreat at Lake Grapevine, northwest of Dallas. By mid-January, they were on the move, some to Iran, the rest to other assigned locations overseas. Those who went to Tehran with Simons stayed in a "safe house" rather than a hotel. They all wore black stocking caps and had let their facial hair grow in order to blend in with Iranians as much as possible.

As Bull Simons set his plan in motion, it brought back memories of those days before Son Tay. The setting and mission might have been different, but the emotions were just as real, the fear just as palpable. And his feelings about his team ran just as deep.

Speaking of Son Tay, Simons said, "Trained soldiers get pretty cool after a while. They are born skeptics; they're always looking for what you are *not* saying. The goal of the mission, to rescue POWs, made them want to do the thing so bad they could taste it."

And what of his team for the Iranian mission? "I had that same sensation. That this is something important to do, more important than anything else you've ever done, because you are so emotionally involved in it."

When Simons arrived in Tehran, he was put up in a private residence belonging to another EDS World employee, Keane Taylor, who then checked into the Hyatt Regency, where other members of the team were staying under the guise of "negotiators." With Simons and his Tehran team in place, Perot decided to fly to Iran—against the advice of his attorney, Tom Luce, and virtually everyone else, including Simons. The question was how to get there, since commercial air traffic into Iran was not feasible I contacted a friend at my former network, ABC-TV, who told me that the networks often used courier jets from Amman, Jordan, to fly their film in and out of Iran.

Sounded good to Perot, who headed for Amman and boarded a courier jet that was transporting film for NBC. Using his own name and passport, he walked through Iranian customs with film as if he were a real courier. He checked in at the Hyatt Regency and was then taken to Taylor's "safe house" to meet with Simons. From there, it was on to the massive Gasr Military Jail in Tehran that housed Chiapparone and Gaylord.

The two EDS men had no idea Perot was coming to visit them, bearing letters from their families. Paul Chiapparone recently told me, "We were shocked, elated, overjoyed, misty-eyed, when he handed us letters from our families. He was totally unexpected. His visit uplifted us in a way nothing else could have."

The two men hadn't been mistreated physically, but the experience was harrowing nevertheless, particularly not knowing if or when they would be released. Initially having been thrown into a tank with seven or eight other men, they were later moved to an area above the jail's mental ward, where they were forced to listen to screams from the mindless prisoners below. "Listening to all the sounds from around us and knowing there was a revolution going on—there were some anxious moments," Chiapparone said.

In an hourlong meeting with his employees—his friends—Perot told them that deliverance was at hand. He told them what to expect and where to go when the time came. He also picked up personal intelligence from being able to see, firsthand, the jail where they were being held. Though they had originally been held in a smaller jail, the Gasr Military Jail housed thousands of prisoners. Although it might have been feasible to forcibly extract them from the first jail with a small group of men, Perot quickly saw that would be impossible at Gasr.

"My visit to the prison and my visit with Colonel Simons confirmed what Colonel Simons already knew—our team was too small to extract these men from prison by force," Perot said. "Some other method had to be developed."

Simons counseled patience, noting that with every revolution, the people eventually overrun the prisons to free political prisoners. Nothing like using political unrest to your own advantage—and wise counsel it turned out to be. The Iranian revolution was in full swing, with hundreds of people killed daily in the streets of Tehran. Martial law had been declared, and tanks had been positioned around the city to protect police stations. With unrest the rule, it was a relatively simple matter for Perot to arrange with revolutionary leaders to whip the crowds into a frenzy to storm the prison.

And storm the prison they did, breaking down the doors and

flooding inside, while the prisoners flooded out. Rashid, an Iranian guide working with Simons's team, waited near the prison to lead Gaylord and Chiapparone to the Hyatt Regency, where Simons waited. In the ensuing confusion, Rashid missed seeing them as they tried to blend in with the crowds of escaping prisoners.

"It was very touch and go," said Chiapparone. "The jail where we were held was in a very religious part of Tehran. I blended in with the locals very easily—dark hair, dark skin. But Bill was light-skinned, very American-looking, and that made us move more carefully."

Meanwhile, Perot had returned to Dallas, where he awaited word. As part of the plan, neither he nor Simons would speak on the telephone connection that had been established between Dallas and Tehran, but others would relay information to him. As soon as he knew his friends were safely in Turkey, he would activate his chartered 707 to fly them home. Perot also had two helicopters standing by in Istanbul, ready at a moment's notice to fly into Iran and physically extract the two men if it came to that.

Back in Tehran, Rashid returned to the Hyatt and reported his failure to find the two EDS men. Simons's team was just preparing to fan out into the streets to search for them when they arrived at the hotel, still dressed in prison garb.

"We hitchhiked and made our way through the chaotic bedlam that filled the streets all the way to our hotel meeting place," Chiapparone said. "I don't know exactly how far it was from the jail to the hotel, but it took us more than two hours to get there." [They had traveled ten miles.] We thought we could take a slow, tingling shower, relax a bit and then have a good steak, something we had not had for quite a while. But the Colonel said, 'Let's hitch it up; we've got to move.'"

The two men stripped out of their prison clothes and dressed in dark clothing, then it was immediately off to another safe house, residence of yet another EDS employee. It was a good thing they moved so quickly, too, because less than two hours later, Iranian authorities arrived at the Hyatt looking for them.

The team waited at the new safe house for three days and then headed overland for Turkey in two Range Rovers, guided by Rashid. Things were still a little dicey because neither of the liberated prisoners had his passport—only fake ones. "The picture on mine could have been me if you stretched the imagination," Chiapparone said, "but Bill's picture looked nothing like him. So when we were stopped en route to the Turkish border, we always tried to hold our fingers over the pictures."

In fact, they were stopped several times as their route took them through many tribal areas. Simons had schooled Rashid in what to say and how to handle each questioning, and they ultimately arrived safely at the Turkish border. There, Rashid negotiated with the Turkish border guards to accept the Range Rovers in exchange for passage into Turkey.

Ralph Boulware was supposed to meet the team at the border, but he wasn't there when they arrived. Three tense hours passed while they waited. When he finally arrived, they learned he had encountered difficulties of his own. His transportation had broken down repeatedly during his 1,000-mile journey, and he had traveled the last 600 miles through remote mountains by taxis. One can just imagine what the tip would have been on a fare like that in the United States.

While waiting on Boulware, someone had remembered that thousands of dollars in cash for bribes had been stashed, in waterproof containers, inside five-gallon oil drums in the Range Rovers. Rashid recrossed the border to retrieve the cans, convincing the guards that he and his friends needed the oil to rub on their skin as protection from the sun. The guards bought it and allowed Rashid to take one oil can back into Turkey.

At last the group made it to Istanbul, where Perot's chartered 707 waited to take them to Frankfurt, Germany. Once airborne, Chiapparone and Gaylord were officially free men again.

Champagne flowed as the men ate, and Colonel Simons again fired up his small cigars, celebrating their repatriation. Fortunately, they had not had to use their weapons, although they had been instructed on what to do if the need had arisen. Perhaps Simons had given the EDS team the same instructions he had given his men prior to Son Tay: "You will let nobody stand in your way—nobody. I don't want you to go in there and deliberately murder a bunch of women and children, but you will let nobody stand in your way. I will take the responsibility for whatever you do."

Back in Dallas, the two EDS men enjoyed a tearful reunion with their families at DFW Airport. While watching those family reunions, Simons, who had refused payment, told Perot, "Seeing this makes everything paid in full."

Next came a meeting with the press at EDS headquarters. Perot gave a broad overview of the origins of the Iranian problem and how he had put together the rescue team. He then called on Chiapparone, Gaylord, and Simons for remarks. My guess is that it had been a long time since such a large group of reporters left a news conference so wide-eyed and speechless.

And, truth be told, the ending could have turned out much differently because of the press. The *Dallas Times Herald* had somehow heard of the mission and broken the story *before* the group was out of Iran. The paper said its information was that the men had already reached safety. Endangering lives had not taken a back seat to its zeal to be first with a story, the paper claimed.

After the news conference, Perot asked Tom Marquez, Merv Stauffer, and me to take Colonel Simons to dinner. We headed to Arthur's, at Northpark Center, just a seven-minute drive from EDS headquarters on Forest Lane. Over dinner, as Colonel Simons twirled his double Chivas Regal on the rocks, I asked him what had been the most satisfying thing about the mission. Without hesitating, he answered, "Shoving it up that Iranian SOB's rear who wanted thirteen million dollars bail for Paul and Bill's release."

The Iranian rescue was like a shot in the arm for Simons, breathing new life into him. He spent a lot of time after that at Perot's villa in Vail and also in the guest cottage at Perot's Dallas home. In March 1979, when he suffered a heart attack in Vail, Perot sent his jet, with doctors aboard, to fly him back to Dallas for medical care.

Because the story of the rescue had been played so prominently in the Dallas press, and with a growing contingent of Iranian nationals in the Dallas area, off-duty members of the Dallas Police Tactical Squad stood guard outside the Colonel's door at Baylor Hospital. Simons also kept a .357 Magnum beneath his pillow. When told he couldn't keep a gun in his room, he said, "Who's going to take it away from me?"

As it turned out, no one tried to harm him during his hospital stay, but his heart condition proved to be a lethal enemy. Awaiting surgery, he said, in his own inimitable style, "They tell me I will come out of here walking, or feet-first. I'm ready for either one."

It turned out to be feet-first. Tough as nails to the very end, Colonel Simons died of heart failure on May 21, 1979, at the age of sixty.

—◇◆◇—

"He made brave men braver and proud men prouder. He instilled courage in his men and fear in his enemies. He personified the iron fist in a velvet glove. Compassionate and kind to his friends, he was unrelenting when fighting for his country."
—Brig. Gen. Robinson Risner

After he had returned to Dallas from Iran, I spoke with Colonel Simons about the raid.

"I spent my whole life in the Army," he said, "so I am used to working with people who are used to being in semi-violent, moderate risk at least, situations. I am struck now by two things. I don't know of any other company in the world that would attempt something like this. They would either let nature take its course or the government handle it."

Simons was also impressed with the quality of the team Perot had put together—military experience, sure, but civilians nonetheless. "During all of the training and during the operation, I never heard one of them complain."

That wasn't something he could say about all of his Raiders on the Son Tay mission. "I had some trouble with one man ... I told him I would hang him. I said, 'By God, I'll mount your goddamn head on the wall and stick an apple in your goddamn mouth.'"

That man ultimately came around. "As a matter of fact, he was one of the few guys that was hit by rifle fire as we went into North Vietnam. The demolition pack on his back got hit and it knocked him completely to the ground, and he just rolled over and kept on going."

But Simons never had to threaten to mount heads on the Perot rescue team. "I sent people out to do things that had a very high level of risk to them and they went out without a word of complaint, without asking me why ... and with a great desire to do it. So I felt ... that I had the best people in the world that you could work with. I am somewhat dazzled by that at this point in the game because these people operate with highly sophisticated machines, not submachine guns."

He also found that working with Perot offered advantages he never had while in the military. "Everything that I asked for I got without any bureaucratic quiveling around, without military property officers asking you why you needed it, and without the delays that are inherent within the military establishment because that's the way it operates. Here, anything you asked for you got instantly, and some of what was asked for was over a range of 3,000 miles and was delivered as fast as it was humanly possible to get it there."

Funeral services were held for Bull Simons at Highland Park Presbyterian Church in Dallas. Four former Vietnam POWs and one Iranian hostage—Adm. Jeremiah Denton, Col. George "Bud" Day, Lt. Col. Orson Swindle, Capt. Render Crayton, and Paul Chiapparone—offered brief eulogies. Members of the Son Tay Raiders served as pallbearers for the service, which was also attended by the EDS Iran Rescue team, numerous former POWs, and members of the Dallas Police Tactical Team who had guarded Colonel Simons in the hospital during their off-duty hours.

In his eulogy, Paul Chiapparone said, "Both of my parents passed away a few years ago. I was deeply saddened because I lost the two people who gave me my first opportunity in life. Today I feel exactly the same way about the loss of Colonel Simons. Only a parent would care enough to do for Bill and me what Colonel Simons did."

Gen. Robbie Risner, another former POW, offered this: "Some of us owe our lives to the Son Tay Raiders and to Bull Simons's leadership. Colonel Simons loved his country and his fellow man. He was fiercely proud of our freedoms and repeatedly laid his life on the line for them. His motto might have been, 'I do not choose to be a common man. It is my right to be uncommon if I can. I seek opportunity, not security. I will never cower before any master nor bend to any threat. It is my heritage to stand erect, proud, and unafraid; to think and act for myself, enjoy the benefit of my creations, and to face the world boldly and say *this I have done*.'

"Bull Simons's eyes have seen the glory of the coming of the Lord."

Ross Perot, followed by Murphy Martin, president of United We Stand, leaves North Vietnamese Embassy in Vientiane, Laos, after meeting with North Vietnam representatives in December 1969.

126

Ross Perot, seen talking with Peggy Wheedon, producer of ABC-TV's Issues and Answers, prior to start of program in Washington in 1970. At top of picture, bending over, is Murphy Martin; ABC's Ted Koppel is between Martin and Perot. The program was hosted by John Scali, seen with back to camera at left.

Murphy Martin and his wife, Joyce, are seen here with three of the four POW wives they escorted to Paris for the first meeting ever with the North Vietnamese peace delegation. Wives seen here are Joy Jeffrey, Sandy McElhanon, and Paula Hartness. Not seen is Bonnie Singleton.

Murphy Martin and Ross Perot discuss plans for meeting with North Vietnamese en route to Southeast Asia in December 1969. They carried thirty tons of cargo, which they hoped to deliver to the POWs held in North Vietnam.

Ross Perot eats from box lunch aboard charter flight carrying 100 newsmen from Saigon to Da Nang to inspect POW camps in the south in 1970. South Vietnamese Officer Thanh is on Perot's left.

Four POW wives hold news conference in Paris Chamber of Commerce offices following meeting with North Vietnamese peace delegation seeking information about their husbands. Left to right: Mrs. Robert Jeffrey, Mrs. Gregg Hartness, Mrs. Jerry Singleton, and Mrs. Michael McElhanon. Murphy Martin, who with his wife accompanied the wives to Paris, is seen standing at the right.

Perot arriving in Vientiane, Laos, in 1970 to meet with North Vietnamese seeking information about American POWs held in North Vietnam. Murphy Martin is immediately behind Perot.

Ross Perot and Martin, 1970, inside POW camp in South Vietnam, where North Vietnamese and Viet Cong prisoners were detained.

From left: Murphy Martin, Ross Perot, Father Matt Menger, and Perot assistant Sharon Holman leave Pathet Lao headquarters in Vientiane, Laos, following meeting with Soth Pethrasi regarding POWs in 1970.

Mr. and Mrs. Murphy Martin meet with Le Phu Hou, head of the North Vietnamese News Agency, at the North Vietnam compound in Choisy le Roi, outside Paris, in 1969. This was the initial contact that opened the doors for subsequent meetings with the North Vietnamese about American POWs.

Ross Perot and Murphy Martin answer questions from the press following efforts to deliver film of North Vietnamese prisoners held in South Vietnam. The meeting in Choisy le Roi, just outside Paris, was in April 1970.

From left: (front row) Murphy Martin with briefcase, Tom Marquez and Major Ma Son Qui, camp commander of POW facility being inspected by Ross Perot in short-sleeved shirt behind Martin, and POW wives seen to the right of Major Qui.

130

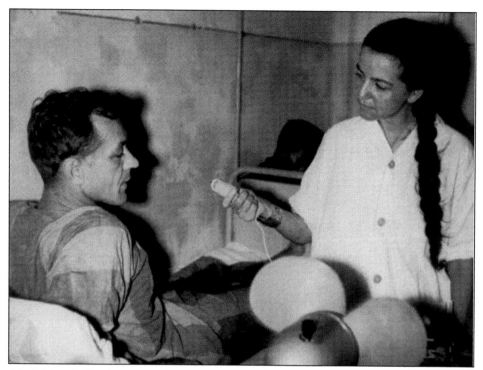

Madeleine Riffaud, communist reporter, one of many Murphy Martin dealt with while working the POW problems for Ross Perot, is seen talking to downed U.S. pilot Colonel Kasler.

Murphy Martin with South Vietnamese officer in Da Nang, 1970.

Seaman Douglas Hegdahl sweeping yard in North Vietnamese prison, where he was detained after being captured at sea. Hegdahl received an early release and worked with United We Stand in trying to obtain additional information about American POWs.

Martin interviews Col. Samuel Robert Johnson, Air Force pilot who was a POW for nearly eight years in North Vietnam. Johnson's reunion with his family at Sheppard AFB in Wichita Falls, Texas, provided Martin with what he calls "the most rewarding moment in my career."

Col. Samuel Robert Johnson speaks at Memorial Day Service in Dallas in 1973. Murphy Martin is seated in lower right of picture.

Martin proposes a toast to just released POW Col. Samuel Robert Johnson in Plano, Texas, which Johnson now represents as a U.S. congressman.

Col. Bull Simons led rescue of EDS employees from an Iranian jail.

Ross Perot (left) and Col. Bull Simons (right) meet the press in Dallas following rescue of EDS employees Paul Chiapparone and Bill Gaylord from Iranian jail, where they were being held for $13 million bail.

The colonel briefing his men prior to the Son Tay Raid in North Vietnam. After his retirement, Simons helped Ross Perot gain release of two key employees from Iranian jails.

133

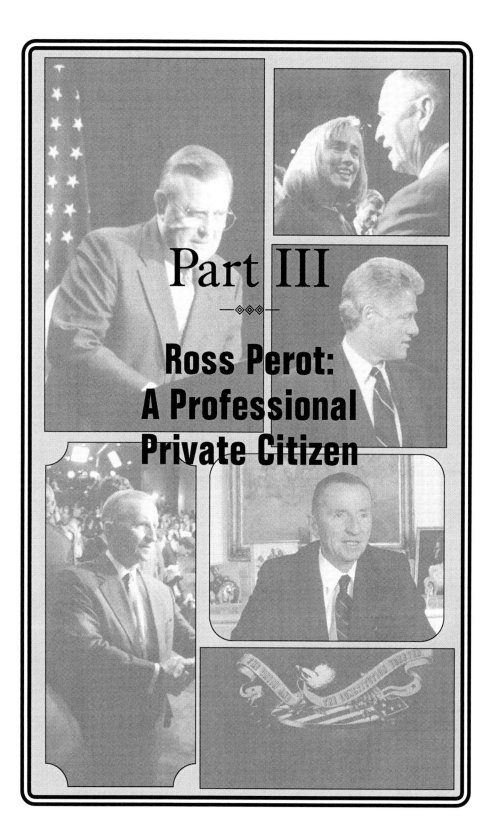

Part III

❖❖❖

Ross Perot:
A Professional
Private Citizen

CHAPTER 7

What's $100 Million, More or Less?

> *"We were wooed, lured, and attracted, and, if that's seduced, then yes, I would say we were certainly wooed, encouraged, and pleaded with to put money in the Street. Then, once we had the money in the Street, the Street had no obligation to keep its arms around us."*
> —H. Ross Perot

Hello, Wall Street, good-bye $100 million. Sound familiar? The eight-year bull run of the 1990s and the bursting of the tech bubble in 2000 hit a lot of families right in the stock portfolio, where it hurts. A lot of well-known names in industry lost hundreds of millions of dollars, but chances are no one really mourned for them. Their affliction, at least as viewed by the average American, was greed, and, perhaps, they got exactly what they deserved. After all, the cynic would say, $100 million isn't what it used to be. Certainly not what it was in 1970, when Ross Perot's $5 million investment in Wall Street brokerage firm F.I. DuPont quickly snowballed into a nearly $100 million loss.

Today's venture capitalists who lost big in the stock market simply gambled and lost along the way to obscene wealth. But Perot's loss was different. He hadn't invested just to make a buck. No, he had been *asked* to invest by folks from Wall Street to Pennsylvania Avenue who played on his patriotism. His goal? He was trying to save Wall Street.

Was he successful? Well, had trading volumes inched upward just slightly in the early '70s, Perot would probably have been hailed as the "Savior of Wall Street" instead of being castigated for being in over his head with his inexperienced management team. But the bottom line is that here we are, three decades later, and Wall Street is still alive and kicking.

So what happened back then? What led Perot to get involved with DuPont in the first place, and why did it turn out so disastrously for him?

To understand exactly what happened and what Perot was trying to do, you must first understand the situation that existed on Wall Street at the time. The market had been through a huge bull run at the end of the 1960s, perhaps not unlike that of the 1990s. As an outgrowth, the Street had also experienced unprecedented run-ups in the amounts of shares traded publicly on a daily basis. Although the numbers pale by comparison to today, they were considered almost unbelievable at the time, culminating in volumes of 20 million shares a day—a record that wouldn't be reached again for another decade.

Unfortunately, the "back rooms" of Wall Street brokerage firms, where the day's trades were cleared and the books balanced, were ill-equipped to process the paperwork that accompanied those huge run-ups in volume. In fact, the New York Stock Exchange was even closed early on some days to allow traders to catch up on the backlogs of orders and to allow the back rooms to try to catch up on balancing the books. But, as it turned out, the volumes continued to outpace the firms' abilities to catch up, and the problems simply mushroomed. Soon the brokerage firms found themselves unable to reconcile trades, and there were even concerns that some firms had begun inflating their capital figures just to keep up with the demands.

About that time, the bears came out of hibernation—and with a vengeance, just about knocking the props out from under Wall Street. With the problems already created by the rapid increase in trading volumes of the bull market, coupled with fears of inflated capital, a group of leading Wall Street executives established a "Crisis Committee" to solve the Street's problems and save their own firms in the process. Felix Rohatyn, prominent in the world of Democrat politics and a partner at the brokerage firm of Lazard Freres, chaired this self-regulating body. Another member of the committee was Bernard "Bunny" Lasker, chairman of the New York

Stock Exchange and close personal friend of Republican President Richard Nixon. The looming disaster on Wall Street had created strange bedfellows indeed.

By the time the Crisis Committee had been formed, five smaller firms had already gone into liquidation while larger firms had been, or were being, forced to merge in order to survive. One venerable old firm, Hayden, Stone & Co., which had been around for eighty years and which serviced more than 100,000 customers, now teetered on the brink of collapse, a grave concern for the committee. Rohatyn feared, and was even quoted as saying, that if one of the major firms went under, the whole Exchange might collapse. And so the committee set a high priority on regaining stability in the individual firms on the Street by finding merger partners or investors to bail them out.

Another of those in trouble was F. I. DuPont Company, one of the largest and most respected brokerage firms in New York. Like so many firms, its back room had become a mess and its capital position precarious. In an effort to save itself, it merged with two other, also financially shaky, firms in July 1970: Glore, Forgan and Staats & Hirsch. And so, at least for the time being, DuPont escaped liquidation.

It was against this backdrop that Rudolph Smutny first approached Ross Perot to help clean up F. I. DuPont's back room and halt its financial skid. Smutny was familiar with Perot and EDS, having been a partner at R. W. Pressprich & Co., the New York underwriting firm that had taken Electronic Data Systems public in September of 1968. Smutny also had been in close contact with DuPont and knew of their problems. It occurred to him that this might be an ideal opportunity for EDS, which had been quite successful with data processing in other industries such as insurance and banking, to make its first foray into Wall Street.

Perot had not been immune from the ravages of the new bear market, either. On one day in late spring, his EDS stock had dropped from $150 per share to $90 per share, creating a paper loss of more than $400 million in one day. Nevertheless, at the suggestion of Rudy Smutny, in May and June of 1970 Perot sent in a team, including EDS Systems Engineer Mort Meyerson, to review the DuPont back-office data processing. DuPont had contracted with one of its subsidiaries, called Wall Street Leasing, and was paying it

$3 million per year to perform its back-office data processing. Following his review, Perot traded shares of EDS to buy Wall Street Leasing and took over the data processing for DuPont with an eight-year, $8-million-per-year contract.

In the meantime, Wall Street continued to stumble, keeping the Crisis Committee busy. In September 1970, through close monitoring and some hands-on help, the committee successfully saved Hayden Stone. In October, the committee arranged for Merrill Lynch to rescue Goodbody & Company, the fifth largest brokerage firm in the nation. The committee then turned its eyes back to the radar, looking for the next target to salvage.

And DuPont limped onto the scope.

Although EDS had been successfully salvaging the mess in DuPont's back room under its data processing contract, DuPont's mergers with Glore, Forgan and Staats & Hirsch had not solved DuPont's capital woes. By early November, it needed an infusion of fresh capital; however, the DuPont family refused to contribute. In an unprecedented move, the New York Stock Exchange censured DuPont and fined its management for allowing its capital to deplete so rapidly.

DuPont then turned to the billionaire in its back room, looking for capital. As Mort Meyerson said later, "We were not intrigued with the idea. As a matter of fact, we thought it was a terrible idea—but then the pressure was on." And, indeed, pressure there was, as the members of the Crisis Committee called in their markers in Washington, D.C., the New York banking community, and the Stock Exchange community.

Perhaps the most severe pressure came to bear from Richard Nixon's White House, playing on Perot's patriotism. After all, Perot was the man who had made sacrifices, financial and otherwise, to try to bring the POWs home from Hanoi. Who better to bail out Wall Street? And so Perot was deluged with calls from 1600 Pennsylvania Avenue—calls from, among others, Peter Flanigan, formerly a top executive at the Wall Street brokerage firm of Dillon Reed and now on Nixon's staff; Secretary of the Treasury (and former Texas governor) John Connally; and Attorney General John Mitchell—all pressuring the Texan to "do the patriotic thing." After all, they were only talking about $5 million, weren't they? Surely that was nothing to the man who had once told Braniff Airlines he'd buy them a new airplane.

Could Perot, the ultimate patriot, resist that kind of pressure? Could anybody?

—◈◈◈—

"The initial reaction to us when they were trying to seduce us to put money in the firm is that we were intelligent, bright, hard-nosed, and the only people in the world capable and brave enough to make an investment. As soon as we made the investment, that quickly shifted into we were the dumb guys, didn't know the business, and should rely on their judgment."
—Mort Meyerson, EDS Systems engineer

Five million dollars should do it, Perot had been told. And, according to Meyerson, Perot had also been told repeatedly that if DuPont failed, Wall Street itself might collapse. Talk about pressure! As Meyerson said, "The markets had been good to us. We had been products of the American systems ourselves, and we wanted to make a contribution. In addition to that, we thought that we owed some allegiance . . . to the firm. We had been a data processing contractor and we were at that time very sympathetic with their principles.

"Now, those are the altruistic reasons. In addition to that, it did make business sense for us to try to protect a customer."

So, in December 1970, Perot loaned DuPont $5 million. Problem solved.

Or was it?

In early 1971, the New York Stock Exchange sent a team of auditors under Jeff Adler to evaluate the capital structure of DuPont. The news wasn't good. According to Adler's team, DuPont's capital was in much worse shape than anybody, including the EDS folks, had been led to believe. Not only were millions more needed, the auditors froze the initial investment, prohibiting Perot from seeking repayment of his loan. Meyerson said they were told, "You've just been stuck."

In order to save his initial investment, Perot turned the money tap on, pouring capital into DuPont. Now committed financially, he also moved to consolidate control. If he was going to be "stuck," he was at least going to be in a position to try to fix the problems. On

May 14, 1971, he named Meyerson, who was only thirty-two years old, as president of one of the largest and oldest companies in the United States. Almost immediately, Meyerson commissioned an audit to "determine where all the bodies were buried." He even hired Jeff Adler away from the Stock Exchange and added him to the audit department.

The "bodies" included an additional $50 million necessary to keep DuPont alive, which Perot put up. Even that didn't do the trick.

For Perot, continually pouring money into DuPont must have seemed like a losing proposition. Why didn't he cut his losses and pull out? Recalling what he and Perot had been told early on in the "seduction dance," Meyerson explained it this way: "The New York Stock Exchange and the Wall Street community, the leaders of the community—those people told me specifically that, in the event DuPont failed, Merrill Lynch would unwind their Goodbody transaction and that they felt that there was an excellent chance that the capital markets as we know them in New York would cease to function."

Hyperbole? Perhaps, but that wasn't a risk Perot was willing to take. In hindsight, the question arises whether Perot, or anybody, could have turned DuPont around. Not that he didn't try, but the obstacles were formidable—not the least of which was his being viewed as an outsider by Wall Street's stodgy, old money aristocracy. To counter that, Perot had brought in experienced people, like Wally Auch, who had been a fixture on Wall Street since the mid-1950s, and Bob Dunwoody, an "old school" DuPont employee and former branch manager.

Perot even learned to play the merger game. As he said, "Once we were there and they realized the size of the financial resources we brought to the Street, and when they saw us clean up the books, balance the books, clean up the vault and get it back under control, turn the firm around, they realized there was only one thing left to do and that was rebuild the sales force."

In the early part of 1973, under Perot's leadership, DuPont merged again, this time with Walston & Company, a respected New York brokerage house. Perot had invested $4 million in Walston, contracted for EDS to handle its back-office work, and put several EDS representatives on its board of directors. With the financial outlook for DuPont still grim, and hoping to avoid making yet additional cash infusions, Perot wanted to merge DuPont's and Walston's sales and back offices. That way, he could cut costs and increase revenues.

The result, after a heated session with Walston's board, which had to approve the merger, was the second largest retail broker in America next to Merrill Lynch (at least on paper) with 140 branch offices, 2,800 salespeople, and more than 300,000 customers.

But it proved to be too little, too late. World events had combined to make it unlikely that the investing public would move back into the market in sufficient volumes to allow DuPont to again become profitable, at least in the near term. Perot said, "Basically, all the people who were running the firm felt that, in the face of the news of the oil boycott, deteriorating markets, Watergate investigation, Agnew resignation, war in the Middle East, and on and on and on, there was every reason to anticipate a continuation of light volumes in the market."

And so, after an all-day meeting with Wally Auch and Mort Meyerson, Perot finally decided it was time to shut down, take his losses, and move on. "We dug into each other's hearts and souls as far as we could," Auch said. "Finally, Ross Perot looked at me and he asked me just one question: 'Do you believe that you can go out of business and protect our people and make sure that the public doesn't get hurt?'

"I looked at him and Mort looked at him, and Mort and I looked at each other. We said 'yes.'

"And with that he said, 'You got my vote.'"

"I think the feeling was that there was time, at that point, to close the firm in an orderly way to protect the investors," Perot said. "If we ran out the string, so to speak, to see if the market did turn and improve, we could have reduced the capital in the firm to the point where adequate funds would not have been available to close the firm."

That was vintage Perot, wanting to ensure, first and foremost, that the customers would be protected.

And long after he had left Wall Street and DuPont was but an unwanted memory, Perot staffed an office in Dallas with Wall Street people, with only one goal for the office: making sure all DuPont customer accounts, which totaled nearly $3 billion, were transferred without the loss of one single dime.

—◆◆◆—

"Of course, nobody really knew the extent of the DuPont problem. I, at first, thought it was a $5 million problem; I guess it ended up costing Ross $100 million."

—PETER FLANIGAN,
AIDE TO PRESIDENT RICHARD NIXON

The question is still open as to who sold whom a bill of goods while Perot was being enticed into bailing out DuPont. What is not open for debate, however, is the urgency with which others enticed him to act, nor the fervor with which he acted. As I had seen in the late '60s, when he first got involved with the POW-MIA campaign, Perot's love for his country and his patriotism run deep, and he is, and was, willing to back it up with time, money, and effort. Those who singled him out to come to the aid of Wall Street knew this and, I believe, that's exactly why they targeted him.

Over the years, the term "seduced" has often been used to describe the process that started Perot on the way to losing almost $100 million. In late 1976, I asked Peter Flanigan, one of those who had been doing the seducing from the White House, about the use of that term. I found his response particularly interesting—and unsettling.

According to Flanigan, "I think that it was naive to suggest that he was seduced. He went in there to make money, and they wanted him in there to solve a problem. And the fact that he didn't make any money didn't really cause anybody a lot of heartburn, particularly when he said this place was run by a bunch of old stiffs, and that he had a *Fortune* magazine article saying he had one billion six hundred million dollars. The feeling is 'What's a hundred million dollars, more or less?'

"So I don't think there was any excess of nobility on either side, and there wasn't an excess of avarice on either side, either."

I came away from that interview feeling stunned. *What's a hundred million dollars, more or less?* I found it hard to believe that anyone could be that cavalier about *someone else's* money. Sure, Perot is wealthy—but the arrogance of treating his loss as worthy of nothing more than a shoulder-shrug is mind-boggling. This is particularly so when Flanigan was among those playing on Perot's patriotism to solve a $5 million problem that ended up costing almost twenty times that—and Perot did so without flinching because he saw it as his patriotic duty. At least the seducers got that part right.

Was EDS hoping to make money on its investment? Certainly. After all, the company's management had an obligation to its shareholders as well. Does that justify the shoulder-shrug from Flanigan?

Absolutely not. Perot deserved better than that.

And he deserved better than what he got from some in the American press, too.

"It's an ironic commentary on this leadership state of the securities industry that the most visible representative of Wall Street to the nation at large these days is a pint-sized, crew-cut Texas evangelist named Ross Perot—the Billy Graham of American industry."
—THE WALL STREET LETTER, JUNE 11, 1973,
IN AN ARTICLE HEADLINED
"MEET MR. WALL STREET: ROSS PEROT"

I have often wondered, after reading some of the negative stories that appeared in the press after Perot's Wall Street efforts, if that slant contributed to Perot's distrust of the media during his 1992 presidential campaign. If so, I'm not surprised.

Just as Wall Street insiders and politicos such as Peter Flanigan failed to give Perot his due, so, too, did much of the American media. In fact, there is considerable evidence that the media, particularly the financial media, contributed to the failures that cost Perot so much money.

Who does Perot consider the major culprit? Richard Rustin of *The Wall Street Journal*. It is Perot's opinion that Rustin damaged DuPont's ability to get its sales force stabilized—the single largest factor in the snowballing losses. Perot said, "They couldn't hurt us around balancing the books, or getting the vault under control, but in terms of damaging the image of the firm, I think if any scholar ever did an analysis of the intensity of the fire that they directed on us, as opposed to other firms, in a comparable situation, you will see a measurable difference."

Others also had strong opinions about Dick Rustin. Wally Auch, who had a long background in Wall Street, and who became president of DuPont-Walston in July 1973, agreed. "The plug that was pulled on DuPont-Walston was from an article written by Dick Rustin. Conjecture in the press about the financial condition of the firm just became self-fulfilling prophecies. And, I must say, DuPont Glore Forgan and DuPont-Walston got more adverse press than any brokerage firm in the thirty-one years that I have been in this business."

Bob Dunwoody also agreed that the real adverse effect of the press came to light after the merger with Walston & Company. "Once we got down to DuPont-Walston, it was a disaster. I mean, the press really exacerbated our problem. Just article after article after article, most of which, in my opinion, were half-true."

The big question is why. Why did Rustin single out DuPont and Perot for this treatment? "Why they did it, I don't know," Perot said. "Rustin made his living selling newspapers, and spectacular stories sell more papers, gain more recognition for people like Rustin. And ... he is the king of anonymous sources. I just wondered if any of those people's parents ever bothered to name those who talked to Rustin, because if you go through Rustin's stories, if he ever had anybody stand up on his back legs and allow himself to be quoted, I don't recall it.

"I think I was just a piece of raw meat that Rustin could chew on," Perot said.

Which is not to suggest that the coverage was all bad. There were some who had good things to say. For instance, as described in Chris Welle's book *The Last Days of the Club*, Bernard "Bunny" Lasker told the New York Stock Exchange Board of Governors, "As long as there is a Wall Street, we owe a debt of gratitude to Ross Perot. I, for one, will be, for as long as I live, forever grateful."

William Salomon of Salomon Brothers later told me, "I thought he did something that, literally, was an act that took a lot of courage and certainly a lot of money." Salomon felt that Perot simply took up the challenge thrown down by both the Street and Washington, with an eye toward solving a problem. He concluded, "I think his motivation was a very good and fine motivation." And *Barron's*, which had not been a big Perot supporter, ran a lengthy editorial after Perot closed DuPont. A banner headline to that story read: "Don Quixote Unhorsed—The Fall of Ross Perot Leaves Wall Street Poorer."

In February of 2003, I asked Perot, looking back, about his

DuPont experience. He summed it up this way: "We helped them get through a critical period. We stabilized it. And then, unfortunately, the market was bad and stayed bad for a long time, but at least the Street got stabilized.

"I was asked to get involved by our government—some senior officials. They said it would cost me a maximum of $5 million. Sixty days after I got involved, it was way above that. We stayed with it, but it was one of those things that didn't work out. That's all part of life. Timing was bad. The best time to sell umbrellas is when it's raining."

— ◇◇◇ —

"The biggest thrill in my career will be the day we put cars on a ship and begin selling them in Japan."

—H. ROSS PEROT

Ross Perot, all five feet seven inches of him, has traveled many a road since his first business venture, throwing newspapers from horseback in Texarkana, Texas, at the age of thirteen. A lot of those roads have been rocky—unpaved and filled with pot holes—but a few turned out to be paved with gold. Perot gold, that is. Hard-earned gold.

Strangely enough, Perot used the same road maps to discover both kinds.

He found one of those gold-paved roads in 1984, when General Motors, the ultimate American "big business," bought Electronic Data Systems for $2.6 billion. Because Perot owned forty-five percent of the EDS stock, the sale meant $950 million in cash for him—for the same company he had founded on his birthday in 1962 with $1,000 borrowed from his wife's savings account.

It also gave Perot a seat on the General Motors board of directors. And if he had his way, he would jumpstart GM to new all-time highs in business, to start putting those cars on ships to sell in Japan.

But something happened along the way to stall those dreams. Maybe it was a personality conflict, or maybe it was simply differing business philosophies, but Perot soon tired of what he considered to be bad business decisions by General Motors brass, while Roger

Smith, GM's chairman, quickly tired of Perot's suggestions for improvement.

Perot, at least, couched the differences in terms of business philosophies. "At EDS, snakes are dealt with directly," he said. "At General Motors, first thing you do is organize a committee on snakes. Then you hire a consultant on snakes. Then you talk about it for a year. At EDS, if you find a snake, you kill it."

Perot also had suggestions for improving employee morale, suggestions again based on EDS philosophies. "In my opinion, we need to get rid of the fourteenth (executive) floor. I would get rid of executive dining rooms. I would urge the senior executives to locate their offices where real people are doing real work. Live with them, listen to them, spend time with them. Find out straight up what it takes to win and do it."

Perot was motivated by a desire to save the world's largest business entity from what he saw as disgrace at the feet of the Japanese auto industry. He felt that only through a rededicated, reenergized work force could General Motors restore itself to its rightful position in the world manufacturing community. But, as Perot described it, trying to bring positive changes to General Motors was "like teaching an elephant to tap dance."

The stormy twenty-four-month marriage ended in divorce in early December 1986, with General Motors buying out Perot from his position on the board of directors of GM, as well as his decision-making positions at EDS. As payment, GM paid Perot and three other top EDS executives (Senior Vice President Tom Walter, Vice Chairman Mort Meyerson, and Corporate Vice President William Gayden) $850 million for their subsidiary shares of stock. The buy-out agreement also included a clause that would impose fines of $7.5 million if either Perot or GM Chairman Roger Smith spoke negatively about each other, and included a three-year non-compete agreement.

The General Motors chapter of Ross Perot's life brought an already wealthy man more money than he could ever imagine seeing, much less owning, in his early Texarkana days when he was breaking wild horses for one dollar each. And so Perot found himself wealthier than before, and with nothing but time on his hands.

Could the world of politics be far behind?

CHAPTER 8

In and Out of the Race for President

"Would you run if your name was placed on the ballots in all fifty states?"
—LARRY KING TO H. ROSS PEROT

In his parting agreement from General Motors, Ross Perot also agreed that he would not start a competing company to EDS within the next eighteen months. So, with even more wealth than before, Perot had time to kill. He could have spent it at his Bermuda retreat piloting his cigarette boat or saddling up one of his fine Tennessee Walking Horses. But Ross Perot doesn't spend much time just relaxing. Instead, he was already planning his next information systems company, in the same way he had outlined EDS while sitting on that beach in Hawaii years before.

While waiting to start that new company, which ultimately became Perot Systems, other things filled his days. He made a few speaking engagements and visited a talk show or two. He even renewed efforts he had started in 1969 and 1970 to get information on American servicemen he still believed had been left behind in Southeast Asia. That belief arose, in part, out of a late-night summons Perot, Tom Meurer, and I had received while in Vientiane, Laos, in April 1970, from the U.S. Embassy there, telling us they had new information about missing U.S. servicemen. The three of us immediately went to the Embassy in the dead of night, where the

CIA station chief, Larry Devlin, showed us a map and explained that there was reason to believe about twenty-five white men were being held in caves near Sam Neua, though this was never verified.

In March of 1987, Perot flew to Hanoi and met with several North Vietnamese officials who offered to provide information to Perot on those missing men, but they attached two conditions to their offer: They wanted a certain Vietnamese pianist to play a concert in America, and they wanted one of their top military leaders, General Giap, to be allowed to speak at the U.S. War College. Immediately upon his return to the States, Perot sought a meeting with President Reagan to discuss the conditions.

Unfortunately, Reagan was distracted by the Iran-Contra affair and, perhaps, was beginning to experience the beginnings of Alzheimer's Disease. According to Perot, the president continually referred to a stack of 3 x 5 cards during their meeting, speaking from them as if they were, in effect, cue cards. At one point, he even read the same card twice and never seemed to know. Perot felt this was a lost opportunity to do something to help those twenty-five American servicemen. "It just got lost in the bureaucratic shuffle," he said.

Ultimately, those men were never found or accounted for, a fact that continued to haunt Perot. Later, while testifying before a Senate investigating committee in 1992, Devlin denied ever showing us such a map—although I personally saw it—and the U.S. ambassador to Laos in 1970, G. McMurtrie Godley, called our report "a lot of bullshit." But the very issue that had so driven Perot in those earlier years, and which had first propelled him onto the radar of American consciousness, still drove him almost twenty years later.

Perot got Perot Systems up and running in June of 1988 but continued speaking out on a number of political issues. In November 1990 he was invited to speak at the National Press Club in Washington, D.C., where he spent considerable time talking about problems of growing concern in America, such as the economy and campaign reform, and what could be done to correct them. He was starting to sound an awful lot like a candidate for office. In fact, during the question-and-answer session following his speech, he was asked, "Isn't it time you ran for president of the United States?"

Perot just waved it off, claiming he didn't have the proper temperament for the office. He did, however, fan the fires by asking those who thought he should run to stay in touch. He even gave them a post office box in Dallas they could write. And a grassroots movement was born.

Over the next year or more, Perot found himself on the guest list of just about every talk show: *The Today Show*, *The MacNeil/Lehrer Report*, *The Phil Donahue Show*, *20/20 with Barbara Walters*, and finally *The Larry King Show*. A groundswell of support was building across America, and it was while talking with Larry King on February 20, 1992, that the issue finally came to a head. King bluntly asked Perot, "Would you run if your name was placed on the ballot in all fifty states?"

Perot responded, "If volunteers put my name on the ballots in all fifty states, I would run."

If Perot intended to shock folks with the announcement, he succeeded. I, for one, had no inkling he planned to make such an announcement, nor did his wife, Margot, watching from her hotel room in Washington, D.C. "I could not believe what I had just heard," she later said. But she also expressed surprise at the depth of support for her husband, coming from such a wide variety of people. How could he ignore that?

Perot called me the following morning to talk about his appearance on Larry King. "That was quite a shocker," I said. Talk about understatements.

Truth is, I don't think even Perot himself had known he was going to say what he did. "It just felt comfortable," he said. Then he downplayed the whole thing, cautioning me that it might not happen anyway. Quite a trick to get your name on the ballots in all fifty states. On the other hand, if the American people believed in him strongly enough to get his name on those ballots, he almost felt as if he had no choice. "I just want to help the people who want me to help them," he said. Vintage Perot.

Having now committed himself, Perot threw himself into the project with his usual vigor. Less than two weeks later, he called to ask if I would be available to help if and when the time came. I replied that I had a couple of consulting agreements, but that they were not overly time-consuming and that I could be available if he needed me. Mostly I was just putting him off because I had serious questions about whether I had the time to commit that I knew Perot would demand if he successfully found himself on the ballot.

By the middle of May, I still hadn't decided, so Perot met with me to discuss in more detail my potential role. He understood my time concerns and tried to assuage them. Shouldn't require more than twenty or twenty-five hours a week, he told me, and most of that would be pulling together interviews for television spots. I thought I could spare that much time, so I agreed. He then asked me to set up an office in the Perot Systems headquarters on Merit Parkway in Dallas rather than in the campaign headquarters a few blocks away. He wanted me close by, he said, and even assigned me the office adjacent to his. I should have known then that virtually all my waking hours were soon going to be his.

I officially went to work for the campaign on June 10. As it turned out, I don't think I ever spent less than fifty hours on the campaign in any given week in the months that followed. In fact, much of my time ended up being consumed by an unexpected problem that had been spawned the last week of May by an unlikely source—political campaign professionals.

Or maybe that is, in fact, a very likely source.

By the end of May, Perot had much of his campaign team in place. Jim Squires, former editor of the *Chicago Tribune*, was already on board handling inquiries from the press, while attorney Tom Luce had been appointed campaign chairman, with Mort Meyerson assisting. Perot's son-in-law, Clay Mulford, an attorney, spent much of the campaign trying to learn about purchasing television time but never quite got a handle on it; his legal efforts, though, were helpful. And Sharon Holman, a former secretary at EDS from Perot's hometown of Texarkana, with little or no experience, became Perot's press secretary. A quick learner, she charmed her way through many a tough question.

Knowing that elections are often won or lost in the public relations wars, Perot and his closest advisers discussed bringing in outside help for that aspect of the campaign. Tom Luce and Mort Meyerson championed the idea of bringing in former Jimmy Carter campaign guru Hamilton Jordan and his counterpart for Ronald Reagan, Ed Rollins. Meyerson, in particular, felt they needed Rollins to assist Jordan since he had been out of politics for some time. Squires, an old print media guy, opposed Rollins. He feared that Rollins would be more interested in publicity for his own ends. But Squires was outvoted, and Ed Rollins came on board—in retrospect, one of the biggest mistakes Perot made.

In fact, the way Rollins came on should have been a harbinger of things to come. If nothing else, it lent credence to Jim Squires's powers of prophecy, because Rollins himself leaked the news to *The Wall Street Journal* without waiting for Perot to make the announcement. That didn't sit well with Perot, a team player, who voiced his displeasure to a duly chastened Rollins. Unfortunately, as I was soon to learn, it didn't take.

On June 8, 1992, I spoke with Peter Jennings at ABC-TV, with whom I had worked for a few years after he joined ABC in 1964, and who was curious about my involvement, if any, with Perot's campaign. Because I had not officially gone to work for the campaign nor had there been any official announcement from Perot, and learning from the Rollins faux pas, I simply told Peter I was considering it. Peter told me he believed that Perot had captured the imagination of the American people, then wished me well. Two days later, I officially went to work for the Perot campaign.

One of Rollins's first moves was to bring in Hal Riney from San Francisco to assist in the campaign. Riney and his ad agency had put together President Reagan's successful "Morning in America" campaign. On Friday, June 12, I met with Rollins, Mort Meyerson, Tom Luce, Perot, and Riney in what was supposed to be a get-acquainted session between the candidate and the Rollins/Riney team. Looking back, I see that this is when the trouble started. Right away, I got the sense that Perot was a little uncomfortable with both Rollins and Riney, who seemed to have their own ideas for the campaign and seemed equally determined to implement them whether anybody else liked it or not.

A few days later, along with Tom Luce and Jim Squires, I met with Ed Rollins and Hamilton Jordan to talk about getting interviews under way to use in television commercials. By now, I was beginning to share Perot's discomfort with the "outsiders." My discomfort increased when, almost immediately, Rollins made it clear he had big-time Hollywood type productions in mind rather than simpler, Dallas-based material that in my opinion was better suited to Perot.

My concerns at this point were twofold. First, as I said, I was concerned Rollins and his team would unnecessarily run up the costs for the campaign. But, second, it didn't seem as if Hal Riney had a clue about the kind of man Perot was and the kind of candidate he wanted to be. Rather, he had come in with preconceived notions of how Perot *should be* as a candidate and was determined to bend Perot around to his way of thinking rather than acclimating himself to Perot's. I worried that, if he continued, it wouldn't work for Perot, a man who fits very few preconceived notions.

I also felt that this wasn't sitting well with Jim Squires either. Squires, a former newspaperman, believed in "print" promotions and hadn't yet accepted the strength of television ads. He, too, could see where the conversations were headed. And, as with the hiring of Rollins, he had already proved to be a man of foresight.

Later, I found out that Riney and Rollins had been just as concerned about me as I had been about them. After the election, Rollins was quoted in *Time Magazine* as saying that Perot more and more became dependent upon longtime friend and former ABC anchorman, Murphy Martin, and that "Martin was in over his head." From my vantage point, though, it appeared that neither Rollins nor Riney ever lowered their heads far enough to see what the campaign was really all about.

Out of those early meetings, we ultimately determined that we would establish three production units, with my unit operating individually to prepare the "people spots." A separate unit would work exclusively on a bio of Perot, while the third, Riney's, would produce the television commercials. And so there was a plan—of sorts, but with no real central strategy. Things continued to be uneasy between the Perot people and the "outsiders."

And, apparently, there was some uneasiness among the outsiders themselves. On the afternoon of Friday, June 19, less than three weeks after coming on board, Hamilton Jordan called to tell me that he was withdrawing his involvement with Riney. Apparently, Jim Squires and I weren't the only ones unhappy with Hal Riney.

In the latter part of June, Peter Jennings and ABC produced a documentary on Perot, to be followed, when it aired, with ninety minutes of live questioning for Perot from ten different cities across America. The format would be a "town hall" type meeting, with Jennings hosting. I reminded Peter that he had not achieved his good reputation as a reporter by doing "hatchet jobs" on his subjects.

He replied, "I have integrity, and I plan to keep it intact." He wasn't defensive or offended when he said it, just matter-of-fact. I intended to hold him to it.

In the midst of all this, I was subpoenaed to the Federal Building in Dallas on June 24 to give my deposition to a Senate Investigating Committee looking into those missing servicemen in Laos. Ironically, the issue which had arguably started Perot on his road to the presidency now threatened to disrupt his campaign. The committee, under Senator John Kerry, wanted Perot to come to Washington, D.C., to testify in a series of hearings, but Perot had been able to convince the senator to delay that until after the election. In a compromise, the committee still sent attorneys to Dallas to take depositions from those of us who had been involved.

My deposition ran almost four hours, after which I drove to the Westin Galleria to be interviewed on *Frontline* as part of a program on Perot to be aired shortly before the election. Those twenty to twenty-five hours per week were looking more and more like a fantasy.

On June 26, the day before Perot's birthday, I spent most of the afternoon trying to reach Peter Jennings to talk about the upcoming prime time special and some of the candidate's concerns. Perot's worries about the media were nothing new, tracing back, I believe, to his experiences on Wall Street with DuPont. Often he referred to that statement he had originally made regarding *Wall Street Journal* reporter Dick Rustin: "I'm just a piece of raw meat to him." He was determined not to be raw meat for anyone else, including Peter Jennings. It seemed as if the few might have tainted the many in Perot's mind.

Peter finally called me from his car, en route to enroll his son in summer camp. He said that virtually everybody in the Perot camp had been trying to track him down, apparently concerned about the network promos for the program. I hadn't seen the promos, but several who had seen them were concerned that the documentary portion of the program might question Perot's business practices. Though he also had not seen them, Peter assured me that the promos were "benign."

I then reminded him of one of our previous conversations in which he had asked me to assure Perot that he was a good guy and not to worry about the program. I told Jennings that I had done just that. "Don't make a liar out of me," I said.

As it turned out, there was no need for concern. During the live questioning portions, Perot handled himself as the strong orator he has always been. The only problem was that ABC had tried to use too many cities for the questioning, which tended to jump around, and made it difficult for Perot to establish a rhythm on a train of thought. All in all, though, it went quite well.

The rest of the campaign, however, wasn't running as smoothly. A lot of different people were working on film pieces for commercials, but there was still no central plan that had been presented and approved by Perot himself or even by his most trusted advisers. Everyone was waiting on Riney to come up with that unifying theme, but in my opinion all he seemed interested in was spending Perot's money. Finally, Perot dictated that I should stick close to Riney day and night to keep an eye on what he was doing and where all the money was going.

Easily said, but not so easily done. The morning after this Perot edict, I arrived at campaign headquarters, and Riney was nowhere to be found. Perot immediately called Ed Rollins and laid down the law: "I told you I wanted Murphy totally involved with Riney. I don't want to have to say this again."

I quickly found out that Riney was out spending more money. A huge luncheon had been organized at the Anatole Hotel for state coordinators for the campaign, which Riney wanted to film for a television spot. Unbelievably, he had ordered four 35mm cameras to cover the event and, immediately afterward, headed to San Francisco to process the film. Needless to say, that didn't sit well with Perot, who again unleashed his venom on Ed Rollins, the man who had hired Riney.

Trying to smooth things over, I then headed over to Rollins's office, only to walk into a wall of profanity as he lashed out at Perot through me. It was as loud and profane an explosion as I had heard since I left ABC in New York. "I gave up a million goddamn dollars a year to come down here for this shit," he said, which might have been the most cordial thing he said. From there, it was all downhill.

After letting him spew for a few minutes, I said, "The real problem is this: Neither you nor Riney ever got on the same page with Perot. You keep trying to make him into your preconceived image instead of taking the candidate as he is and working with him. You have not made any effort to take Perot's strengths and utilize them. You have not taken the things that the grassroots movement finds so inviting in this man ... Unless and until you make a real effort to get on the same page with the candidate as he is, it is not going to work."

We left on friendly terms, and Rollins even apologized for venting his frustrations at me. I hoped that our conversation had smoothed over the problems, but it was only a few days later when I discovered that my message had fallen on deaf ears. I arrived at Perot's office for a meeting with Riney and Rollins to discuss the TV spots. When Perot inquired as to costs, Riney told him that network TV spots could range from $400,000 to $1.25 million, and that the best film production crews got up to $175,000 per day.

Perot thought about that and then said, "Mr. Riney, I appreciate your efforts, but I am afraid you are trying to put me in a Rolls Royce when all I need is a Volkswagen." With that, Perot dismissed Riney from the campaign. After the meeting, he told me to take over all production duties and to proceed with whatever needed to be done. And, less than a week after dismissing Riney, Perot fired Rollins as well.

"Now that we have gotten rid of the Pentagon," he said, "we can get something done."

"If we cannot win in November, the election will be decided in the House of Representatives, and since the House of Representatives is made up primarily of Democrats and Republicans, our chance of winning would be pretty slim. Now that the Democratic Party has revitalized itself, I have concluded that we cannot win in November and that the election will be decided in the House of Representatives. So, therefore, I will not become a candidate."
—H. Ross Perot, July 16, 1992

No one was more surprised than I was when Ross Perot told me, on the evening of July 15, that he was considering withdrawing from the race. After all, he had shown a steady rise in the polls, we had gotten rid of the costly advertising team, and the campaign could now get really cranked up. All our efforts were just starting to gain momentum, and, with the election less than four months away, all systems were finally "go." Why would he even think about pulling out?

I still don't know the full answer to that question. But I do know one thing: No one loves his family more than Ross Perot loves his and, when he told me that he had gotten word that people were trying to humiliate his daughter, I could see immediately the protective father in him take over the candidate.

Perot's daughter, Carolyn, was soon to be married. According to Perot, a "trusted" adviser had told him of a campaign by a Republican "dirty tricks" group to embarrass Carolyn by doctoring photographs to put her face on another person's body in a compromising situation. There were also reports that the dirty tricksters planned to disrupt the wedding, though Perot had no details as to how. He was not, however, going to permit anyone to harm his daughter. He had always put his family first and, he told me, he would do so again. I could see the pain in his face and hear the anguish in his voice as he said, "I may make the decision tonight to shut the campaign down."

I didn't really believe he would shut it down. I just thought he was venting and would be back on track the next morning. So firmly did I believe that, in fact, that when I left, I went to our production studio in Las Colinas and edited film for campaign material until 2:00 A.M. Following that with four hours sleep, I arrived at the office the next morning at 8:00, ready for another day of campaigning. Imagine my shock when Perot told me he had met the night before with Tom Luce and Mort Meyerson and had, indeed, determined to shut the campaign down.

I reminded him how far he had come and told him I believed he had a great chance at winning. If he stuck with his decision, I feared it could scar his credibility terribly. That fear increased when he showed me his withdrawal speech. The Democrats were looking better, it essentially said, and Perot didn't think he had a chance to win. So, rather than throwing the election into the House of Representatives, he had decided to withdraw.

Not a single word about dirty tricks against his family—something every parent in America could have understood. No, simply a political statement that he had gauged his chances to win, determined he couldn't, and was shutting it down. In my opinion, that failure to mention the real reasons would come back to haunt him later, and I told him so.

"This is sufficient," he said. It turned out it wasn't.

—◇◆◇—

Tears and frustration flowed at campaign headquarters when Tom Luce broke the news to the workers. These were people who believed in Perot, who had dedicated themselves to an incredible grassroots movement that had swept across the nation and propelled Ross Perot onto the ballots across America. People who saw democracy in action, not just as a civics lesson in a classroom. People who had devoted their time, money, and tireless efforts to making their dream come true—putting a man in the White House who truly cared about, and believed in, them.

And now he was dropping out.

The next morning, I sat with Ross Perot, Jr., in my office, Monday-morning-quarterbacking the campaign up to that point. The problems had first started, we decided, when the "outsiders" had come in and tried to take over—people who didn't understand Ross Perot, the candidate, and who certainly didn't understand Ross Perot, the man. Despite those early problems, the outsiders were now truly outside, the campaign had just started to run on all cylinders—and now this!

As Ross, Jr., and I talked, Ross, Sr., called en route to New York. I filled him in on what his son and I had been discussing. Not too late to get back in, I told him. We had commercials finished and ready to go. All he had to do was say the word.

That evening, in an appearance on *The Larry King Show*, Perot hinted that he might be back in the race. "We have commercials in the can," he said. Later, on *20/20 with Barbara Walters*, he had an almost playful aura about him. He seemed to tease with an "I could, but I am not planning to" attitude when she asked if he would get back into the race.

My ears perked up as I listened. My guess is that ears perked up all across America. Could it be? But we would still have to wait a while to find out.

In the meantime, life went on. On August 10, 1992, Perot, Tom Meurer, several others, and I testified before Senator John Kerry's committee looking into the affairs in Southeast Asia. We were still trying to convince the committee that there were American servicemen unaccounted for in Laos. Presidential candidate or not, the best interests of Americans still ruled Ross Perot's heart.

And, truth be told, Perot was looking and acting like anything but a non-candidate. After his withdrawal speech, *Newsweek* had come out with a cover photo of Perot with the words *"THE QUIT-TER"* emblazoned across it. That had to be galling to a man who so often had quoted Winston Churchill's famous line, "Never give up! Never give up!"

Or did he simply miss being involved?

On October 1, 1992, barely a month before the election, Ross Perot reentered the presidential race.

"I know I hurt many of you who worked so hard through the spring and summer when I stepped aside on July 16. I thought it was the right thing to do. I thought that both parties would address the problems that face the nation. We gave them a chance. They didn't do it."
—H. ROSS PEROT, OCTOBER 1, 1992

Perot's withdrawal from the race had raised a lot of questions; some had been answered, others had not. But people were about to see the real strength of Ross Perot, the candidate. He did not build successful companies by accident. He was one of the world's great salesmen, and he was about to go on display for all to see. The presidential debates were just around the corner.

I was to act as point man for Perot for all three debates. I arrived in St. Louis early the day of the first debate, October 11, and checked out the facilities at Washington University, including the lectern height, lighting, cameras, where Perot's family would sit, and made sure the green room stocked his favorite light foods, pasta and chocolate chip cookies. Perot arrived on his Lear jet about two hours before broadcast time. Mark Blahnick and I picked him up, then followed a single unmarked police car to the auditorium.

At the auditorium, I walked him through the debate to follow, including taking him up on the stage. Under the debate rules, the candidates were permitted to keep three yellow legal pads on their lecterns, but there could be no notes or writing on those pads until the debates began. Then the candidates would be free to take notes if they desired. After checking out everything in the auditorium and making sure the legal pads were in place, we returned to the green room.

Already prepared for the debate, Perot didn't need to study. He wasn't hungry, wasn't tired, but seemed restless—so why not visit? I followed him twenty feet down the hall to Bill Clinton's green room. Perot opened the door, and there sat Clinton, being "made up" for television. Before Perot could speak, Clinton's aide, Mickey Kantor, rushed over and gently ushered him back outside the room. "I'm not wearing makeup," Perot told me.

From there, Perot wanted to go over to President Bush's room, which was guarded by Secret Service agents. After some small talk with Jim Baker and Brent Scowcroft, it was back to the auditorium, where his family had now gathered. After he visited with them for a few minutes, we went back to his green room and he took a short nap.

At fifteen minutes before debate time, he nibbled on a chocolate chip cookie while dressing in a freshly starched shirt and newly pressed suit. Unlike Clinton, who had looked so at ease in his chair having makeup applied, Perot still refused to wear any. I finally convinced him to at least dab a little powder over his beard area, and, at three minutes to air time, I escorted him to his entry spot.

Lights ... cameras ... action ... and H. Ross Perot knocked 'em dead. Well-thought-out challenges for the other two candidates, witty analogies, even self-deprecating jokes about his big ears. Bottom line: Perot kicked some serious tail, and even his harshest media critics awarded Round One of the debates to him.

After the debate, we swung by the green room for a quick pit stop, then headed back to President Bush's green room, where Jim Baker and Brent Scowcroft again stood outside. Just as we neared them, the door opened and Barbara Bush swept out. Normally quite cordial, she brushed past us, ignoring Perot's greeting.

"Why is she mad at you?" I asked him.

"She's not mad at me," he said. "She's just upset because George got his butt kicked tonight."

Well said, Mr. President-to-be, I thought.

In a *Newsweek* poll, 43 percent scored Ross Perot as the debate's winner; 31 percent picked Clinton; and only 19 percent sided with Bush. Maybe Perot had been right in his assessment of Barbara Bush's mood.

A couple of nights later, the vice-presidential candidates squared off, pitting Democrat Al Gore, Republican Dan Quayle, and Independent Adm. James Stockdale against each other in the Theater for the Arts at Georgia Tech University in Atlanta. Although Admiral Stockdale, the Congressional Medal of Honor winner from his agonizing years as a Vietnam POW, hadn't been out front much during the Perot campaign, and wasn't a skilled debater, he did score points with his opening remarks:

"Who am I? Why am I here?"

After laughter and applause at the opening, he continued, "I am not a politician—everybody knows that, so don't expect me to use the language of the Washington insider. Thirty-seven years in the Navy and only one of them up there in Washington. And now I'm an academic. The centerpiece in my life was the Vietnam War. I was there the day it started. I led the first bombing raid against North Vietnam. I was there the day it ended, and I was there for everything in between. Ten years in Vietnam, aerial combat, and torture. I know things about the Vietnam War better than anybody in the world.

"And I know how American governments can be courageous and how they can be callow. That's one thing I'm an insider on. I was a leader of the American pilots who were shot down and were in prison in North Vietnam. You should know that the American character displayed in those dungeons by those fine men was a thing of beauty. I look back on those years as the beginning of wisdom, learning everything a man can learn about the vulnerabilities and the strengths that are ours as Americans.

"Why am I here tonight? I'm here because I have in my brain and in my heart what it takes to lead America through tough times."

With growing momentum, the Perot campaign rolled into the second and third debates, in Richmond, Virginia, on October 15 and East Lansing, Michigan, on October 19. The procedures were generally the same as at the first, and Perot performed well, but he was particularly strong in the final debate. It almost didn't start out that well. Just minutes away from start time, Perot changed into his fresh suit for the debate. Turning to me, he asked, "Do I look all right?"

"You look great," I said. "But I think you should zip up your fly."

Following the debates, a CNN/Gallup/*USA Today* poll reflected that Perot's favorable rating had jumped to 70 percent. In just a few days, he had dramatically turned around public opinion with aggressive, almost spellbinding performances in the debates. The Bush and Clinton teams certainly were having second thoughts about having approved Perot's participation in the debates.

But how was Ross Perot dealing with his newfound success?

> *"The point is you guys hate that I am in the race. You guys hate the fact that the American people put me on the ballot. You guys have less respect in this country than Congress. You'll do anything for a 'gotcha' story—anything that will get you a headline—anything that will get you a high five with your peers."*
> —H. ROSS PEROT, OCTOBER 19, 1992

When Perot had dropped out of the race on July 16, communications director Jim Squires wondered, like so many other people, why he had really pulled out. What was the real reason? He wondered if, perhaps, Perot's relationship with the press had something to do with it. After all, Perot had never had what one would call a warm relationship with them during the campaign—not like he'd had in 1969 and 1970, when he had been able to focus the world's attention on the POW issue. And the things Squires had seen from the press during the Perot campaign—well, he didn't much care for what he saw.

In a column in *The Plain Dealer* August 29, 1992, Squires wrote:

"Watching the press cover the Perot campaign underscored my growing conviction, shared by many veteran journalists, that the traditional institution of the press of which I was so proud is no more and that the news media that had replaced it are so rife with careerism and incompetence and so driven by marketing compulsions that they have ceased to be a positive force in the democracy."

Maybe it was fueled by what he knew was a successful performance, but when Ross Perot finished visiting with his supporters following the third debate and walked into the press conference with members of the media, he wasted no time releasing his pent-up feelings.

"Is it gonna be the usual?" he asked when he reached the bank of microphones on the podium. "Does someone want to know what food I feed my cat? I love all the things nobody wants to talk about— bank failures, foreign paid lobbyists, indecision over military action in Panama, pre-war dealings with Saddam Hussein."

I stood at the back of the room with Sharon Holman, Perot's press secretary, not wanting to believe my ears. We exchanged stunned looks as Perot continued his tirade. It wasn't that what he was saying was wrong; it was that at that moment he was choosing to say it at all. He still refused to play their game.

"The point is you guys hate that I am in the race. You guys hate the fact that the American people put me on the ballot. You guys have less respect in this country than Congress. You'll do anything for a 'gotcha' story—anything that will get you a headline—anything that will get you a high five with your peers."

What I was hearing was totally opposite from the warm, charming demeanor that had served Perot so well on camera throughout the debates. When someone asked whether he thought reporters intentionally distorted the news, he replied, "I have never met a more thin-skinned crowd in my life. You all can dish it out; you ought to be able to take it. You can't take anything."

As I listened, I could almost envision the headlines that would appear in the next day's newspapers. The debate itself, where Ross had been so successful, would probably be relegated to a secondary story next to what I saw playing out before me. I yearned for the days of the POW campaign, when the media seemed to keep Perot on a pedestal, almost adoring his every move. Back then he was the multi-millionaire spending his money to help others, with no strings attached. After a trip to Southeast Asia and Europe in 1970, he had once been asked, "How can you not call your activities political?"

"I will not run for political office. I will not hold an appointive office. I just don't think I would be good at it. I'd have to check my plans out with too many people. I think I can do more with my own resources."

But twenty-two years later, he stood as a politician seeking the highest elected office in the land, seemingly intent on antagonizing the press.

Thinking back over the campaign, I wondered whether his displeasure at what he perceived as a deteriorating line of questioning by reporters—ignoring the real issues to focus on the private or the sensational—had led to his decision to make fewer public appearances than the other candidates. I wondered, too, whether that had backfired by actually leading to the very kinds of questioning he detested. If he had just played the "press game" a little more throughout the campaign, would I be standing there watching him level his broadside at a room full of reporters? As good a salesman as Ross Perot is, and he's one of the world's best, could he have used a bit of his sales talent on the press?

Looking back now, I also wonder whether that *Newsweek* cover that labeled him a quitter played any role in his decision to reenter the race—to prove the media wrong. And could his attempt to use the media to justify his decision to withdraw—his appearance on *60 Minutes* in which he raised, publicly, for the first time the "dirty tricks" charges that he had not mentioned at all in his withdrawal speech—have backfired? In that appearance, he spent almost as much time arguing with his interviewer, Leslie Stahl, as he did answering questions. At one point, he even threatened to terminate the interview when he didn't like the tenor of the questioning, accusing her of misrepresenting what he had said. Could all that have worked against him?

I don't know.

—◇◇◇—
"If you have to categorize me, call me a professional private citizen who loves his country."
—H. ROSS PEROT, 1970

When the election was over, Ross Perot had captured 19 percent of the popular vote. Given the problems of the campaign, starting with the turmoil created by the advertising issues, Perot's withdrawal and reentry into the race, and his publicly lashing out at the press just as his popularity was peaking, that 19 percent represents something truly remarkable. And one of the more amazing things was that, in the day and age of outrageous sums spent on campaigns, Perot did it for less than some gubernatorial races cost today.

He even did it despite the media's refusal, at least early on, to take his campaign seriously. CBS Television Vice President Mary Lou Jennerjahn had refused to sell us advertising time because, at the time, Perot had not yet been placed on the ballots in all fifty states. "We do not allow deep pockets to control America's thinking," she said.

I wonder if she ever questioned whether CBS's Dan Rather or Mike Wallace, both of whom have fairly deep pockets, ever controlled or influenced America's thinking.

After the departure of "the Pentagon," Rollins and Riney, some truly magical work was done for Perot by longtime friends Liener Temerlin and Dennis McClain, who helped bring together a magnificent advertising campaign. Working on short notice, they presented to the American people the Ross Perot that Rollins and Riney never captured.

Ironically, after the election, Perot received numerous offers to essentially become a member of the media. He was asked to appear regularly on television, write syndicated columns for newspapers, do network radio programs, even do semi-entertainment/documentary weekly programs. I had more than one conversation with Bob Wright, president of NBC-TV, and his News Division president, Michael Gartner, about Perot appearing weekly on the *NBC Evening News*. And the list goes on: John Brewer, president and editor-in-chief of *New York Times* Syndication, offered Perot a high six figures for a weekly column, and William Colston, chairman of the *Los Angeles Times* Syndication, also offered big bucks for a bi-weekly column. Disney Productions was even interested in doing a show with Perot. The man who couldn't get along with the media now found the media to be his biggest suitor.

All in all, our efforts garnered Ross Perot nearly 20 million votes—more than any third-party candidate in modern history, and almost triple the number of votes he would receive in 1996 when we were not involved. Had Perot been able to properly court the press during the 1992 campaign, things might have turned out different. And had Temerlin McClain been on the scene from day one, before Ed Rollins and his crew arrived, Perot would have made a more productive run at the White House. There are many people who believe that if Perot had not been so distracted by the "outsiders," he might well have been elected president.

I am one of those people.

—◇◇◇—

"The world wants things done, not excuses. One thing well done is worth a million good excuses."
—GABRIEL ROSS PEROT

Gabriel Ross Perot personally typed a list of thirty-six maxims for business success on his Cotton Sales Office letterhead that he gave to his son, Ross, to help him succeed in his boyhood jobs. Now past his seventy-third birthday, seldom does a day go by that Ross doesn't check those suggestions even today. And every day in between, he has tried to live by them.

Here are some of the others:

- Diamonds are chunks of coal that stuck to their job.
- Your services will not command a premium if your word has to be discounted.
- It may be further around the corner of a square deal, but the road is better.
- You cannot dream yourself into a character; you must hammer and forge yourself one.
- The trouble is we spend too much time thinking about what is going to happen and too little time making things happen.
- If you must make mistakes, it will be more to your credit to make a new one each time.
- Use what talent you possess; the woods would be very silent if no birds sang but those which sing the best.
- If you are not afraid of failure, failure will be afraid of you.

Who, looking at those, can't see a little bit of Ross Perot in each one? He prides himself on being a man of action, and a man who does things well. Some cases in point·

- He spent millions of his own money in the POW/MIA campaign;
- Even while losing almost $100 million trying to save Wall Street, he bought twenty Tennessee Walking Horses for the New York Police Department's mounted police;
- He chaired the War on Drugs Committee in Texas in 1980 at the urging of Governor Bill Clements;

- He chaired the Select Committee on Education in Texas in 1983 at the request of Governor Mark White, which led to what became known as the "no pass-no play" rule requiring students to pass all coursework in order to participate in extracurricular activities;
- He gave hundreds, if not thousands, of non-public gifts for medical and social needs;
- He donated $15 million to help build the Mort Meyerson Symphony Hall in Dallas;
- He gave millions for research at Southwestern Medical School; and
- When a friend was hospitalized in intensive care, he showed up regularly at the hospital to check on the patient. More than once while I was undergoing radical heart surgeries, I awakened to find Ross standing with my wife at my bedside.

I met many interesting individuals during my television news career. Many of them I interviewed; others I covered from various distances. More than a few of the interesting people I covered were disciplined. More than a few were dedicated. Lesser numbers were comfortable around the media, consistent in their demeanor, had their priorities in order, and even fewer numbers of those I met wanted to really give back more to this country than they were able to extract from it.

Ross Perot is one of perhaps a total you could count on the fingers of one hand whom I felt had most all the positives, fewer of the negatives, and by far the most desire to put something back into our country.

Was he perfect? Far from it. Did he have a temper? Of course. Did he demand maximum effort from those around him? Always. Was he a tough and demanding businessman? Without a doubt—and fair. Did he have genuine concern for others? More often than anyone knew. Did he share the fruits of his labors with good causes? More than $120 million and still giving. Was his family always first? Without exception.

Ross Perot is still going strong.

Murphy Martin checks podium and set-up prior to Perot speech in 1992 presidential campaign in Dallas. Martin was Perot's television adviser for the campaign.

Ross Perot visits with Bill Clinton and audience members following first presidential debate, St. Louis, 1992. Perot had surprised the nation by dominating the debate.

Bill Clinton checking what his wardrobe should be just hours before first presidential debate, St. Louis, 1992. Clinton and his aides carefully checked how various apparel would look on camera. Ross Perot just brought a freshly pressed suit, clean shirt, and tie and wore no makeup.

Perot waits at rear of auditorium with his television adviser Murphy Martin, to be introduced for the second presidential debates in Richmond, Virginia, 1992.

Ross Perot visits with Barbara Bush following third and final presidential debate in Michigan, 1992.

Martin shows Perot where his family will be seated during the debates at Michigan State University.

Ross Perot emphasizes a point during first presidential debate, St. Louis, 1992.

Ross Perot at his desk at
Perot Systems in Dallas.

Sharon Holman and Murphy
Martin at news conference,
Perot Campaign
Headquarters, 1992.

Portion of capacity crowd at Perot's final speech at Reunion Arena in Dallas the day
before the 1992 presidential election.

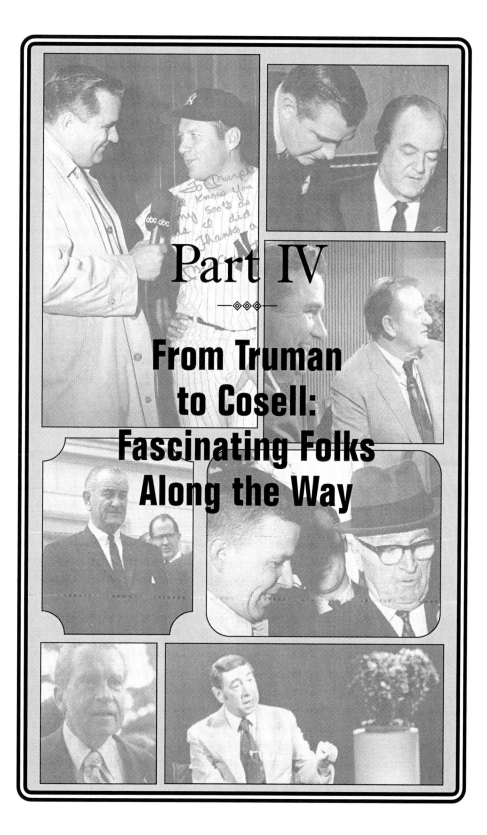

Part IV

❖❖❖

From Truman to Cosell: Fascinating Folks Along the Way

CHAPTER 9

Presidents and Would-Be Presidents

"I sent the Japs word that I had the most powerful weapon in the history of the world and I expected to use it, and the best thing for them to do would be to surrender. They told me to go to hell. Well, I didn't go."

—PRESIDENT HARRY S. TRUMAN

Few political analysts will argue that the presidency of the United States has undergone profound changes since the days of George Washington. Today's presidents are, to a large degree, products of the media. In a country obsessed with popularity ratings and polls, we are most likely to elect the candidate who best looks and talks the part. Still, whatever the capacity to govern, the president must also be a human being committed to an almost superhuman effort.

Larry Grove, a friend of mine, once wrote: "The greatest task of a President is not that of Commander-in-Chief or party leader or legislative leader or director of foreign policy or chief of the executive branch or head of state. Each of these is important, of course, but if a President is to be a great leader of a morally great nation, he must do something that transcends these jobs. He must speak to the United States as well as for it."

I wholeheartedly concur with this assessment. The president

must find the right words to lift men and women above themselves. He or she must be this nation's conscience and its chief teacher. Such leaders are rare, and we have a tremendous task of finding one every four years. Some are better than others.

The man from Independence, Missouri, was one of my favorite White House occupants. I never had the good fortune to cover him during his presidency, but in April of 1967 I found Harry Truman to be just as feisty at age eighty-one as he had been thirteen years earlier when someone criticized his daughter's singing.

Long before he entered the Oval Office, Truman possessed, in his background and personal makeup, great political qualifications. During World War I, he served as a first lieutenant in an artillery unit and was later promoted to captain. Following the war, he opened a clothing store in Kansas City, where he learned the perils of the business world firsthand. His business failed and he lost about $20,000. It took him ten years to repay the debt his business disaster created, but he did repay it.

It was Tom Pendergrast, the Kansas City Democratic boss of the time, who first recognized Truman's political potential. Pendergrast, recognizing Truman as a salt-of-the-earth Baptist with a keen awareness of people and their problems, urged Truman to run for county judge, setting him off on a journey that would end at the White House. He was elected presiding judge in Kansas City in 1926, a position he held until he was elected to the United States Senate in 1934.

Though Pendergrast was a man of questionable reputation who served prison time for income tax evasion, Truman's political report card was spotless. He quickly established a public record of honesty and integrity seldom questioned by his peers. In 1944, President Franklin Roosevelt, concerned that his vice president, Henry A. Wallace, was a Russian sympathizer and therefore a political liability, dumped Wallace from the ticket and put out a call to Harry Truman, who answered. And, when Roosevelt died on April 12, 1945, Truman became the thirty-third president of the United States.

Throughout his tenure, Truman wrestled with decisions that might overwhelm most people, not the least of which was the decision to use the atom bomb to end World War II. But Truman acted decisively on each occasion, without regard to how his decisions might affect his personal popularity. For him, the country's well-being came first. He was a man of unbending courage and grit, crusty and often profane. But he was exactly what the country needed at the time.

I, along with several other newsmen, had the privilege to speak to Mr. Truman in April of 1967 during one of his early-morning walks while he was in New York to accept an award. Dressed in his well-tailored best, consisting of hat, suit, tie, and topcoat, he walked like a man on a mission. The rest of us found it hard to keep up. His years away from the White House had changed him little, as far as I could tell.

The Truman candor was certainly still present, as our conversation turned to one of the prime topics of the day—the civil rights struggle. He had done a great deal for black Americans at a time when it didn't advance him politically. Who, I wanted to know, had been the black leaders he had listened to during his presidency?

He considered my question for a moment, then said, "In those days, we had several good nigger leaders. And there are plenty of leaders among the colored people now, decent people, just the same as we are. Of course, there are also a lot of damn fools among them—just like Martin Luther King."

Unlike today's journalistic climate that thrives on exposing the gaffes and the politically incorrect statements of public figures, those comments, although heard by my editors at ABC Radio and TV, never aired. I knew it wasn't the first time Truman had used that word, and I doubt it was the last. I also doubt that Truman meant to insult the black race. He was simply one of those people who had been brought up in an environment in which a disgusting label was accepted without passion, used simply to denote a different race. But one can remove such words from his vocabulary with a little awareness, of that I am certain. I speak from the experience of having grown up in rural East Texas.

I asked Mr. Truman to elaborate on his thoughts about Dr. King. After all, this was a man who had won a Nobel Peace Prize for his work in supporting peaceful demonstrations throughout the South and elsewhere rather than utilize ugly confrontational politics.

"I think he is a troublemaker and acts like a damn fool," Truman said.

Surprised, I asked, "Mr. Truman, are you saying Dr. King is a damn fool?"

"No, I said he acts like one—and you make damn sure you quote me correctly."

I reminded Truman that he was speaking of the man who had won a Nobel Peace Prize. "Well, I didn't give it to him," Truman snapped.

In that same conversation, I asked Truman to name the toughest decision he'd had to make as president, fully expecting him to identify the dropping of the atom bomb. "Korea was the most important decision I made," he said. "That affected the whole free world, and that was the reason for that."

"This was a tougher decision than the atom bomb?" I asked.

"The atom bomb wasn't any decision at all," he said. "The atom bomb was a weapon of war and I used it to end the war ... wasn't anything heart-breaking about using the atom bomb. Saved, I guess, about 150,000 of our kids from getting killed, and as many on the other side, and probably five times that many from getting injured for life."

And just like that, with moral clarity, the decision had been made. I wondered whether it had been a military decision or a joint presidential-military decision. Surely it wouldn't have rested in the hands of one man alone.

"Of course I had to make a decision," he said. "Who else could make it?"

Any regrets? "Not the slightest. I haven't dreamed about it since."

I next asked whether, looking back, he would have done anything differently as president.

"No, and I'll tell you why I wouldn't have done anything differently. Because when conditions came up at that time, I had to make a decision on the spot. And any man that's going to do the job would have to do the same thing and when things came along, I met them as best I knew how. And that's all there was to it and that's what I'd do again."

But back to the atom bomb decision. How did that come about?

"While I was at Potsdam, I got a telegram about, oh, I don't know how long. It was a full-page report on the testing of the atom bomb. Then I put it on Admiral Leahy's desk. The Admiral told me that the damn thing wouldn't go off. He was wrong, along with a lot of other people. So it became a weapon of war just the same as the long rifle or anything of that kind that's used in war. When it came time to use it, I ordered it used and that's all there was to it. Wasn't anything heart-shaking or heart-rendering about it."

I reminded him that, while the bomb may have saved lives, it also took a lot of lives.

"Of course," he said. "It had to. They had plenty of notice it would be used if they didn't stop, and they told me to go to hell, and I sent them there, and that's all there was to it."

So going back to the decision he identified as his most important while in the White House, I asked whether he had done a lot of soul searching about his decision to commit troops in Korea.

"No," he said. "Korea had a situation that had to be met. You don't have to do any soul searching when you're president of the United States."

"All I have I would have given gladly not to be standing here today."
—PRESIDENT LYNDON BAINES JOHNSON,
FIRST ADDRESS TO CONGRESS

Probably no president took office under more stirring and dramatic circumstances than did Lyndon Baines Johnson. Having already spent more than two decades on Capitol Hill, he found himself elevated to the presidency by one of this nation's greatest tragedies, the assassination of John Fitzgerald Kennedy. A man more tolerated than accepted in Kennedy circles, Johnson was crude, sometimes earthy, but always the master politician.

Born the son of a Texas Hill Country farmer and state legislator, LBJ first encountered politics when he left Texas for Washington as secretary to Representative Richard Kleberg in 1931. Within six years, Johnson was himself a member of Congress and on the road to the White House.

After serving out the remainder of Kennedy's term, Johnson won reelection in 1964 against Arizona Senator Barry Goldwater in a landslide victory. The victory probably came as no surprise, but the *margin* of victory was another story. And there were moments during the final days of that campaign when I felt about as defeated as Goldwater must have felt when all the votes had been counted.

Spending Election Day at his Texas ranch on the Pedernales

River, Johnson and Lady Bird had cast their ballots together at Johnson City. At the opportune time, they would then drive to Austin, where crowds were already beginning to gather at the Driskill Hotel. Along with Bob Clark and our camera crew, I had been assigned by ABC to cover the president's campaign during its final six weeks, and so I waited along with other newspeople at the Driskill for Johnson's arrival. The entrance had been roped off, leaving an eight-foot-wide aisle for the president and his party. Clark stationed himself inside the Driskill, near the Presidential Suite, while I camped outside, eyeing my competition.

I spotted Dan Rather of CBS on one side of the aisle and, opposite him, Nancy Dickerson of NBC. Knowing that if Johnson stopped to talk with anyone, it would be Nancy, I positioned myself next to her. Soon the victorious president arrived from his ranch, smiling broadly with what I always felt was simply a frozen exercise of well-trained facial muscles. Not wearing his glasses, which he seldom did in public, he strode confidently toward the hotel, waving and nodding.

I boomed, "Mr. President! Mr. President!"

When he turned, he zeroed in on Nancy, as I had known he would. I pointed my microphone out alongside hers.

"Nancy," he drawled, using that down-home tone of affection he saved for certain reporters, "I've been watching your coverage on television and you've been just great."

Not exactly what I had expected. Praise for NBC going out over ABC's airwaves through my microphone from a president who seemed to be pointedly ignoring me.

Not one to be ignored, I asked, "Mr. President, throughout this campaign you have been calling for a mandate from the American people. Do you feel you are receiving that mandate?"

He leaned close, to about twelve inches, looked me in the eye, and said, not in the down-home tone, "I'll talk with you about that later." Then he turned again to Nancy and cooed, "Now, Nancy, what was it that you wanted?"

I lost the rest of what he said due to the screaming in my earpiece—the voice of my producer expressing his loud displeasure. I prayed that ABC had cut away to Howard K. Smith or Edward P. Morgan anchoring back in the New York studios, but I hung in there in case it hadn't.

"Mr. President," I said in my best you-didn't-just-embarrass-me-on-national-television voice, "have you talked to Mr. Humphrey tonight?"

"Yes," he said, "and he'll be arriving here early tomorrow morning. And we're going to honor all you nice press people with a party at the ranch."

A short time later, I asked a Johnson press aide, Liz Carpenter, to please remind the president that there was more than one network in the United States. She must have passed the message along, because Johnson later gave my associate, Bob Clark, an exclusive interview. And, of course, he came across as the good ol' Texas boy as only LBJ could.

—◇◇◇—

"Fire that ———!"

—President Lyndon Johnson

During the final, hectic six weeks of the 1964 campaign, I had the chance to view the president from a variety of vantage points, which allowed me to learn something more about this private man and his unparalleled intensity. At the end of one of those marathon days of campaigning in California, the president, making his final speech to a group in San Diego, had stumbled a number of times while reading from the teleprompter. A man who prided himself on his public speaking, he was furious over those mistakes.

From San Diego, we were to fly directly to Salt Lake City for an overnight stay, then on to the East Coast, then to Houston and Austin. As one of five pool reporters for the flight, I was awaiting the president's arrival at the bottom of the ramp to Air Force One. Standing off to one side, I saw the young woman who had typed the speech for the teleprompter. She was clearly nervous. When the president started up the ramp, he looked in her direction. He then turned to the supervisor of the teleprompter operations. Without the slightest change in expression, he pointed at the woman. "Fire that ———!" he said.

She did not board Air Force One.

Such was the harsh, all-business side of LBJ. On the other hand, there were moments when he could be as likable and thoughtful a man as you could hope to encounter.

Earlier in the campaign, I had been riding with a group of pool reporters in the second car behind the presidential limousine while his motorcade traveled through Milwaukee. Several times he stopped the motorcade to speak to the crowd through a bullhorn and shake hands with those lining the streets. As we approached one intersection, I noticed Johnson looking in the direction of a small "mom and pop" grocery store. When he had the limo stop, I got out of the press car and headed for the doorway to the store, anticipating his next move.

He didn't disappoint. Within seconds, Johnson had entered the store, which was owned and operated by a middle-aged Polish couple. The president introduced himself to them, as if they didn't know who he was, then headed in the direction of the meat counter where he asked for bologna and cheese. The dazed owner laid out a stick of bologna, from which the president cut an ample serving. Then he sliced some hoop cheese and ate and chatted for a few minutes.

As he prepared to leave, Johnson said to the young Secret Service agents who had accompanied him, "I don't have any money. You got some so we can pay this man?"

The store owner, proud to have fed the president, insisted he wanted no money, but LBJ pressed a borrowed ten-dollar bill into his hand, then left. As he exited, he saw me for the first time and smiled warmly.

"How are your folks back in East Texas?" he asked.

I told him everyone was fine and thanked him for asking. He pulled an LBJ tie tack from his pocket and gave it to me. "I'd like for you to give this to your daddy next time you see him."

I doubt if anything ever pleased my father, a man who had voted a straight Democratic ticket since 1918, more than that gift from President Johnson. And Dad wore that tack on his 100th birthday celebration in Lufkin a few years back.

Then there was the evening of the '64 election when Senator Goldwater refused to concede despite the one-sided vote coming in. LBJ and Lady Bird emerged at 4:00 A.M. from their waiting area in the rear of the city auditorium in Austin to drive back to the ranch. Even at that time of the morning, people waited near the rear entrance, hoping to get LBJ's autograph. When he saw them, the president took a piece of paper and began repeatedly signing his name.

Then he tore the paper into strips and distributed the signatures to the waiting folks.

The scene impressed me. I asked him if he ever got tired of giving autographs.

"No," he said. "I learned back during the World War Two war bond drive that you never get in too big a hurry to sign for the people. It was Jack Dempsey, the heavyweight boxing champion, who taught me that. I asked him one time why he took so much time to sign autographs and he told me, 'Congressman, it has been many years since I was the heavyweight champion of the world. But when someone asks me for my autograph, it tells me they still remember. And it makes me feel good. I figure the day they don't ask, I've got a problem.'

"I look at it much the same way," Johnson said.

The last time I saw LBJ, he had retired to his beloved ranch in the Texas Hill Country. He knew of Ross Perot's efforts on behalf of the POWs and sent word to Ross that he wanted to help. Tom Johnson, a former Johnson aide, extended the invitation to the LBJ ranch, but made it clear that the former president wanted to keep his involvement, if any, secret.

So Perot and I flew down in a private chartered plane and found LBJ waiting for us at the landing strip on his ranch in one of his white Lincoln Continentals. For much of the day he talked about the Vietnam problems, offering to help but continually stressing the need to keep his involvement secret. "If the North Vietnamese knew I am supporting you," he said, "they will turn down everything you ask."

It was, to put it mildly, an interesting day. Johnson held court, reflecting on his days in the White House, the Vietnam War, and the current political climate. He even hinted that he would like to trade some stock in his Austin television station for some of Perot's EDS stock—something which didn't interest Perot. Periodically, Johnson would yell, "Bird! Bird!" Each time, Lady Bird would come to the door and he'd say, "Bring us something to drink, please."

At the end of the day, he took us on his customary ranch tour, driving through pastures where roads never existed. He obviously loved the land. He also was obviously lonesome for the high-paced political life he had mastered for so many years and the spotlight that accompanied it.

After Perot and I boarded our plane to return to Dallas, we watched as our host drove away in his white Continental.

"I wonder why he wanted to talk to us?" Perot asked.

I didn't have an answer then. I still don't today. I can't help but think the fact that he seemed so lonely had something to do with it.

—◇◆◇—

"Thank you, Mr. President, and God bless America."
—ADM. JEREMIAH DENTON FOLLOWING HIS RELEASE FROM CAPTIVITY IN NORTH VIETNAM

As lonely and isolated as Lyndon Johnson may have felt in his retirement years, those feelings must surely have paled next to those of Richard Nixon after his troubled departure from the White House. Although my professional exposure to Nixon dates back to interviews I did with him in 1964, when he was stumping on behalf of various Republican candidates, it was not until he had retreated in disgrace to San Clemente that I came to really know something of the man.

Despite the controversy that swirled around his head arising out of Watergate, he nevertheless remained one of the most admired men in the world by the returning Vietnam POWs. I'll never forget Adm. Jeremiah Denton's emotional speech after he finally arrived at Clark Air Force Base after so many years in captivity. He ended the speech by saying, "Thank you, Mr. President, and God bless America."

In 1978, Nixon hosted a POW reunion at San Clemente, one of the first times he saw anyone publicly following his resignation. The POWs invited Joyce and me as their guests, and so we accompanied them to the Nixon home for a reception. On that day, there were no reminders of Watergate or the cloud under which Nixon had left office. Instead, he opened up his home graciously, served wonderful food and drink, and extended warm hospitality. One of Nixon's aides told me he had not seen Nixon so relaxed and happy since he had left Washington.

The POWs, in a show of gratitude, presented the former president with a painting and, following the visit, Nixon sent each of them an autographed copy of his memoir. I think it can be safely said that, with a few exceptions, those men and their families who were in attendance that day will still tell you that Richard Milhous Nixon was one of America's greatest presidents.

In retrospect, I wonder: If Nixon had destroyed the damning White House tapes, history in general might have regarded him in a much kinder way.

"In the position I'm in, I should not see it even though the president offered it to me . . . It might be used by me, if I were so inclined—which I'm not—ill-advisedly."
—VICE PRESIDENT GERALD FORD

President Gerald Ford, to this day, conjures up the image of an awkward, uncoordinated bumpkin. Hundreds of political cartoons have portrayed him that way, as has virtually every comic who impersonated him. Who can forget the pratfalls of Chevy Chase on *Saturday Night Live*? Ironically, Ford was, perhaps, the most athletic of all our presidents, having played center on the football team at the University of Michigan.

That athleticism and his participation in team sports often dominated his thinking. I talked with him while he was still vice president, and I was hardly surprised when I asked him to name the greatest single disappointment in life. He said it was his failure to be named captain of the Michigan football team, even though he had been named the team's Most Valuable Player.

The other great disappointment, he said, was not being elected Speaker of the House of Representatives. When I suggested that being appointed vice president must surely have removed some of that sting, he conceded only that being vice president might be the *equal* of being Speaker. "I would have a hard time differentiating," he said.

He left me with the impression that becoming vice president was nothing more than a consolation prize. When Nixon's later resignation would propel him into the White House, I wondered if he still felt the sting of dissatisfaction. After all, he hadn't been elected to the presidency.

For someone with his sports background, the lessons learned in team sports were a way of life. So, too, were sports metaphors, which he applied to virtually every aspect of political life, right down to how he treated members of Congress.

"You can't take every competitor on a football team and get the best out of all of them by treating them the same," he said. "You have to treat individuals on a person-to-person basis. You treat members of Congress on a personal basis, not as a big mass of individuals. So the combination of playing the competition, the teamwork, the understanding that you win some and you lose some—all of these things made a big impact on my life."

As we talked, I turned the conversation to President Nixon, who was then trying to fend off association with the growing Watergate scandal. Nixon had just announced that he would turn over documents to the Judiciary Committee that had previously been produced to the Grand Jury, and he had also agreed to answer written questions and, if necessary, oral questions.

In my mind, this was the beginning of the end for Nixon. He might have survived in another time. Had he played his cards differently, he might even have been able to outlast his detractors then. But, I felt, such was not to be.

"I know he feels he's entirely innocent," Ford said. "I happen to think he is, too. And I believe that this step he has taken as an indication of cooperation will, beyond any doubt whatsoever, convince not only this Committee but the American people that he is completely innocent."

Clearly, Ford was being the loyal soldier—or the inveterate optimist. History, of course, would prove him wrong.

I wondered, though, why he felt so strongly in Nixon's innocence. Had he seen the evidence that Nixon claimed would totally exonerate him? Turns out he hadn't, nor did he want to.

"In the position I am in, I should not see it even if the president offered it to me. In the position I'm in, it might be used by me, if I were so inclined—which I'm not—ill-advisedly. I would rather see the evidence when it is presented to the appropriate body."

Throughout our conversation, Ford gave no hint that he thought Nixon's resignation was even a possibility, or that he himself harbored thoughts of becoming president. At least not that way. But if he were to take on the job, he believed his brief stint as vice president was a good training ground.

"If I should become president, I consider the job I'm doing now, this work as vice president, preparation for any additional responsibilities. Certainly I have been given more responsibilities than any vice president during my lifetime in Washington."

And although he had been vice president for two years as of that time, he had no aspirations to run for president in 1976. Too many other logical candidates in the Republican Party, he said, including New York Governor Nelson Rockefeller, California Governor Ronald Reagan, former Texas Governor John Connally, and Senators Baker and Percy. He spoke very highly of all those men.

In fact, I was hard pressed to find anyone in politics of whom he did not speak highly or at least like on a personal basis. Even his predecessor, the disgraced former governor of Maryland, Spiro Agnew, he viewed as "an unfortunate victim of circumstances that prevailed in the state of Maryland historically."

How would he characterize his then-current boss, Richard Nixon?

"One of the most able people in the history of America in handling foreign policy matters and maintaining peace after it was achieved."

And what if he turned the microscope on himself? What would he see?

"I hope," he said, "that I'm a decent, hard-working, honorable, dedicated individual as a member of the Congress or as vice president, giving my very best to the responsibilities that I have."

Certainly he was that.

"Well, I think the people of America today are hungry for a spiritual revival, for an adherence to traditional moral values."
—Ronald Reagan

Then there is Ronald Reagan. In 1974, as California governor, Reagan was a guest on my *Face to Face* show while in Dallas to address a Crime Convention assembly. The country was still deeply embroiled in Watergate, its leader accused of wrongdoing but steadfastly refusing to acknowledge it. I asked Reagan what he would have done had he been president and faced a similar problem.

"I always hate to answer a question in that framework," he said. "It always sounds like the 'If I were king' line."

"Not king," I reminded him with a smile. "Just president."

Little did either of us know then that six years later he would, indeed, move into the White House. But in 1974, he was still a governor facing, as were all Americans, an upcoming phenomenon history would record as the Energy Crisis. Was it really a crisis?

"I think it's very real," Reagan said. "I think all the evidence indicates that . . . We Americans, if you remember things in the past of this kind, we don't really believe the worst is going to happen until it happens. And we've had plenty of warning. Most people have forgotten a man named Molly Malone back in the '50s, a senator from Oklahoma. His colleagues thought he was a pest. He kept hammering at this fact that there was going to be an energy shortage in this country if we didn't do something about it.

"If you look back now on the report he finally turned over to the Congress of the United States, it was as prophetic as a book in the Old Testament. He told us exactly what was going to happen, but everyone literally laughed him out of Washington. Around 1947, a congressional committee on the Interior did a study on the energy requirements and predicted an energy shortage by 1972. And eight of those men are still in the United States Senate."

When the conversation turned to welfare in America, Reagan had strong opinions, and an interesting tale to go along with them.

"There was a columnist writing in an eastern newspaper ... about a part-time welfare recipient working for a part-time farmer and who stole a smoked ham from the farmer's smokehouse. Then he took the ham to the grocer and sold it for $27. With $20 of the $27, he bought $80 worth of food stamps for which he was eligible by reason of being on welfare. Then he bought the ham back for $29, and he bought $51 worth of groceries. Then he put the ham back in the smokehouse.

"The columnist concluded in what is too much the flavor of today ... that the grocer made a profit, the welfare recipient had $7 cash and $51 worth of groceries, and the farmer had his ham back, with no one being the loser."

Then, with the fervor of a tent meeting evangelist, Reagan said, "Well, I think the people of America today are hungry for a spiritual revival, for an adherence to traditional moral values."

He went on to say that he felt it was our responsibility, as adults, to instill those values—such as truth, justice, and honor—into our children. Of course, he reminded me, that belief was nothing new. He was simply agreeing with Thomas Jefferson.

"When Thomas Jefferson was advising his nephew what path he should follow to achieve success," Reagan said, "he told him that men must always pursue their own and their country's interests with the purest integrity, the most chaste honor. He said, 'Make these your first object. Give up money, give up fame, give up the earth itself and all it contains rather than do an immoral act. Never suppose that in any possible situation or under any circumstances that it is best to do a dishonorable thing, however slightly so it may appear to you.'

"I'm afraid that all of us, to some degree, contributed to the erosion of time-tested moral principles such as that one enunciated by Jefferson."

I often wished I could have interviewed Mr. Reagan while he was president, but that opportunity never happened.

> *"I don't think there's any deep-seated resentment of any kind because I think people know that this was really an individual act of a person who was disturbed. And, though I haven't had a chance to visit Dallas, I have visited Texas and look forward to doing so again."*
> —SENATOR TED KENNEDY

One can only wonder how different the electorate would view Senator Ted Kennedy had he been an only son rather than a man loaded with massive family responsibilities because of the deaths of his brothers. Although he may well be the ablest of the family members, history will always view him through the prism of all that has happened to his family.

In 1973, when I asked him whether he intended to run for president in 1976, he told me that his family responsibilities overrode any personal ambitions. "My first reasons are for the responsibilities that I have to my family and to my brothers' families," he said. "That really is an overriding consideration which will dictate my decision. Not to be aware of the tragedies which befell them would be rather unrealistic. But to be obsessed with the possibility would really compromise one's ability to be effective in public life. So one continues to do the best he can."

I turned his thoughts toward Dallas for a moment, anxious to know his feelings about my town, as my producer had called it in 1963. I asked him if he felt any bitterness toward the city that some still blamed for the death of his brother. Although I believe his reply was sincere, I knew I had tapped a deep and unpleasant well of emotion.

"I think the members of the family are aware that President Kennedy had been well-received in Dallas by a great majority of the people before the time of the tragedy," he said. "And I think the members of the family understand that. I don't think there's any deep-seated feeling of resentment of any kind, because I think people know that this was really an individual act of a person who was disturbed. And, though I haven't had a chance to visit Dallas, I have visited Texas and look forward to doing so again."

The Kennedys are as well known for their wealth as they are for their public service. There are still those today who believe Joseph Kennedy "bought" an election for his son, John, in 1960. While there is some truth to the notion that people of wealth have certain political advantages that others do not, I nevertheless believe that we should commend their tendency to offer themselves for public service. The real question, as I see it, is whether the wealthy can truly understand the problems of the average citizen.

Senator Kennedy, certainly quite wealthy, believed they could. And for him, politics truly was all about "service": "Trying to speak for the thousands of people in my state and perhaps in other parts of the country who really haven't felt that they had a real voice in the important legislative enactments of the Congress or had their views expressed at high levels of government."

Kennedy also had, unsurprisingly, strong opinions on a number of other topics. Surprisingly, though, he had some good things to say about President Richard Nixon. He believed that Nixon had made some "extremely important gains" in the areas of foreign relations. He also didn't believe that Nixon, during the crisis moments of the Watergate scandal, should resign before the House Judiciary Committee had fully examined the case. "If there's insufficient evidence to justify impeachment," he said, "then that ought to be the end of it with regard to any presidential involvement."

Putting a positive spin on Watergate, he also believed that the experience actually provided an opportunity for America to shine in the international community. Definitely expressing a "glass-is-half-full" attitude, he said, "I try to explain it to friends from abroad that it really is the greatest day in the history of the country for a free press. I don't know any other country in the world that would have had this kind of examination.

"And I think, rather than saying this is a harsh day for the presidency, I'd rather believe that it's our system that will be stronger for all this once the action is taken by the House Judiciary Committee and finally is resolved in the House of Representatives and the Senate of the United States.

"And we shouldn't apologize for it."

"Mr. President, when I walk in these boots, I feel just like the man we just defeated, because I'll be taking two steps forward and one step back. Maybe we had best get some that fit."
—VICE PRESIDENT HUBERT HUMPHREY
FOLLOWING THE 1964 ELECTION

I interviewed Vice President Hubert Humphrey on *Face to Face* in February of 1968, at a time when he had no inkling that LBJ would not run for a second full term and that he would be the Democratic candidate, on short notice, later that year. At the time, the Vietnam conflict was in full swing and Humphrey—always upbeat, always optimistic—spoke enthusiastically of our progress in the war. He cited figures from governmental sources that listed over 26,000 Viet Cong dead and 6,000 more detained as prisoners of war against American casualties of less than 700—a number that would blossom into the tens of thousands before the war ended. But, at least at that time, there was still room for optimism.

Lurking beneath the surface of his cheerfulness, however, I sensed that the vice president may have been a bit afraid of being in Dallas, the city in which JFK had been killed scarcely more than four years before. It could have been something else, of course, but I definitely detected nervousness as we sat before the cameras.

Just before we started, longtime WFAA-TV employee Tommy Gosnell entered the set to straighten the vice presidential seal that was attached to Humphrey's desk. As Tommy went about his job, Humphrey and his Secret Service contingent caught a glimpse of a shiny metallic hammer that he carried. Just then, a still photographer snapped a picture, capturing Humphrey with a look of absolute terror on his face.

It took several minutes for Humphrey to regain his composure, but regain it he did as the cameras rolled. Then the darnedest thing happened. One of the overhead lights exploded, echoing like a cannon blast through the studio. Had Humphrey been prone to heart attack, his political future might have ended right there.

I'm sure the incident must have remained on his mind throughout the thirty-minute interview, which I shared with Dick West, then editorial director of the *Dallas Morning News*; Jim Lehrer, the capable and incisive Dallas reporter who now anchors Public Broadcasting's *Lehrer Report*; and Travis Linn, Channel 8 news director.

At one point, I asked the vice president about an attack that had taken place on the grounds of the U.S. Embassy in South Vietnam. Although the Americans knew the Tet attacks were coming and were on alert, nineteen Viet Cong managed to penetrate security at the Embassy. How could something like that happen?

His answer, which lasted for three minutes, is just as relevant today, regarding the Middle East, as it was then about Vietnam. I can't vouch for the syntax, however, of the very nervous and recently startled vice president:

"May I say that when men are disguised as civilians, when they're wearing the camouflage, as they were in this instance, of the South Vietnamese police, when they undoubtedly had been infiltrated into the community of Saigon for weeks, if not for months, and when they all pretty much look alike, if you're willing to pay the price, no matter how many Secret Service I have around here, no matter how many police, if they are willing to come in here loaded with explosives, as they did, and willing to sacrifice their lives, they can blow a hole through this studio, too, no matter how many police you put in here, not if they plan it long enough."

That wasn't all he said, of course, but that was all he could get out in one breath.

No doubt about it, the Happy Warrior enjoyed life, which was too soon taken from him. The job of vice president wasn't well suited for him and, though he tried his best to be the number-two man to

Lyndon Johnson, he found that it could sometimes be the toughest job in the world.

Following the '64 election, Johnson followed through on his promise to throw a party at his ranch for the press corps. The ABC assignment desk sent me to the Austin airport to cover Humphrey's arrival, then we all went "off duty" for the party. Inclement weather had moved in, so the party was held inside a large barn near the ranch house. Red checkered tablecloths covered bales of hay that had been stacked against the walls, and Cactus Pryor, one of LBJ's favorite personalities, served as master of ceremonies.

During the party, LBJ auctioned off the bullhorn he had used during the campaign, which went to the high bid of NBC's May Craig. You may remember her as the woman who always wore a hat during her years on NBC's *Meet the Press*. Then Johnson gave Humphrey a pair of cowboy boots. When the newly elected vice president from Minnesota put them on, they were a bit too big.

"Mr. President," he said, "when I walk in these boots, I feel just like the man we just defeated, because I'll be taking two steps forward and one step back. Maybe we had best get some that fit."

"I think the world is sophisticated about the weakness of human beings. I think that the world looks on this country perhaps not as they did earlier; they now see that we have human weaknesses, too."
—NELSON ROCKEFELLER

Perhaps no one ever wanted to be president of the United States more than Nelson Rockefeller, and arguably no one was ever more qualified to hold that office. But despite his desires, his efforts, and his unlimited financial resources, he never really had a chance. I guess it's only fair that he at least got to serve for a while in the number-two spot to Gerald Ford.

During my days in New York, I often interviewed then Governor Rockefeller. I was even briefly assigned to his campaign for one of his runs at the presidency. But it was after my return to Texas that I found him at his most relaxed. After resigning as governor of New York, he came to Dallas in February of 1974 for a meeting of the

Commission on Critical Choices for America. One of the first things I wanted to know was why he had stepped down from the governorship.

"The problems we are facing now were increasingly national and international problems beyond our capacity to deal with as a state," he said. "Having been in national and international affairs in earlier years, I wanted to get back where the action was."

And the action then was Watergate, something he believed would force the country to focus once again on moral issues.

"It may awaken the country to the fact that . . . we have lost a sharp focus on what is right and what is wrong. Too much cutting of corners for all of us, whether it's trying to fix a ticket or deal with the mob, or cheat on an exam, or whatever it is. I think this country is going to have to return to fundamental values. Moral, spiritual, ethical values in all phases of life if we are going to preserve the strength and vitality and greatness that's been America."

I knew Rockefeller had been watching the whole Watergate affair with keen interest. After all, the scandal was playing out in the office he had long yearned for. I found his observations very interesting.

"Well, now, the basic question is did he know about it or did he not know about it. We just have to assume that he did not . . . maybe this will dramatize for America that you can't cheat and you can't cut corners. I think the only tragedy about Watergate that still exists is that those who had human weakness have not been brought to trial and the matter ended. But I think the world is sophisticated about the weakness of human beings. I think that the world looks on this country perhaps not as they did earlier.

"They now see that we have human weakness, too."

"I say that the people of Texas and the people of Alabama and California should determine the policies of democratic domestic institutions such as schools, hospitals, the appointment of legislatures, the matter of house ownership. There simply is no logic in any argument that there is somebody in Washington, D.C., who can run them better than they can be run locally."
—ALABAMA GOVERNOR GEORGE WALLACE

George Corley Wallace was the consummate politician, and a fascinating individual. Reviled by many as a racist, he certainly was a man of strong opinions, not all of them popular. And not all of them as black-and-white as have often been painted.

While at ABC, I covered his first campaign for president as a third-party candidate. While campaigning in Chicago, I watched firsthand as pro-black demonstrators broke through a police line around a television station where Wallace had been taping an interview. Just as he and his Alabama State Trooper bodyguards in civilian clothes exited, a demonstrator headed straight for Wallace. Someone shouted, "Stop him! Stop him!"

One of the bodyguards unbuttoned his coat and put his hand on his .357 Magnum. "No," he said, "let him come on."

The demonstrator quickly melted back into the throng from which he had come.

Such was the campaign of George Wallace.

During my many visits to Alabama covering the civil rights struggles of the '60s, I spent a lot of time talking with Governor Wallace and also got to know his wife, Lurleen, who would later be the stand-in governor for him when he was prohibited by statute from running for another consecutive term. George Wallace offers a study in the differences between the actual politician and the way the politician is perceived by the public. In public perception, the word "bigot" probably comes immediately to mind. One of the preeminent images of the man is that picture of him standing in the doorway to prevent young blacks from entering school following court-ordered desegregation.

But to so lightly cast Wallace aside as anti-black misses the deeper point. I found this out in one of my conversations with him that touched on a number of terms his opponents used to label him: racist, bigot, segregationist. I discovered, to my own surprise, a much deeper man than that, one whose principle failing may have been his inability to properly identify himself with what he was really passionate about—states' rights.

"I've talked about states' rights and local government for a long time," he said. "Some governors in other regions refer to this matter as 'territorial democracy.' There is a growing concern about the government of our country taking over the policies of domestic democratic institutions. I say that the people of Texas and the people of Alabama and California should determine the policies of democratic domestic institutions such as schools, hospitals, the appointment of legislatures, the matter of home ownership. There simply is no logic in an argument that there is somebody in Washington, D.C., who can run them better than they can be run locally."

Hard to argue with the sentiment. So why was he misunderstood—if, indeed, he was? Wallace had an opinion on that as well: "Now, the liberals in the country and much of the news media have written the people of the individual states off by just saying people who want to have their rights on the local level are hate-mongers, racists, or fascists. Since they can't make a logical argument against our position, they just say, 'oh, he's a hater.'"

He staunchly defended his record and denied that he was a racist. As proof of the righteousness of his stance, he pointed out that when he was barred from running for a third term as governor, voters not only elected his wife in his stead, but black voters in Alabama gave her a majority over both opponents. In other words, in his eyes, the black voters validated the Wallace position.

"I never, in all my life, made a speech that reflected on anybody because of race or religion, national origin or creed. You know, it's ironic that they make racists out of people who have been honest. When we talk about schools, I could care less what kind of schools the people in Dallas or Indianapolis or Tulsa have because I know they'll have good schools because they're all good people."

But what about that image of him blocking the doorway to the school? Wasn't he protesting desegregation?

"I don't recommend segregation of anything to anybody in the United States as far as public schools are concerned. I recommend only that the people of California, New Hampshire, Texas, and Alabama and other states run the schools themselves and not have them run from a central source in Washington," he said.

When that interview aired, I was certain that many people saw a more logical and articulate George Wallace than they had previously as he defended the rights of individual states to run their own institutions. Unfortunately for him, by that time public opinion outside Alabama had already been set. He had allowed himself to be drawn into the struggle for states' rights on the wrong issue at the wrong time.

Some years later, when the federal government had extended its reach even farther into Americans' daily lives, his message probably would have sounded almost welcome even outside the South. But not in the 1960s, and not on the issue of segregation. Given that, it was a wonder that he was able to be any kind of political force at all in his run for the presidency. A run that was, for all practical purposes, ended by a would-be assassin's bullet in a Maryland shopping center in 1972, leaving him wheelchair-bound.

In reviewing the transcript of one of my interviews with the governor, I found that he had spoken of assassins long before he, too, was felled. "The death of Dr. Martin Luther King was regrettable and tragic," he said. "It was unsensible for someone to take the law into his own hands and shoot someone. Whether I agree with someone or not, they're entitled to live and not be shot down. That's a typical example of the breakdown of law and order in this country. I hope that whoever's responsible for the death of Dr. King, or anyone else who is shot down, is apprehended and that we get to the bottom of why it happened."

That was George Wallace—misunderstood, perhaps, but a fighter.

A man who wanted to be president.

"I take the basic position that my duty is not to a party, but to my country. The parties are only a vehicle through which you serve your country."
—Former Texas Governor John Connally

Many political observers seriously questioned the timing of former Texas Governor John Connally's switch from the Democratic Party, of which he had been a lifelong member, to the Republican Party in the early 1970s. After all, notwithstanding that there was a Republican in the White House, the Republicans were still in the minority in Congress and throughout the country. And that Republican president was becoming more and more deeply embroiled in the Watergate controversy. Questionable timing indeed.

I talked with Governor Connally in September of 1973 and asked him about that switch. Why now?

"Well, I don't think Watergate casts a dark cloud over the Republican Party," he answered. "I think when we get to this point, when we want to take the acts of a few people and smear a political party, then we get into a question of class indictment. And that's not very far from a race indictment or a religious indictment. It's very un-American, so the fact that I made the decision when I did had nothing to do with what was transpiring in the country."

He went on to say, simply, that he felt the Republican Party offered a more satisfying position to him than did the Democrats. "I think the Republican Party today is the more moderate party of the two. I think it more nearly reflects the broad spectrum of American political philosophy, although, numerically, it's still smaller than the Democratic Party. I think it still espouses a belief, a fundamental belief in government and the functions of government and how government should operate that is more nearly attuned to the feelings and desires and the hopes of most of the people in this country. Basically, it is that government ought not try to run everything in the country, that there can be too much government, and we have too much government—and that the government is too centralized in Washington."

He was starting to sound a little like George Wallace.

"On the obverse side," he continued, "as I said when I changed parties, I think the Democratic Party as I have always known it has changed very radically. I think it is in the hands of people whose philosophies certainly are not in accord with those I have always known that directed the Democratic Party .... I take the basic position that my duty is not to a party, but to my country. The parties are only a vehicle through which you serve your country."

But surely Connally understood that Watergate did have a negative impact, not only on the Republican Party but also on the country as a whole. Yes, in fact, he did. "It's resulted in a diminution of respect that people have for politics and for politicians and for government," he said. "I think it is something that will be overcome, but it's going to take time."

But Watergate had another negative impact, as well—this one related not to the scandal itself but to how the scandal had been handled and reported on. Connally said it this way: "The press, properly I think, insist on the freedom of the press, on their rights, on the rights of people to know. But with every right goes responsibility. And the press is just as responsible and should be just as responsible and held just as accountable as any politician. Because in many ways, the press today is as powerful as all of the politicians put together. The press interprets the politicians to the people and to the public. So, I think the press has a very great responsibility in these times."

How can I disagree with that?

I must admit to being one of those American citizens who holds the office of the president in awe. The job demands create tremendous pressures beyond my ability to comprehend. Even after having met and gotten to know a few who have held the office or aspired to it, I continue to wonder at their remarkable ability to cope with the responsibilities. It is a job for only a special breed.

As President Truman once noted, the kitchen in which they work often gets quite warm. Those who have enjoyed success have simply ignored the heat.

CHAPTER 10

Never a Dull Moment

In addition to being able to see history in the making from a front row vantage point, one of the great rewards associated with the business of journalism is the opportunity to meet a wide variety of people. I know of no other line of work that allows you to know a perfect stranger so quickly and to ask the personal questions no one else would dare. If done properly, it can result not only in thought-provoking stories, but also the beginning of long-term relationships.

Of all the benefits I received from my years in front of a television camera, one of the greatest was the opportunity to develop friendships with people I wouldn't otherwise have even known. They came from all walks of life, pursued different causes, and each made their respective marks in a variety of ways. But they all had one thing in common: they fascinated me.

Please allow me to introduce a few of them to you.

"I don't think it's well for people to be spending their money foolishly because it can be proven that they do, and that is fodder for communist propagandists. They should be spending their money for the benefit of humanity."
—HAROLDSON LAFAYETTE "H.L." HUNT

I've always marveled at the lifestyles of gamblers, men who awaken each day to the challenge of making it or breaking it on a longshot. For some, it is the roll of the dice or the play of a card; for others, it is a business decision. For each, the motivation is the same: to thumb their noses at caution and to risk everything on the chance to make something out of nothing. As legendary hustler/con man Titanic Thompson once said, "It's not the money that's important, really. That's just the way you keep score."

That philosophy, I think, embodied itself in billionaire Haroldson Lafayette "H.L." Hunt. Cherub-faced and balding, this biscuit-bodied man from Lafayette, Louisiana, may have at one time been the richest man in the world, with assets variously estimated at between two and seven billion dollars, during a time (the 1960s) when a billion dollars was real money. Yet for all his wealth, Hunt loved few things more than joining a group of ancient farmers in games of nickel-and-dime dominoes on shade-tree-lined county squares and eating sandwiches on bread made from wheat grown in Deaf Smith County, Texas.

I first met H.L. Hunt in the mid-1960s and probably got to know him as well as any newsman did. I couldn't tell you if he was indeed a billionaire or merely a multi-millionaire, nor did he ever bother to clarify that point for me. He did tell me, though, that he was "willing to take credit for being a billionaire if it pleased my creditors."

That was part of his charm—to evade your queries about his wealth without chastising you for asking. I knew of one saucy gold digger at a social affair who worked hard to engage Hunt in conversation, then cooed, "I hear you're very rich."

"I am," Hunt said, and that ended the conversation.

Hunt was never flamboyant in the way that many outside Texas choose to caricaturize Texans. True, he lived in a luxurious home on White Rock Lake in Dallas, built to resemble George Washington's Mount Vernon—only larger. And true, the furnishings were expensive, but not spectacular considering his wealth. What shocked me the most was learning that he kept the plastic coverings on the sofas in his sitting room.

Growing up in East Texas, I had heard all the stories—or perhaps "legends" is a better term—about how Hunt acquired his wealth. Perhaps the most common story involved a free-wheeling oil operator from Arkansas named Dad Joiner. Somehow Dad had managed to end up on the right side of the Balcones Fault, which had, by movement of the earth in antiquity, left a giant pool of oil twenty-three miles wide and ninety miles long in three counties of East Texas. According to legend, Hunt had won the oilfield from Dad in a poker game.

Other legends had Hunt finding Dad on his death bed and dealing him out of the field for a paltry sum, coupled with a promise to pay off a pile of debts Dad had incurred in his fruitless pursuit of the big strike.

Probably closer to the truth is simply the fact that Hunt had a great deal of business acumen and, more importantly, had found a source of loans to finance his buying of oil leases at a time and in a place that was extremely short of cash. When production in that pool proved to be the largest in the world up to that time, he simply held the best cards.

Then, without publicity, he continued to build his fortune. He bought up leases in Louisiana that were rich in natural gas, although natural gas was, at the time, considered almost worthless because it had glutted the market—a status that reversed itself soon enough. He also bought vast expanses of farmlands in Wyoming and Utah that ultimately turned out to possess rich uranium ore deposits.

By the time I came to know Hunt, he had already raised his family, and his sons had taken over the day-to-day business operations. Although Hunt fathered thirteen children, he seemed to favor one above all: his son Hassie. Hunt once wrote concerning his efforts to support the war effort during World War II: "My son, Hassie, and I produced and marketed to the Allies more natural hydrocarbons than all of the Axis nations combined could ever secure during World War II, but I doubt our oil reserves exceeded theirs."

Hassie, most conceded, was mentally impaired. But Hunt claimed he had certain powers the others didn't possess, including a knack for finding oil.

I had the chance to talk to Hunt about his "common man" appearance, which some believed to be a façade. He admitted that he took his lunch to work each day in a paper bag, but only because it allowed him to eat his favorite health foods and further because it was a time-saver for him. He also admitted that he usually bought his clothes off the racks of a department store, and he didn't change his cars every year like so many of his peers did.

Was this all a contrived effort to retain his common touch, or to be eccentric?

"I don't believe it's well for people to be spending their money foolishly," he told me. "Because it can be proven that they do and that is fodder for communist propagandists. They should be spending their money for the benefit of humanity."

That wasn't the first, nor the last, time Hunt mentioned communists to me. He fervently believed that the most important thing he could do with his money was to fight the threat of communism. He funded a foundation called LifeLine that produced tracts and broadcast anti-communist materials to more than 100 radio stations around the country. Due in part to those broadcasts, many people perceived Hunt as an ultra-conservative; yet Hunt considered himself a Jeffersonian liberal. He felt cheated, he said, because socialists had stolen the word "liberal" and twisted it for their own purposes.

He believed he had found a solution, though, in a world where tags tended to oversimplify political thought. The word was "constructive." The only problem, of course, was that no one used the term that way except Hunt, who frequently signed his personal letters, "Constructively yours."

He even wrote and privately published a book called *Alpaca* that outlined some of his political theories, including a few that might properly be labeled preposterous. For example, in the imaginary Republic of Alpaca, the number of votes a citizen might have varied depending upon the service he provided to the state, such as the payment of taxes. Obviously, in such a system, a wealthy man's voice would be heard loudly at the polls. Some say it is anyway.

I can vouch for the fact that Hunt knew that Alpaca lived only in myth, but others took it more seriously. That noted conservative William F. Buckley, Jr., somehow got hold of a copy of the book, which he called "silly" in an article in the *Saturday Evening Post*. Not content to stop there, he called Hunt's understandings of public affairs "eccentric" and lambasted what he termed Hunt's "yahoo bigotry" and "appalling bad manners."

Hunt quickly fired off a heated response that made its way into the public press. "I do not, nor am I reputed to have, any sexual deviations," he wrote. "I have not given capitalism a bad name and, for more than fifty years, I have actively and effectively extolled capitalism and the individual initiative system. My understanding of public affairs is extensive, and I am not eccentric in my views and statements, all of which are courteous and construc-tive. My acquaintances do not consider me bad-mannered and boorish.

"Buckley egotistically uses unusual words . . . 'Yahoo' is 'a race of brutish creatures,' and denotes vicious, crude, and bumpkin; if not egotism, this may be a clever form of double-talk. However poor are the books I have written, they cannot be classified as silly."

Hunt told me that he was actually offered $600,000 for the movie rights to *Alpaca*, but he turned it down. Any other writer would have jumped at the offer, but his rejection must be placed in perspective: The offer represented approximately the amount of his normal salary for three days.

Although a registered Democrat, not unusual at the time in Texas, which was then a one-party state, Hunt often voted Republican in the general elections. After supporting the Kennedy-Johnson ticket in 1960, he later became a firm supporter of Richard Nixon for what he perceived as Nixon's recognition of the commu-nist menace in the United States, although he also took Nixon to task for his past failures.

Following Nixon's defeat in the 1962 California gubernatorial race, Hunt wrote him a stinging letter, taking the opportunity to out-line a string of Nixon mistakes over the years. He accused Nixon of "assuming the role of a middle-of-the-roader" and "supporting to an unnecessary degree President Eisenhower's tolerance of commu-nism." Hunt went on to chastise Nixon for "wearing the wrong color shirt in the first TV debate (with Kennedy)," "stepping down to run for governor when you had lost the Presidency by only a few thousand votes," and "failing to accept the defeat for the governorship grace-fully."

When I interviewed Hunt for my *Face to Face* program, we talked about his political ideology and his shift to Nixon. During a break to change tapes, we engaged in what I thought would simply be idle chit-chat until we were ready to roll again. He surprised me by saying he had once asked Joe Kennedy how much it had cost to get his son, John, elected president.

"Twenty million dollars," Kennedy told him.

"That's too much," Hunt said. "You'll never get it back." Always the businessman.

"I already have," Kennedy replied. He then explained how, after

John appointed Bobby Kennedy as attorney general, Bobby filed anti-trust actions against a number of corporations, driving their stock prices down. "I bought some of it," Kennedy said, "then a little later Bobby dropped those actions and the various companies' stocks shot back up in value—and I sold all of it. I already have the twenty million it took to get John elected."

Priceless stuff. When we rolled tape again, I tried to get Hunt to repeat that story, but he refused.

I believe that, in his fashion, Hunt desperately wanted to give back to his country as much as he could, out of the belief that the capitalist system had worked well for him. Late in his life, as his steps slowed and his mind sometimes strayed, he was no longer the bashful man I had first met more than a decade earlier. He had come to be at ease before the television cameras, yet he seemed aware that he came across to viewers as eccentric. That was one reason he was never able to make the media work for him, even after he became convinced that television was the medium to rally public opinion to the "constructive" policies he espoused.

The end came quietly for H.L. Hunt in December 1974, when he died at the age of eighty-five in a Dallas hospital bed. His fortune passed on to his wife, Ruth, and ten of his children, including sports entrepreneur Lamar Hunt, owner of the NFL's Kansas City Chiefs and founder of the World Championship of Tennis; Herbert and Nelson Bunker Hunt, who carry on as before in oil and uranium, and who cornered the world's silver supply in 1980—until prices dropped so precipitously they had to scramble to make good almost a billion dollars in loans; and real estate developer Ray Hunt, who sparked redevelopment in downtown Dallas with his splendid Hyatt Regency Hotel and Reunion Tower.

Unlike their famous father, the sons seem more heavily engaged in civic affairs than politics. Still, I believe their father would be pleased.

"I believe if you do anything to excess, it's a sin. But as for people gamblin' and losin' their money, some people are determined they're going to lose it. Put 'em off somewheres, away from everybody, and they're gonna look for a

*mail-order catalog so's they can send away their
money somewhere else and lose it."*
—BENNY BINION

While the financial legend of H.L. Hunt was built primarily in
the boardrooms of big business, another Texan carved his place in
gambling history in a different manner. Benny Binion was the kind
of man Damon Runyon spent his literary life writing about. Though
he started small, he dreamed big as he walked the darker streets of
society, building what he called his "bidness."

Benny Binion's Horseshoe Casino in downtown Las Vegas always drew the no-limit gamblers, and had ever since Benny left
Dallas shortly after World War II. Over the years, Benny won and lost
countless fortunes, and even spent some time in Leavenworth
Federal Prison when his tax statements didn't agree with the figures
the Internal Revenue Service came up with. But Benny was also a
legend in Texas long before an ambitious prosecutor chased him
west—a legend spawned by his running dice and poker games, and
the policy numbers in a state and city that officially frowned on such
activities.

With little formal schooling, Binion developed his business savvy at the knee of a horse-trading father in rural Texas places
like Whitewright, Bonham, Denison, and Sherman. He was still a
boy when he finally arrived in Dallas in the 1920s, but even boys
could run errands. And that's exactly what he did for Warren
Diamond, operator at the old St. George Hotel of a no-limit crap
game for oil men from the patches around Burkburnett, Longview,
Tyler, Texarkana, and Kilgore—men with dollars in their pockets
and gambling in their blood.

There were some interesting times at the old St. George. "I'll
tell you what I heard," Benny said. "One of the first really well-to-do
oil men threw an envelope on the table in Warren Diamond's place
down in Dallas—this was back in the late teens or early '20s as I recall—and said, 'Diamond, I'm gonna make you look.'

"Diamond said, 'Pass him the dice.' The Texarkana oil man
rolled the dice, caught a quick point and missed it. Diamond took
the envelope to his office and opened it. Inside were 178 one-thou-
sand dollar bills."

From the St. George, Benny's legend grew. He started "operatin' a li'l ol' policy bidness" in 1928 and really hit the jackpot in 1936 when the State of Texas temporarily opened up and allowed liquor and gambling in order to make itself more attractive to visitors to the Texas Centennial Celebration. Of course, that encouraged competition, as well, and there was plenty of competition by Benny's reckoning. "I don't claim no titles," he said. "But if there was ever a battle for control, I'd want to take care of ol' Benny."

Sitting at a table reserved for Benny and his family at one of the restaurants in the Horseshoe, Benny talked with me about his days in Dallas and his abrupt departure for Las Vegas just ahead of the law. Although he and his family had become respected citizens of Nevada, with a record of generosity to charitable causes and good works, legends are written in indelible ink. One of those legends has it that, in his rise to the top of Dallas gambling in the 1930s, Benny may have had something to do with the bloody demise of a reputed rival, Herbert "The Cat" Noble.

When I asked, Benny merely shrugged, denying any involvement. It was the same way he denied having knowledge of any of the Dallas "establishment" engaging in games of high stakes poker and dice. He said he was only "doin' what came natural to me. I can't subtract or multiply even now. But I have some people who can. And that's what all the trouble was about in Dallas. I've got people who can take care of all that for me now."

While legend has it that Benny went to Vegas in late 1946 with a suitcase full of cash and simply decided to open a gambling casino, Benny described it this way: "Fred Merrill had won $160,000 at Reno. A fellow propositioned him to bankroll a gambling house, so we came out. And we opened for business on the first day of 1947."

The nattily dressed Binion, who enjoyed wearing a gold nugget watch and shirts with solid gold buttons, quickly developed a reputation as one of the most successful entrepreneurs on the Las Vegas scene. "I got a good bidness here," he said. "But I ain't counted the rest of 'em's money."

Over the years, people of every stripe have passed through the Horseshoe, ready to try their hand. And, to hear Benny tell it, every one of them had his own story.

"There was this preacher once, came in here in '47," Binion said. "He was sharp, well-dressed. I'll tell you, he looked like a cheater." The preacher ended up losing $11,000 in the casino and then went to pieces. It turns out the money he lost belonged to his church. He cried a bit and said he was going to pray about it, then ask his church for forgiveness.

Benny remembered telling him, "'You can talk to the Lord about it, but I don't think I would mention it to that congregation.' He didn't have a dime to get home on. I told him, 'I don't know what the Lord's gonna do, but I know what I'm gonna do. Here's a thousand.'" Then Benny sent him on his way, saying, "I don't want to see you out here again."

But, as with most Benny Binion stories, this one ended with a twist. "Sometime later, I got a check for one thousand dollars from that preacher. I didn't even want it back." The preacher also included a note that said he had asked his congregation for forgiveness, and they had forgiven him. He was still pastor of that church.

Binion always insisted that the money wasn't that important to him. Even so, he enjoyed the ranchland he accumulated in Montana (over 200 sections), and his cattle feed lot in Texas kept a steady flow of steaks coming to the Horseshoe.

"After you get what you need for your family, what good is it except to have some fun with?"

And fun he did have. He even had a million dollars he used just for show. An average of 600 people per day used to pose in front of that million dollars in $10,000 certificates framed in a giant horseshoe in his casino. Did he realize how much money in interest he was losing every day on that money?

"I figure if it costs me a coupla hunnert each day, that's a small price to pay for having it there. We give away about 600 pictures each day of couples who come in. No tellin' how many other people they show that picture to. It's what you call public relations."

Benny's sense of public relations wasn't something you'd find in a college textbook, but it worked. "That's what Benny Binion's thing was," his son Jack, who always referred to his father as "Benny Binion," said. "Benny Binion did not always think so much about profit and loss but rather what would the customer like—what appeals to the customer, because his theory was if you appeal to the customer, he'll come in and we'll make some money off of him. So he didn't think about doing cost studies. He concentrated on 'will the customer like this?'"

Benny was an innovator in things like that. "You know Benny

Binion was the first guy to start giving away free drinks?" Jack said. "Before, they might have said don't charge a particular person for a drink, but Benny Binion opened it up to all players. He was the first one to do it. All the comp things that are standard in the industry today, Benny Binion was ahead of the industry in starting them."

Public relations also included starting the World Series of Poker a number of years ago. The table rules are simple: Each player starts with $10,000 and play continues until someone wins it all. And over the years, the best poker players in the world have passed through the Horseshoe to compete.

"Amarillo Slim, when he won, was younger and in better shape," Binion said. "He just outstayed everybody. It lasted forty-eight hours, so a young feller had the advantage. He got a lot of mileage out of winning. But the best player of them all was Henry Hodges. Everybody called him Society Red. He went to San Francisco once and won all their money. Had it when he died, too, right there in Dallas."

Benny himself claimed to be no better than an average poker player. In his opinion, dice offered the casino patron the best chance of winning, but "with so many distractions, people don't get the chance to get the experience with dice like they used to."

I asked him if, in his later years, he had become a religious man. He had once told me, "I believe in God awful strong. It's all a mystery too deep to doubt." So how, I wondered, could he reconcile his life's pursuit of gambling with that?

"I believe that if you do anything to excess, it's a sin," he said. "But as for people gamblin' and losin' their money, some people are determined they're going to lose it. Put 'em off somewheres, away from everybody, and they're gonna look for a mail-order catalog so's they can send away their money somewhere else and lose it."

And his philosophy of life?

"Somebody told me once, 'Don't ever look back, or holler *whoa!* in a bad place.'"

So when all is said and done, how would he like to be remembered?

"Just bein' a good guy. You can't get through life without hurtin' somebody. You can just hope that you didn't hurt anybody real bad and that you kinda made up for any hurtin' you left behind you."

My association with Benny, which started with an introduction from another fabulous character with a Texas background, Chill

Wills, developed into a close friendship with his entire family. When Ross Perot wanted me, on short notice, to arrange a grand retirement party for Gen. Robbie Risner, a former POW, I quickly flew to Vegas only to find that all the major hotels had long since been booked. It was the Binion family that helped pull everything together for Risner's big send-off—something for which I will forever be grateful.

When Chill Wills died, Benny sat with Gene Autry at the funeral. Chill was to be cremated, and the thought was too traumatic for Benny, who bolted out, caught a cab to the airport, and flew back to Vegas. "Something came over me when it dawned on me that they were going to take Chill's body and burn it," he said later. "I had to hurry out of the chapel. I know that Autry and the others thought I was crazy, but I couldn't take that."

Shortly before Benny died, I was visiting with him in his suite at the Horseshoe when he received a call that Bunker Hunt, one of H.L.'s sons, was downstairs to see him. This was after the Hunt Brothers' disastrous foray into the silver market, so Benny and I were both amused when Bunker arrived and asked Benny if he knew of any abandoned gold mines in Nevada. As the conversation continued, Benny asked Bunker how much the IRS claimed he owed them over the silver problems.

"About seven hundred million," Bunker said.

"They claim my old buddy Willie Nelson owes them twelve or thirteen million. Why don't you just have them put Willie's little bit over there with yours? It won't make much difference to you, and ol' Willie can start over clean again."

As I said at the start of this chapter, never a dull moment.

"Well, I think the Alamo represents Americana. It could be any state. It isn't the fact that it's Texas. It's the principles and the integrity of the men involved."

—JOHN WAYNE

The world needs more men like John Wayne, a man of principle. At a time when heroes were hard to find, thank God there was always the Duke. When he died in the summer of 1979, I felt the loss personally. I believe millions of others did as well. Not because he was such a great actor. He never claimed any particular distinction for his acting talent, nor did the critics, who usually saw him as merely playing himself—a slow-talking, ambling man of courage and strength.

No, what I would miss about John Wayne was his off-screen honesty. In my meetings with him, I found him to be the same unassuming and warm man I had applauded as a boy in the Pines Theater in Lufkin, Texas. I watched as he battled cancer to the finish with the same unconquerable will as the Davy Crockett role he played in *The Alamo*. He left us feeling the immortality of man's spirit.

The best interview I ever had with Wayne occurred in 1969, exactly ten years before he died, and five years after his first bout with cancer in which doctors had removed a lung. Still, he looked robust as ever when he arrived at the WFAA studios in Dallas for an appearance on my *Face to Face with Murphy Martin* show.

Wayne never made any bones about his affinity for Texas people, and his popularity continued strong in the Lone Star State even though many of its college students had vilified him for his outspokenness in support of the Vietnam War. This was a time when the nation's college campuses had become refuges for hippies who rejected their country's call to battle in Southeast Asia but who lacked the energy to flee to Canada, and John Wayne represented qualities that embarrassed them. Qualities like integrity, patriotism, and responsibility.

When I first sat face-to-face with Wayne for that 1969 interview, he was just coming off his role as Rooster Cogburn in *True Grit*. He had even tried to buy the movie rights to the Charles Portis bestseller when it was still in galley form, but producer Hal Wallis outbid his $300,000 offer. Wallis had also hired Henry Hathaway to direct, which led in to my early questioning.

"How does a director work with John Wayne?"

"I don't think I get any special care," he said. "They bawl me out sometimes and let me go at other times. When they hire a personality, they're hiring a color—the director needs a certain color. If he uses that color right, you look good on the screen. If he overdoes it, sometimes the chemistry comes out bad. I've luckily been working with men who know me—Howard Hawks, Ford, Hathaway—they know what they have in me. They know my limits and keep me within them."

As Harry Callahan once said, "A man's gotta know his limitations."

Wayne had already made 175 movies by then, but television was starting to cut into the movie industry's profits and talent base. Movie theaters were no longer the gold mines they had once been. Wayne attributed part of the decline of movie-going to "the kinda dirty pictures, the sex and violence they are putting on."

He continued, "Violence never bothered anybody. It's the manner of showing the violence. We're in the business of illusion and you can take Lubitch pictures in the old days—they couldn't have been more risqué than his pictures, yet they had charm and they were pleasant to see and you could send your children or anybody to see his pictures.

"But today, it's something called 'realism'—they have to show you the blood and gore and sweat and hair and whatnot. It's made it necessary for parents to be careful of the pictures their children go to. Now, when [movie studios] put these out, they say, 'Jesus, we're getting a new dimension and we're drawing in a new audience.' They are drawing in a new audience, but they are losing their big audience. I'm afraid this will affect our business to the point that the mother and father won't just turn their kids loose to go to a picture."

Well, what's so bad about realism? As the head of the Motion Picture Association had once told me, what we were starting to see in movies and television "mirrors the society in which we live."

"Well, I don't think people go to a motion picture to see a mirror of their life," Wayne said. "They go to escape what they have in everyday humdrum, the vulgarity of living. They want something to lift them up and give them a pleasant evening. No, I can't quite go along with this excuse for the type of picture they are making."

I then turned the focus to the state of the country, which was in the grips of an unpopular war and rising dissension from within. Was there room for optimism? Sure, Wayne said. "I think it'll get back to where we might even applaud if a kid makes A's in school instead of burning down a building."

Wayne also believed that much of the domestic dissent was being flamed from beyond America's borders. Never shy about his feelings on communism, he said, "Well, it's quite obvious that their line of chatter backs up *The Daily Worker*. I don't think you can prove those things. This is like a few years ago, you knew a fellow was a communist but you couldn't prove it. You didn't have the card. It's quite obvious that organizations causing the trouble are communist-infiltrated. But some people in our country don't think this is a menace.

"Hitler wrote *Mein Kampf* and told us what he was going to do. The communists have told us time and again what they intend to do. They are our enemies, but somehow or another we've heard this so often that we try to avoid it. We sit complacently while our kids are getting killed for us over in South Vietnam in a cause that was certainly as strong as going to war with Hitler."

Wayne then weighed in on hippies, yippies, and the "New Left." "I think most of these dirty-footed kids are just afraid to face the future and they've found a way they can group together and escape. When I was a kid, we used to grow our hair long, too, but not like girls. When we were the top body-surfers down at the beach, we thought we were great—but we got over it. I think these kids will get over it in time if they aren't made so important and so provocative by people in the news capacity."

Well, that touched a nerve. After all, aren't we in the news business supposed to report the news? I asked him, "What do we do if we ignore them and six months later they burn the campus, and you haven't reported the same thing six months before?"

"They won't burn up that campus if you don't bring that camera out there so they can make a big scene. The thing, Murphy, I find irritating is the teacher who is so immature that he will back kids who are rebelling with anarchy in their country. And this is why the majority of the kids haven't thrown those fellows out of school anyway . . . [T]he average student wants a certain amount of authority over them. They need a certain amount of discipline; everyone needs discipline. You can't get it unless someone inculcates it in you."

Despite his strong views, he expressed no interest in entering politics. He just wanted to keep on with his acting once the "doctors and The Man Upstairs" had helped him through his lung operation. "It was a terrible shock, I'll tell you that," he said. "I had no cancer effects that they speak of. In three months, a little spot on my lung had come to almost fist size. It had caused me no pain, no reaction at all. But the most embarrassing part was to tell my kids and wife without being dramatic."

With his private health problem splashed in the media by virtue of his being a public figure, he laughed about some of the other things that had been written about him over the years. "There is a fellow at *The Enquirer* in New York, he's very good to me. I always win every fight—but he has me in a fight every week. I'm always the hero of the story, but I'm afraid that people will think that every time I go out, I belt somebody.

"I don't think I've hit anybody in ten years."

I wrapped up the interview with some thoughts on his years in the movie business. Favorite leading lady?

"I like them all. I've done quite a few pictures with Maureen O'Hara, and we've had a good, lusty, rough relationship that I think the audiences have liked."

Favorite movie roles?

"There are two or three. I'll tell you, the hardest job I ever had was *The Quiet Man* because I had little or nothing to do in that. I was the only straight man, and that is hard. I think probably Captain Bridles for *She Wore a Yellow Ribbon*—I had an Oscar nomination for that—and Sergeant Striker from *Iwo Jima* were two pretty good jobs. I thought I did a pretty good job in *Red River* and *The Searchers*. I don't know."

This time, John Wayne had a winner in *True Grit*, which brought him his first and only Academy Award win for Best Actor. And of my conversations with him over the years, I liked this one the best.

—◇◇◇—

"The name Lester Townes sounded a little too interior-decorator on a marquee, and I wanted to be a regular guy. Bob was about as solid as you could get."
—BOB HOPE ON WHY HE CHANGED HIS NAME

Perhaps no civilian was closer to the war in Vietnam than Bob Hope, the man most people called the World's Number One Showman. Throughout the war, he spent his Christmas seasons entertaining the troops and knew better than any that his show was threatening to become one of history's longest running.

When I talked with Hope in the early summer of 1969 while I was at WFAA-TV in Dallas, the Paris Peace talks had already begun, but no prospects for peace loomed on the horizon. Fighting still raged, and young men were still dying. By then, Hope had started seriously questioning the American presence in Vietnam. And believe me, there is nothing more serious than a funnyman who turns serious.

"Last year," he said, "when we did the show in Vietnam for the First Division, they didn't laugh. I asked about it later and these boys had just come in off eight major skirmishes that had been really bad. The morale was way down. They were just tired—and they didn't laugh."

And so, he had concluded, maybe it was time to end the war. But more than a showman, Hope was also a patriot, and he sensed that those who were the loudest and most violent in their dissent against the war were actually damaging this country's efforts to end it. He worried, particularly, about the extent of student dissent on the nation's college campuses, where protests, arson, and building takeovers had become commonplace.

"I worry about the direction some of them are taking," Hope said. "This burning of buildings, things like that. Everyone that age protests something—that's the name of the game. The difference that I worry about is the outside help, and I mean the outside-the-country help. It would be a terrible thing if dissent were allowed to destroy the system that allows it."

Our free-ranging conversation then moved on from the war to such issues as the state of television and movies. Who better than one of its longest-lasting stars to weigh in on the controversies that surrounded changes in those industries that had taken root by the late '60s? Changes that introduced new levels of sex and violence, shocking to many in mainstream America, with movies like *Bonnie & Clyde*, *The Graduate*, *The Wild Bunch*, *Midnight Cowboy*, and *Easy Rider*.

"You look at the paper which is advertising the pictures in New York today and it looks like a nude art gallery," Hope said. "I'm surprised I'm still in pictures, that I can pass the physical. It's not whether you can act; it's the size of your appendix scar."

He predicted, wrongly as it turned out, that the pendulum would soon swing in the other direction. "Where else can it go?" he reasoned. "The great Walt Disney, if he were alive today, would really be cleaning up with this situation. He'd come out with a couple more of those *Mary Poppins* [movies] where you could send the kids."

He reminisced that when Elvis Presley first appeared on the *Ed Sullivan Show*, the cameras only caught him from his waist up, to avoid showing his pelvic wiggle. "Now the whole world's rocking," Hope said. "Look at the clip of Elvis now and he looks like an altar boy."

So what was the answer? Censorship? Even to this day, the word sends shudders down the spines of entertainers and First Amendment advocates. But it didn't to Bob Hope.

Noting the squabble between the network and the Smothers Brothers over their show's content, Hope said, "What else could the network people do? The Smothers Brothers got themselves on a kick that was sort of anti-American and they got themselves in trouble. They were very good, but they're playing to a broad base when they're on television. You can't just let these guys go.

"It was nothing new—I mean going to the limits of taste. When I started out in radio, we just loved to get out these jokes that were right on the border, to grab attention, and we drove a couple of NBC censors right out of their skulls. But somebody's got to keep it in line. If you're not a good editor, you're not going to be on television very long. And if the industry doesn't do something, Washington will have to—and what's wrong with that if the industry doesn't clean itself up?"

Hope also touched on another bugaboo for many television entertainers: ratings. Many an actor has assailed the system that dictates whether you or your show returns for another season or whether you are relegated to the unemployment lines. I had had my own experience with ratings while at ABC, dropped from my anchoring duties because, at least according to the network party line, ratings had improved but not dramatically enough. So I expected Hope to attack the ratings system as so many others had.

He surprised me.

"What other standards do they have to measure it by?" he asked. "You see it reflected in the way they seat you at the Brown Derby. If you come in with a low rating, you might even wind up in the parking lot. They don't even call you by your name, just, 'Hello, 20J4, how are you?'"

Of course, Hope could afford to defend the ratings system. After all, his shows consistently soared in the ratings stratosphere.

It seemed as if everyone wanted to claim Bob Hope, who had as many "hometowns" as anyone I ever knew. Cleveland, of course, was one of them, which explained his support of baseball's Cleveland Indians. Others, as you might expect, included Los Angeles, Hollywood, and Palm Springs. Somewhat surprisingly, he also counted Dallas as one of his homes.

In his less prosperous years, the story goes, Hope was employed by the late R. J. O'Donnell, who owned Interstate Theaters in Dallas. O'Donnell provided an outlet for Hope during his vaudeville days, something that Hope never forgot. On his frequent visits to Dallas, he could almost always pick up a little spending money in a friendly game of golf on one of the city's many courses, and he has raised more money for more causes in Dallas than you'd care to see listed. He gave far more than his great name to the Bob Hope Theater on the campus of Southern Methodist University, and the theater is now the center of a nationally recognized drama department.

With all those hometowns, not many knew that Hope actually hailed from England, where he was born as Lester Townes. He was often asked why he changed his name, and he rarely gave the same answer twice in a row. I, of course, had to ask, too.

"The name Lester Townes sounded a little too interior-decorator on a marquee, and I wanted to be a regular guy," Hope said. "Bob was about as solid as you could get."

From there, he segued into his history—every subject a source of humor. "I left Britain when I was very young. I knew there was no chance of my ever becoming King, though a little later I could have gone right across the Channel and become a Queen. No, I went into vaudeville and dancing ..."

And on it went.

Bob Hope was, without a doubt, the king of show business. He deserved every honor that a nation he taught to laugh during some awful times could bestow. America lost an entertainment treasure in July 2003, when Bob Hope died two months after his 100th birthday.

— ◈◈◈ —

"Heaven help us if the American people ever get to the point where they will not believe the press. If there's a credibility gap, if they heartily dislike it, or reject it completely, that would be tragic. Because if we stop to think about it, the national press—including print, radio, and television—is the only thing there is. There's no other alternative to the business of letting people know what their leaders and idea-makers are saying and doing."

—CHET HUNTLEY

Few men I've known combined the qualities of a gentleman and working newsman so comfortably as Chet Huntley. When NBC looked for a different way to cover the 1956 political conventions, the team of Chet Huntley and David Brinkley was born. Their nightly sign-off—Huntley reporting from New York, with Brinkley in Washington: "Good night, Chet ... Good night, David"—became a familiar mainstay of American culture. And their magic together continued for twenty years, until Chet finally chucked it to return home to his beloved Montana.

Before finding an audience as NBC's co-anchor, Chet had paid his dues as a wartime correspondent during World War II's island-hopping engagements in the Pacific. Even after securing his seat at the anchor desk, his yeoman-like work habits continued, with days spent at his NBC newsroom desk from 9:00 A.M. to 5:00 P.M., or, worse yet, changing planes in airports and spending yet another night in some strange hotel room.

Although those may have been the times that ultimately wearied him of the chase, he could use the time to think about fishing and raising purebred Hereford cattle, or his dreams for his beautiful Montana. One of his biggest dreams, one he was never able to see totally fulfilled, was to build a resort called The Big Sky, complete with landing strip, fishing, golf, and anything else that might lure tourist dollars to the Montana economy.

I never thought of Chet as a rival, but rather as a senior colleague from whom I might learn. I found that we saw eye-to-eye on most subjects we discussed, including the importance of the news business. Not that we, personally, were important, but that our jobs were. He had seen a great deal of America and what made it tick and, I think, was himself changed by many of the events he saw.

When I last talked with Chet, after he had retired and returned home to Montana, among the things we discussed was the importance of being objective in our reporting of straight news accounts. I asked him, as I have often asked myself, whether it is truly possible to maintain that kind of objectivity sitting as an anchorman with a major network.

"Murphy," he said, "sometimes a piece of news comes in and it absolutely kills me to be objective about it because my conviction runs so strong the other way. Sometimes you have to repeat something with a very straight face and cool demeanor that you are convinced is a downright lie. But if you're doing news, you've got to go ahead and say it and give all sides and all sections of opinion a fair shake."

At that time, some news journalists, such as Harry Reasoner, Howard K. Smith, Eric Severeid, and even Chet's old partner, David Brinkley, had started the practice of giving editorial comment within their news programs—a practice that greatly troubled Chet. He preferred watching a half-hour of what he called "good, hard, straight news in the old fashioned who-what-where-when journalism, keeping separate periods of the day for comment, debate, and opinion."

Otherwise, he believed, people tended to remember the opinion or personal attitude of the reporter and gauge everything else the reporter might say through that bias. "When you comment along with your hard news, you're kind of messing up your own shop," he said.

Chet had tired of the news business by the time he retired, but he still loved journalism and lamented some of the changes he had seen over the years. Through an era of assassinations, wars, and violence, he had seen how the media, particularly television, could be manipulated. During the riots in Newark, every time the lights went on for filming, crowds gathered for another outburst of violence. Protesters on college campuses called the news media to invite them to cover staged riots. "Smart little publicists," Chet called them.

While he had been working in New York, I knew that Chet secretly aspired to run for the U.S. Senate from his native state. But, with retirement, he abandoned that aspiration. After all, he knew he couldn't beat popular Senator Mike Mansfield. He left, instead, to build his Big Sky resort and provide light commentary on a syndicated radio show.

As I look back over his career and the things he shared with me, I remember how eloquent he could be. I also remember how incisive he could be in his appraisal of the events and individuals he covered. For example, as a Texan, I had been particularly interested in his assessment of the style of President Lyndon Johnson, whom he viewed as a latter-day Andrew Jackson.

"Americans have become too sophisticated and urbane to tolerate an Andrew Jackson in the White House," he said. "Let's face it, Murphy, I suspect the people can no longer tolerate a man who may have a little manure on his boots and who sometimes uses rough language and has no particular sophisticated style and doesn't subscribe too enthusiastically to the fine arts and all these things. And he had the misfortune to follow probably the most urbane and sophisticated president we ever had."

And then, as if to remind me that we're all human and we all make mistakes, Chet let me in on what he considered his most embarrassing moment in journalism.

Returning to Los Angeles after a Pacific junket during World War II, he received a radio assignment to interview movie stars on Pershing Square who had been marshaled in support of a war bond drive. "At the time," he said, "there were two women named Adler: Stella Adler, who had written a book I enjoyed, and the other Adler, Polly—who was the famous madam.

"I got the two confused; the one I was talking to that day was indeed Polly Adler, and I thought she was Stella. I said to her, 'Miss Adler, I just want you to know how much I have enjoyed your work.'

"Oh, boy! She wouldn't let me up. She said, 'Honey, what are you talking about? Come with me,' and she wouldn't let go.

"They sent me back out to the Pacific."

I still miss him, and I am happy to have been a part of the business in which he worked and the times in which he lived.

Good night, Chet.

CHAPTER 11

Fame, Faith and (Mis)Fortune

"Sure, I go out on that balcony right there and say, 'My God, I'm just a little Jewish kid from Brooklyn and everybody in this town knows me and I'm important to this city.' I wouldn't be human if I didn't think that."

—HOWARD COSELL

What came to be known as the revolution of the '60s was more than a single movement—much more than a revolt of a young generation against established authority represented by parents and institutions. It was a time of expectations so high that nothing could have fulfilled them. Sex, drugs, and rock and roll.

Even our sports heroes of that period seemed to be cut from a different cloth. Older generations associated greatness and depth of character of its sports heroes with modesty. It was supposed to be about the game, and not the player. After all, Lou Gehrig, the Yankee "Iron Horse," had been a modest man who let his Louisville Slugger do his talking. Likewise, football coaches were expected to assess each opponent with respect and to concede only that they'd be lucky to keep their opponents from running up the scores each week. Braggadocio and "trash talk" did not yet pervade as they do today.

But sometime in the '60s, that began to change. It's hard to put your finger on any one event or time, but a lot of people think it can be traced back to a brash young man from Louisville, Kentucky, who berated his opposition before each fight and sang his own praises. It was bad enough that he behaved that way, but he also backed up what he said. How do you criticize a man who simply speaks the truth?

But when Cassius Clay had the audacity to change his name to Muhammad Ali and ignore the military draft—well, to borrow a boxing metaphor, the gloves came off. Many sportswriters continued to call him Cassius Clay, and even Gaseous Clay. Sure, he was an adept fighter, but couldn't he have the grace to be modest about it? Or at least quiet about it?

Ali was a new breed of athlete, and it took a new breed of sportscaster to see it first.

Howard Cosell had been doing radio when I first arrived at ABC-TV in 1963. Always unconventional, he did the unconventional even then, calling the champion "Muhammad Ali" without smirking.

"Why do I do it?" he asked. "Law. Common law from the United States out of Blackstone. A man is entitled to be known by the name of his choice unless by change of name he seeks to escape lawful obligations and creditors. That's why I don't call Archie Leach, the stilt-walker from Coney Island, Archie Leach. I call him Cary Grant. That's why I don't call Betty Weintraub, who went to Erasmus High, Betty Weintraub. I call her Lauren Bacall."

Hard to argue with an American tradition. Howard also had harsh words for those who refused to respect Ali for his religious beliefs, particularly some of those in the print media. "I think it's one of the sad commentaries on print journalism in this country that they steadfastly refused to call this man Muhammad Ali after he had adopted a religion that probably was the most important thing in his life and continued to call him Cassius Clay. Such men are not journalists; they are vulgar and they are crude."

Ironically, it was his criticism of the print media, his frequent pronouncements suggesting that only he "tells it like it is," that gained him notoriety in the very media he criticized, making him far more newsworthy than he might otherwise have been. Accident or design? With Howard, one never knew.

I remember talking with him one evening about his station in life as he and I sat with his wife, Emmy, in their high-rise apartment on Manhattan's East Side. I wondered, did he really deserve the notoriety and attention he had garnered? And the wealth? As it turns out, Howard wondered that, too.

"Sure, I go out on that balcony right there and say, 'My God, I'm just a little Jewish kid from Brooklyn and everybody in this town knows me and I'm important to this city.' I wouldn't be human if I didn't think that.

"I'm comfortably fixed," he continued. "But if you ask me if I had reached my ambitions as far as materialistic values, the answer is no. But at the end of my contract, if God grants me good health, I will have reached that point. And I know that Emmy and my two daughters and two grandsons and my son-in-law, who is doing very well without ever any help from me, will be taken care of."

Then Howard told me what really seemed to be in his heart. "This comes out of growing up in Brooklyn and in the depression, when I remember my father fighting with the porter in the basement to restore our electricity. He couldn't pay the electric bill. There was no disgrace about it. It was happening all over America, but it made a great impact on me. There is no question a part of my continuing drive throughout my life has been for the economic security my dad could never achieve."

Who, especially those who grew up during the depression, couldn't identify with that? And who would dispute that Howard Cosell achieved that security? But, I wondered, did it really make him happy? Wealth and fame are nice-sounding things, and there's certainly nothing wrong with them. But what about the things that really matter, deep down? Things like faith.

"I grew up in Brooklyn of Jewish parents, though I had no formal religion," Howard said. "I grew up ... with the age of Hitler. I grew up part of the time right across the street from a Catholic parish, in St. Theresa's, where every day of my life I climbed the back fence to get to school so as not to be attacked by the Catholic kids.

"This wasn't unique in America in those days. I also remember when I went back to Munich, Germany, for the 20th Olympiad, and there's the tragedy in Building 31. You become—even though your wife is Protestant by faith, and even though your daughter has married a Catholic boy, and even though you have no formal religious training—you become overwhelmingly Jewish."

Someone once dug up the fact that Cosell's forebears were listed as "Cohen" on immigration papers at the time Howard's father immigrated from Poland. Was he, or someone in his family tree, trying to hide their Jewish heritage?

A simple miscommunication, Howard says. "The family name is Cosell and always was. When immigration officials didn't understand the name in the foreign language, they would automatically, if they were people of the Jewish faith, stamp them 'Cohen.' The net result was that my father's division was Cohen, but all the rest of the family was Cosell. My brother and I elected to return to the family name."

As a boy growing up, Howard likely felt great pressure to "amount to something"—that is, to become a professional. It was a natural thing in Brooklyn for immigrant parents to push their sons into either medicine or law, to achieve that which had been denied to them as immigrants: status, prestige, security. Given the hardships they typically suffered, they were determined that their children would not only have those opportunities, but that they would take advantage of those opportunities. The Cosells were no different.

And Howard chose law.

"It was easy for me, with the kind of mind that I have. I had no desire to become a doctor. My father went to the bank every three months to renew the loan to keep me in law school. I think the legal education is the finest education a man or woman can have. It can help to develop a meticulous and orderly sense of analysis in your thinking; it can give you a sense of reasonality, an understanding of two sides to every story. I never wanted to become a lawyer but, despite that fact, I'm grateful for that education."

"Being known and being in a public medium of communication is an awesome responsibility. If there's one thing I've learned, it's that journalism is not now, never was, and never will be a popularity contest."

—HOWARD COSELL

I am certain that, across his years in the business, Howard believed that there had been an improvement in sports journalism. He also believed he had been part of the impetus behind that improvement. And he may very well have been. After all, he had almost daily harped on colleagues in the print media for feeding the American people what he called "pap."

"People probably needed it at one time," he said. "They need surcease from the daily problems of making a living, sickness, wars, hunger, poverty, and racial tension. Sports are an escape. But the way sports had been fed to them by the sportswriters and the old world sport broadcasters was a fairyland, a Camelot where there were no problems. I've traveled a half million miles or more, and there's no Camelot, not even in sports."

He made a strong case that the problems of the real world are also reflected in sports. Problems like strikes, racism, drugs, and greed. After all, athletes are still people, just like the rest of us. Just because they can run faster, hit a ball farther, or jump higher than most of the rest of the world doesn't make them immune from life's ills. Howard felt it was his duty to point that out.

"It's somebody's task to tell the truth about these things," he said. "I've tried to. Being known and being in a public medium of communication is an awesome responsibility. If there's one thing I've learned, it's that journalism is not now, never was, and never will be a popularity contest."

Good thing it isn't, because Howard could never win. But he undoubtedly made mileage out of being the broadcast industry's heavy. At home, though, he showed a gentler side. Even a funny side. He once joked about how he and his wife, Emmy, met. "She's the one who put the move on me," Howard said.

At the time, he was Maj. Howard Cosell, U.S. Army, and Emmy was a WAC, an enlisted soldier working for another officer. "He was a terrible bore," Howard said of the other officer. "But I came in quite often to chat with him and, in less than a year, Emmy and I were married."

"That sums it up," Emmy said, something that Howard always found difficult to do in so few words.

Emmy also added something the world might little suspect about Howard Cosell: He was really just an old softie, who sang nursery songs to his grandchildren and "*koochee-koochee-cooed*" them, just like any other grandfather. That might not square with his public image, but she was just "telling it like it was," she said.

Besides his association with boxing and Muhammad Ali, Howard's real springboard to prominence as the man people loved to hate was his role in the booth on *Monday Night Football*. There he shared the microphone with two of the most likable personalities in all of sports or broadcasting, Don Meredith and Frank Gifford. By comparison, Howard probably came across worse than he might otherwise have. Yet he had no complaints.

I once asked Howard for his off-the-top-of-his-head assessments of his two co-hosts. "Don Meredith is a soul brother," he said. "A man of style, irreverence, and yet a deceptively intelligent man—a much deeper thinker than people give him credit for. He has a sense of where it's at in life, what the values are.

"Frank Gifford is a very decent and hard-working man, not born to talent as a performer, but a man who has given so much of himself trying to make himself a performer that he has achieved professional acceptance of himself as such."

Perhaps since I had once been stung by disparaging remarks simply because I happened to have been from Dallas, I asked Howard for his impressions of my city. I knew he would be candid, and he was.

"Like too many other people, I thought Dallas was a bad city because a man I loved and admired had been assassinated there, and I wrongly blamed the city. The time when I terribly needed support from people, I got it in Dallas, Texas. And it's now one of my favorite cities in all the world."

—◇◇◇—

"Okay, Howard, are you going to bullshit me, or am I going to bullshit you?"
—TRACY STALLARD, NEW YORK METS,
UNAWARE HE WAS ON LIVE TV

"Tracy, my boy, do you have any other pronouncements for the eastern seaboard?"
—HOWARD COSELL

After I left the ABC network anchor desk, I co-anchored local news with Bill Beutel on the ABC flagship station in New York City, WABC-TV. Howard Cosell did the sports on those programs and, for those who may have doubted Howard's recall capabilities, during those years I never once saw him use a piece of prepared copy. He ad-libbed everything.

There are many Howard Cosell stories to tell, but I'll leave you with just a few:

Don Meredith and Howard Cosell had been assigned by ABC to cover one of Evel Knievel's motorcycle jumps, this one in Dallas, for *Wide World of Sports*. Joyce and I had breakfast with the Cosells at DFW Airport the morning of the event, then we all hooked up with Meredith to head to a nearby drag strip where the jump was to take place.

While sitting in Knievel's luxurious trailer, which was more like a living room, Meredith began telling me how Dallas County Judge Lew Sterrett had performed his wedding ceremony. As he talked, Howard kept interrupting with observations and asides. I could see that he was annoying Meredith, who patiently continued his story, but Howard wouldn't stop. It seemed as if he took perverse pleasure in being annoying. In fact, I think he *always* got perverse pleasure out of being annoying.

Finally, though, Meredith had had enough. "Howard," he said, "if you don't stop interrupting, I'm going to tell Murphy what really happened in Philadelphia."

That got my attention. I was dying to know what Meredith was talking about, but figured if I bided my time, I'd find out. After all, what were the odds that Howard would actually shut up?

Sure enough, Howard continued to interrupt. "Okay, Howard," Meredith said. "I warned you." Then he proceeded to tell this story.

On a *Monday Night Football* game in Philadelphia, Howard had begun to noticeably slur some of his words shortly before halftime. After halftime, he was neither seen nor heard again on that telecast. Reports circulated the following day that he had become ill because of an adverse reaction to medication that he had been taking and that was why he didn't work the second half.

Not so, I found out.

"I didn't care if he slurred his words," Meredith said, "but when he puked on my new cowboy boots, that was too much. So I locked him out of the booth."

Howard then hailed a cab outside the stadium and had the driver take him all the way home from Philadelphia to his apartment in New York City.

I recall another incident, this one at WABC, when Howard had New York Mets pitcher Tracy Stallard as his guest for a sports segment around Christmastime. The standard format called for Howard to report sports news for a couple of minutes, then to break to commercials for sixty seconds. After the commercials, the director would come back with a shot of Howard and his guest for the segment, followed by the interview.

This particular night, Howard went to break, saying the usual, "In a moment, I'll be back with my guest, Tracy Stallard of the New York Mets, but first these words."

Cut to commercial. But, for some reason, there were only thirty seconds of commercials that night instead of the usual sixty. When the picture came back up, with Stallard and Howard on screen, we heard Stallard ask, "Okay, Howard, are you going to bullshit me, or am I going to bullshit you?"

Howard saw the red lights on the camera and knew that the mikes were open and the camera was live. "Tracy, my boy, do you have any other pronouncements for the eastern seaboard?" he asked.

Realizing what had just happened, Stallard calmly got up, took off his microphone, and walked out of the studio. Needless to say, Howard spent a lot of time fielding phone calls from viewers after that.

Another Cosell gem took place after Joyce and I had moved back to Dallas from New York, and Howard was in town for a *Monday Night Football* game. Wally Schwartz, then president of ABC-TV, and his wife, Ginny, were also in town. After the game that night, Howard rode with the Schwartzes and us in our car, rather than use the ABC limousine as he normally would. After about fifteen minutes of being locked in the traffic snarl leaving Texas Stadium, Howard, who was in the front seat with Joyce and me, asked, "Murphy, isn't there something we can do to get out of this?"

I told him that if we could get over to the right lane, I could take the next exit and maybe make better progress using surface roads. On cue, Howard rolled down his window and asked a burly truck driver next to us if he would let us in front of him. The driver stared at Cosell, then pulled up, blocking our move.

"Pull up again," Howard said.

I obliged, and Howard again spoke to the truck driver. "Pardon me, sir, would you be so kind as to allow us to pull in front of you so we can make the next exit?"

Again, the truck driver pulled up and blocked our move.

Howard pushed the button to raise the window, then turned toward the president of ABC in the rear seat and said, "Can you believe that? The son of a bitch didn't recognize me."

My favorite Cosell story reflects a warmer and much more human side of the man. Before moving into Manhattan, the Cosells lived in a rambling home in Pound Ridge, New York, complete with swimming pool, which they enjoyed on weekends. One Saturday, as Emmy reclined poolside beneath an umbrella, reading, Howard was in the pool in a floating chair, also reading, martini at his fingertips and Havana cigar in his mouth.

After a while, Howard paddled quietly to a poolside telephone, spoke briefly in a quiet voice, then paddled back out into the middle of the pool. A short while later, two brand new Lincoln Continentals—one white, one black—rolled up the Cosell driveway next to the pool. Emmy dropped her book in her lap and looked at the cars in amazement.

"Sweetheart, which do you like best?" Howard asked.

After she stated her preference, Howard told the drivers to leave the keys to that particular one, then to take the other one and the Cadillac in the garage, keys inside, back to the dealership. "Tell your boss I'll be in to settle up," he said.

After they had left, he turned to Emmy. "Happy birthday, darling."

He had bought his wife a brand new Lincoln Continental and never left the comfort of his own swimming pool.

—◈◈◈—

"Pompous, arrogant, obnoxious, cruel, vain, verbose—I have been called all of these. And, of course, I am."
—HOWARD COSELL

"Howard Cosell was grace disguised by bluster."
—RACHEL ROBINSON EULOGY FOR HOWARD COSELL

Howard Cosell was more than a sportscaster to me; he had been my friend. He once sent me a copy of a book he had written entitled

I Never Played the Game, which contained the following inscription: "To my old, dear friend, Murphy. You will understand the time has come to tell the truth, the whole truth, and nothing but the truth. Journalist that you have always been, you could never play any game at the expense of your integrity. Emmy and I love you both."

Howard died on April 23, 1995, from an embolism. One of his daughters, Jill, invited me to attend a private memorial service on May 25 at the St. Paul and St. Andrew Methodist Church on the Upper West Side of New York. Joining me on the flight from Texas was Bobby Bragan, former baseball great with the Brooklyn Dodgers. We arrived a little before noon and went straight to Mickey Mantle's restaurant on Central Park South for lunch, then on to the church.

Jill Cosell met us there and took us through a rear door to a pew near the front of the church. We took our seats next to Eddie Robinson, the longtime football coach at Grambling. By the time the service began, many notables were seated all around, including actor Billy Crystal in the row behind us, and former New York mayors John Lindsay, Ed Koch, and David Dinkins, and then-current mayor Rudolph Guiliani on the row in front of us. Also in the pews in front of us sat those who would deliver eulogies, including Jackie Robinson's widow, Rachel, sportswriter Frank DeFord, former NFL tight end Russ Francis, and Oakland Raider owner Al Davis. Across the aisle, behind the Cosell family, were Muhammad Ali, Joe Frazier, Floyd Patterson, Jose Torres, and artist LeRoy Neiman.

Representatives of the three television networks also paid their respects, including Fred Friendly, former CBS-TV News president; anchors Peter Jennings of ABC, Dan Rather of CBS, and Tom Brokaw of NBC; former ABC News director Ed Silverman; former ABC-TV network president Walter Schwartz; and Bill Beutel, who had co-anchored the news with me on WABC-TV in New York when Howard was our sports reporter.

The service opened with the Harlem Boys Choir, who sang as only they can, followed by remarks from representatives of Cardinal Cook and a rabbi from New York. As I sat in that Protestant church for the memorial service for a Jewish man and heard music from a black choir and words from Catholic, Jewish, and Protestant speakers, and looked around at the diverse makeup of the small invited audience, I thought, *This is just the way it would have been if Howard had planned it.* And who knows? He may well have.

It had been more than ten years since the man America either loved or hated had left *Monday Night Football*. Perhaps no one has ever radiated such ambivalence as Howard Cosell. However, I doubt if there was anyone in that church who would disagree that Howard Cosell was probably the most articulate, gaudiest, entertaining, smartest, and unforgettable television broadcaster we have known. As Muhammad Ali said to me at a reception at Tavern on the Green following the memorial service, speaking in barely a whisper, "There will never be another Cosell."

I agree.

> "I can be very emotional if I'm just watching a game. But when I'm so involved in a football game, and I've said it so many times, I'm not even aware of the crowd; I'm not aware of anything that's happening, because I'm right into the play. I'm always ahead of the game to see what's going to happen on the next play and the next play."
> —COACH TOM LANDRY OF THE DALLAS COWBOYS

I believe America needs heroes, people we can look up to. I also realize that even heroes are human, and sometimes we're better off keeping our heroes at a distance—far enough away that we can't see their warts. So often, heroes disappoint, but perhaps that's because we expect too much from them. Sometimes it's impossible for them to live up to our standards.

I can think of at least one whom I knew very well, but who never disappointed: Tom Landry, former coach of the Dallas Cowboys. And I think it was because he was a man of such strong faith.

Landry grew up in the South Texas town of Mission, where he was a high school football star who went on to star at the University of Texas, after first serving in the Armed Forces during World War II. From the University of Texas, it was on to a professional career as a defensive back with the New York Giants, then an assistant coach with the Giants before becoming the first—and, for the first twenty-nine years of their existence, the only—head coach of the Dallas Cowboys.

It was when he was coach of the Cowboys that I first met Tom Landry and his lovely wife, Alicia. When Alicia first met Tom back in their college days in Austin, she said she had been impressed by the way he walked—straight as a rod, his head held high. "When I told him he looked like he owned the world," she said, "he told me, 'No one ever told me I didn't.'"

And she never saw much change in him from that day forward, right up until the day he died on February 12, 2000. Well, maybe there was one change, although it might have been mostly inward, not outward. When Tom played for the New York Giants and the team won a world championship, he said he didn't feel the fulfillment he thought a championship would bring. It wasn't until two years later, when some friends asked him to join a Bible study group, that Landry experienced that change.

"I came face to face with the realities of Christ; I accepted him into my heart, then my whole life changed because I had a new perspective. For the first time, I knew what life was all about. I knew we had to find the right relationship with God to find this peace that he has to offer us. Once that happened, then I could really enjoy coaching."

From that point forward, Landry's faith influenced everything he did, both personally and as a coach. "Even in losing football games?" I once asked him.

"I don't think there's any question about it, Murphy," he said. "I think God has a plan for all of us that have committed our lives to him. We must trust in his judgment and his plan. And, therefore, when you get defeated, you're human enough to suffer. And I suffer just like anybody else does after a defeat. But you seem to recover very quickly and go on with the next task."

I revisited that issue with Coach Landry and Alicia in a separate conversation and got the female perspective as well, leavened with a touch of humor. I asked her, "After those defeats, though, do you walk on tiptoes in the Landry house?"

"No, it is never like that," she said. "Some defeats are harder to take than others, but actually I'm not talking much either, so we don't have too much of a problem about that."

"She's being really kind, Murphy," Landry said. "Because I am walking very soft after some defeats."

"I know not to ask any dumb questions," she said.

Over the years, I saw Landry's faith tested on more than one occasion, yet he always seemed to come through the fire with an even stronger faith. I have seen that in other Christian athletes as well, like Landry's quarterback in the 1970s, Roger Staubach, also a man of deep faith. In 1973, Roger walked through a dark valley as his mother battled a lengthy illness. It was during that time that Landry first began the practice of calling the plays for his quarterback, rather than leaving that chore up to Staubach. That practice subjected both coach and quarterback to criticism in later years, and Staubach chafed at the restriction, but Landry stuck by the practice.

I asked Landry if he had started the practice to take pressure off of his quarterback at a particularly vulnerable time in his life.

"Well, I'm sure it was a factor," Landry said. "I just knew that there was something missing in Roger's style [that] year. He wasn't that easygoing. He wasn't the type of quarterback that he'd been before, because every time you looked at him, you knew something was deep in him that was hurting him. And you just felt it all year. And it's something we all hated to see, but there wasn't anything we could do about it . . .

"I think when I did start calling plays for Roger, he felt more relieved. I know that he did things more natural, the way he had before, after I took that off him. And I don't believe too many people could have done what he did without a great faith. I believe that's the thing that sustained him throughout these crises because, even though he saw his mother dying, for those of us who are Christians, we know that this is a reward, you know, when we pass away. And, therefore, that's a comforting feeling for a Christian."

Now this all raises an interesting question, one about which I've heard a lot of speculation over the years. Does God reward Christian athletes on the field for their faith? If that were true, wouldn't every coach and every owner be rushing out to stock up on Christians? And what happens when there are players of strong faith on both sides of the ball? Both sides can't win. I asked Landry about that.

"I don't believe that God intercedes [in a football game]. I often tell people when they ask me whether or not I think God has much to do with the outcome, and I say He does if you have talent. There's a lot of truth in that. I believe what God does in a football game, what He does in your life, He enables you to reach your full potential. When He does that, then if you're on a football team with enough talent, then you're going to be a winner because of what He enables you to do."

Tom Landry had taken his share of criticism over the years—most of it, I feel, unjustified. Unemotional, many said. A "plastic man," one of his own players called him. That player was Duane Thomas, a running back of extraordinary talent, but deeply troubled. For a while, it seemed as if the Cowboys had bent the rules to accommodate him, but finally they shipped him off to another team. Sadly, he never lived up to his full potential once he was outside Tom Landry's sphere of influence.

Did it hurt when Thomas called him a "plastic man"?

"No, it didn't really upset me," Landry said. "When I heard that statement, I thought, well, what Duane was referring to here is not so much that I am plastic, but I'm part of management, I'm part of organization, I'm part of what he doesn't like in this country."

But what about the knock that he's not emotional enough? Did Landry ever consider trying to become more emotional, or at least showing his emotions more, to defuse that criticism?

"I'm what I am, and I'm going to react that way," he said. "I can be very emotional if I'm just watching a game. But when I'm so involved in a football game, and I've said it so many times, I'm not even aware of the crowd, I'm not aware of anything that's happening, because I'm right into the play. I'm always ahead of the game to see what's going to happen the next play and the next play. And I'll go through the game and I'll be so involved, the game will be over, you know, sometimes before I really realize that the thing's over with. I'm concentrating that hard. And when you concentrate, you can't show emotion."

Over twenty-nine years as head coach of the Cowboys, what was Landry's greatest disappointment in a game? "The ice game, against the Packers."

What Cowboys fan could forget that one, played in temperatures that reached 13 below zero, on frozen Lambeau Field in Green Bay? Those Cowboys were "next year's champions," coming off a 34-27 loss to Green Bay in the NFL Championship game the year before, now rematched in the championship against those same Packers. Leading 14-10 with only seconds to play, the Cowboys defense dug in with its back to the Packers goal line. Even now, my heart sinks as I remember Packer guard Jerry Kramer cutting the legs out from under defensive tackle Jethro Pugh and watching quarterback Bart Starr sneak across the goal line for the winning touchdown.

"We were a young, flamboyant team who had just hit the big time," Landry said. "We could have beaten them . . . we were mature enough to win it all. And when we failed, Bart Starr quarterback sneaked to beat us, that was probably the biggest disappointment that I ever experienced."

How about the biggest thrill?

Easy. "The Super Bowl . . . I think the thing that got me in the first one was when I looked at some of those guys that had suffered so many times. The Bob Lillys, the Chuck Howleys, who were really at their last phase of their career . . . boy, to see the excitement in those guys in that one day was worth all the years of frustration."

When I interviewed Coach Landry on my *Face to Face* program in December of 1973, I asked for his impressions on a variety of subjects and people. I found his answers quite interesting.

Sportswriters?

"Honest people who are trying to do their job within their knowledge."

My old friend, Howard Cosell?

"Howard is a great friend of mine. Of course, Howard's a showman more than anything else. He says a lot of things he really doesn't mean; down deep he's sound."

Duane Thomas?

"Disappointment. I think this is probably one of the biggest disappointments in my coaching career. The guy with the great talent, a fellow who potentially could be a great asset to anything he did, but he didn't contribute."

His wife, Alicia?

"Well, I love that girl. She's a great stabilizing influence in my life. She's the thing that really has given me a purpose for everything I do."

And finally, what about himself? "What is your thought," I asked him, "when someone asks you to capsulize Tom Landry?"

"I find it difficult to capsulize me because I never tried to do that. I just believe that God has a plan for me and I don't know particularly what it is, but I believe he has a plan. What tomorrow will bring, I'm not really sure. But I'm not too worried about it, either."

—◇◇◇—

"I do feel like in my position, you know, as the head coach of the Dallas Cowboys, that I don't want to make my players feel obligated to do something that's not spontaneous."

—TOM LANDRY, WHEN ASKED WHETHER HE PUSHED
HIS FAITH ON HIS TEAM

Long ago, when I first started announcing Dallas Cowboys games as a hobby at Texas Stadium, my job was to handle the pre-game announcing, followed by the introductions, then later the half-time show, while play-by-play was done by someone else up in the booth. I did my pre-game work from down on the field level, and therefore I wound up close to the team bench quite often. During one game, when I was near the bench, I watched Coach Tom Landry on the sidelines, neatly dressed in his powder blue Cowboy sport-coat, felt hat, navy blue Cowboy tie, and dark pants. Arms folded, his cheat sheet for the game in one hand, he intently watched the action on the field.

At some point, a penalty was called against the Cowboys—one with which assistant coach Mike Ditka violently disagreed. He jumped onto the playing field and slammed his clipboard down as he proceeded to rage at the officials. One of the referees started for him, reaching for his flag. Landry, unsmiling, paced to where Ditka was, then said just loud enough for Ditka to hear him, "Michael, just settle down. Right now, you're not worth fifteen yards to me."

That was Tom Landry—always in control. Until the very end when a cancer he couldn't control claimed him on February 12, 2000. A private funeral service was held for him at Sparkman Hillcrest Funeral Home in Dallas, attended by dozens of Cowboys players, past and present. Howard Hendricks, who led the chapel services for the Fellowship of Christian Athletes at Cowboys games, presided. As the service ended, he announced that the family had asked everyone to walk to the gravesite, which was only a couple of hundred yards away.

In a very somber procession, a hearse drove Tom's body to the gravesite, while the pallbearers walked immediately behind, followed by the family, then hundreds of mourners. A short graveside service followed, including a military flyover and 21-gun salute in honor of this man who had served America proudly in World War II. As the American flag which draped his coffin was folded and handed to Alicia, taps played. A group of former players stood beside the coffin listening. On an impulse, one of them, I don't know who, stepped up and touched the coffin. That set off a chain reaction as every player walked by, gently touched the coffin, then turned and walked away. Not a dry eye among them.

It was one of those moments you never forget.

—◆◆◆—

"Well, if that's all the guts you've got, come on back to Oklahoma with me and work in the mines. You don't belong in baseball anyway."
—ELVIN "MUTT" MANTLE TO HIS
EIGHTEEN-YEAR-OLD SON, MICKEY

In 1958, I joined a group of people, including longtime friend and former American League batting champ with the Boston Red Sox, Pete Runnels, to build a bowling center in my hometown of Lufkin, Texas. Pete and I drove to Dallas to invite New York Yankee Mickey Mantle, who had just opened a bowling center in Exchange Park, to come to our grand opening. Mickey and his brothers, Ray, Roy, and Butch, accepted our invitation, and I began a friendship with Mickey that continued through my days at Channel 8 in Dallas, to ABC-TV in New York, and back to Dallas, right up to his death in 1996.

When Joyce and I moved to New York in 1963, we leased an apartment just a half block from the St. Moritz Hotel on Central Park South, where Mickey lived during the baseball season. Over the next few years, he and I spent a lot of time together, particularly on weekends when I would go to Yankee Stadium with him, visit the dressing room before and after the games, and then return to Central Park South to his place or mine. If his wife, Merlyn, was in town, we often all went out to dinner. If not, Joyce would often invite Mickey over for some "down home" cooking—the kind a boy from Oklahoma couldn't find just anywhere in the Big Apple. This enjoyable friendship afforded me the opportunity to really get to know one of the great athletes of all time.

Mickey Charles Mantle was the eldest of five children born to the Elvin "Mutt" Mantles in Spavinaw, Oklahoma, in October 1931, right in the midst of the depression. Mickey's dad, a mine worker and avid baseball fan, named his eldest son after the old-time major league catcher, Mickey Cochrane. When Mickey was a mere youngster, Mutt would sometimes take him the 600-mile round-trip from Oklahoma to St. Louis to see his namesake play for the Cardinals.

An outstanding high school player who seemed destined for the major leagues, Mickey skipped his high school graduation from Commerce High School in Oklahoma to play in a baseball game attended by New York Yankees scout Tom Greenwade. Greenwade was actually on his way to Broken Arrow, Oklahoma, to see a different shortstop play, but his stopover in Commerce may have been the best decision he ever made. That night, the seventeen-year-old Mickey blasted three home runs, and Greenwade signed him on the spot, for a total of $1,500, bonus and salary, for the remainder of the season in the Yankees minor league system—not much, even for those days. But Mickey always considered himself lucky to have gotten that. He believed that the hungrier you were, the harder you'd try and the longer you'd last.

The next year, Casey Stengel brought Mickey up from the minor leagues when he was just eighteen. During spring training in Phoenix, Mickey blasted the ball all over the park, unheard of for a shortstop, his position at the time—but not for long. Because Mickey wasn't the best glovesman, Stengel moved him to the outfield, a more natural position for him.

With the lighter air in Arizona, and its great climate, he hit more than a dozen home runs during that spring training. Sportswriters started the drumbeats. The next DiMaggio, they said. But when they rang the bell for the regular season, his bat had cooled considerably. Their high expectations dampened, fans and sportswriters alike started getting on his case, which only made things worse.

Recognizing that the pressures were getting to be too much for the teenager, Stengel sent him to the minor leagues, to Kansas City, for a bit more seasoning. As it turned out, things weren't any better there. In his first twenty-two at bats in Kansas City, the best Mickey could muster was one bunt single. For the first time in his short life, doubts began to creep in. He began to question himself and his abilities, which further undermined his confidence on the field.

When his father came to town to watch him play, Mickey moaned, "I can't play this game." If he was looking for sympathy, he'd come to the wrong place.

"Well, if that's all the guts you've got," Mutt Mantle told his son, "come on back to Oklahoma with me and work in the mines. You don't belong in baseball anyway."

Not at all what Mickey expected or wanted, but it accomplished its purpose. Before long, he had regained his stroke and soon headed back to the big leagues. The rest is baseball history. And who knows how great a career he might have had, had it not been for the injuries that so often kept him from playing at 100 percent?

Throughout his career, Mickey underwent multiple surgeries on his knees and shoulders. On game days he usually arrived at Yankee Stadium two and a half hours early, spending the bulk of that time in the training room. The Yankees had two trainers in those days, known as Big Pete and Little Pete. The trainers would first massage both of his legs with hot linament, then he would get into the whirlpool, to be followed by electric wave treatments. Next, both knees would be wrapped with yards of elastic bandage, and, finally, he would be ready to play. Mickey often said that the lack of cartilage in both knees didn't bother him too much for single games; it was the double-headers that really brought out the aches.

Injuries and surgeries interrupted Mickey's career so frequently that the word "courageous" was often bandied about by the press because of the way he played with pain. But Mickey never bought into that bit. After all, baseball was only a game—a kid's game. No, life was where courage came in, and he quickly told anyone who would listen that the most courageous man he ever knew was his own father.

In 1951, Mutt Mantle came to watch his son play in the World Series. When Mickey injured his knee in the second game against the Giants, the trainers sent him home accompanied by Mutt. The next morning, as Mutt was helping his son out of a taxi in front of Lenox Hill Hospital, Mickey put an arm on Mutt's shoulder to brace himself—and watched in horror as his father crumpled to the sidewalk. That was how Mickey first found out his father was suffering from Hodgkin's Disease. Mutt had kept it from him so it wouldn't become a distraction to the burgeoning young superstar.

Both Mantles were admitted to Lenox Hill Hospital that day.

Later that year, Mickey and Merlyn took Mutt to the Mayo Clinic, and found the prognosis wasn't good. Realizing that Mutt didn't have long to live, Mickey took him back to Oklahoma for his last days. Not long after that, because he didn't want his children to see him wasting away, Mutt and his wife moved to Denver, Colorado, where he lived out his final days in a sanitarium. He died in the spring of 1952 at the ripe old age of thirty-nine.

There are many Mickey Mantle stories. Not all of them involved Mantle directly. One of Mickey's best friends was Billy Martin, the brilliant Yankee infielder whose career also touched fans in Kansas City, Detroit, Cleveland, Minnesota, and Milwaukee before he turned to managing. But it was as a Yankee that he is best remembered, and for good reason. Casey Stengel, who first called Martin up from the Pacific Coast League, once said of him, "That little punk. How I love him."

I got a call late one evening at my apartment in New York from Mickey telling me that Billy, who was then managing the Minnesota Twins, was in town and needed a place to stay for a while. A few minutes later, when they both arrived at our Central Park South apartment, Joyce and I quickly learned why Billy needed a place to stay.

He and his wife, Gretchen, had been in Toots Shor's having dinner. When they left, they were having a small argument as they entered a cab for the ride back to their hotel. The cab driver stopped the cab and chastised Martin for the way he was talking to his wife. As anyone who knows anything about Billy Martin knows, he doesn't take challenges like that very well. And, in true Martin style, he invited the cab driver out of the cab to "discuss" the matter. That was when the cab driver made his mistake: He got out.

Blows were exchanged, the cab driver was left dazed on the sidewalk, and Martin beat it on foot for his friend Mickey Mantle's apartment in the St. Moritz Hotel not too far away. Gretchen headed back to Toots Shor's, alone.

Mickey and Martin decided he'd best not stay at the St. Moritz because that would be one of the first places anybody would think to look, so they headed for our apartment. When they got there, Martin asked me to go down to Toots Shor's and get Gretchen and bring her back. I caught a cab there, where I found Gretchen in a booth alone. I talked to her for a moment, then escorted her out the front door, past police officers who were getting information from a mad cab driver, and back to our apartment, where she was reunited with her husband. All was forgiven, and Billy Martin had dodged another bullet, thanks to his friend Mickey Mantle.

Besides those times, I also had the good fortune to witness a lot of Mickey's baseball exploits firsthand. I suffered with him during those days when he was looking for home run number 500. It seemed as if it would never come. As I recall, he had between 45 and 50 at bats between numbers 499 and 500, which finally came one Mother's Day. As Joyce and I rode to the stadium with Mickey that day, he told us he had talked to Merlyn back in Dallas. He had forgotten to get her a card, but told her he was going to give her a very special present: He was going to hit number 500.

Joyce and I both had tears in our eyes as he kept his promise. And later that day I had one of my greatest thrills as a broadcaster when he reserved his first interview after the game for me. That moment is indelibly imprinted in my mind. Later that season, when Mickey hit his 515th home run against Minnesota, a fan caught the ball, then returned it to him. I now proudly own that ball, autographed to Joyce and me from Mickey, although I keep it in my safe deposit box at the bank with other valuables. It's a treasure—a very dear treasure.

—◇◇◇—

"If I'd known I was going to live so long, I'd have taken better care of myself."
—MICKEY MANTLE

I remember once, not too long before Mickey got ill, talking with him about the amount of money he had been paid for playing baseball. The highest contract he ever received was for $125,000 a year. Later he would make much more than that just going to weekend card-signing events at memorabilia shows, where he would be booked for a guaranteed minimum of $25-30,000 just to show up—far more than he ever made playing baseball.

I asked him about the outrageous multimillion-dollar salaries being paid to current stars. "If you were still playing today," I said, "how much do you think you'd make?"

He thought for a moment, then looked at me with a straight face. "Oh, probably about $500,000."

Fame, Faith and (Mis)Fortune // 241

I said, "That's all you think you'd make? Just $500,000?"

He said, "Yeah, but hell, I'm sixty-five years old."

Then he started in with that seventeen-year-old giggle he had at one time, still a child at heart. And he had the biggest heart I've ever known anybody to have. If he hadn't fought the battles with the bottle and some other problems in life—wow, what could have been!

Because his father had been so young when he died, and because his uncles and grandfather also died at young ages, Mickey worried a great deal about an early death for himself. But, when he finally passed his fiftieth birthday, it no longer seemed to concern him as much. Maybe he quit worrying too soon.

Mickey's last days in life were not pleasant. He'd been through a lot of heartache, a lot of health problems. Alcohol had become a way of life for him, something that finally drove him to the Betty Ford Clinic for treatment. I had seen him under the influence of alcohol and I had seen him sober and, like so many who are imprisoned by the bottle, he was a vastly different person when he was drinking. As his health continued to deteriorate, and after discovering that his liver was gone and he needed a liver transplant, the dark hours set in.

While undergoing the liver transplant at Baylor Hospital in Dallas, his family asked if I would sit with them during the operation, which I gladly did. We waited in the living room area of their hospital suite throughout tense hours. Afterwards, as Mickey was recovering, I would often go back and stay with him from time to time to spell the other members of the family. At first he seemed to respond and things were better for a while, but then they quickly turned. His condition began to really get bad in the summer of 1995, particularly in early August when the doctors discovered that he had developed cancer in the new liver. Then it was just a matter of time.

I visited Mickey a lot during his last days. On one of those visits, when he was at his weakest, he told me he thought the Yankees were going to win it all that year, and that one of his most treasured possessions was a baseball, autographed by the current team, that had been given to him with the note, "Get well, Mick." He showed me the baseball, which was on the table beside his bed. I remarked that if anybody should get an autographed ball, he should. After all, he had probably signed more balls than anybody else had.

We talked of the good old days when the police had to escort him to his car at Yankee Stadium because of the hordes of fans clamoring for his autograph. There were two policemen who made up his escort team, and he said they had recently been through Dallas to pick up a prisoner and had stopped by to visit with him. Old times.

On Thursday, August 10, I found Mickey visiting in his hospital room with his brother Roy and the old Yankee pitching great, Whitey Ford. As the day wore on, more old Yankees began to drop by. They knew that Mickey's last breath was drawing nearer. Second baseman Bobby Richardson was there. A strong Christian, and very active in the Fellowship of Christian Athletes, he and Mickey prayed together and talked about God and Mickey's relationship with him. Faith came late in life for Mickey, but it came.

Later, Moose Skowron and Hank Bauer arrived, and it was just a great Yankee reunion day. I was cornered several times that day in the hospital by members of the press seeking information, but I didn't disclose that the Yankees were up in Mickey's room. This was their time with Mickey, and his with them, and I didn't think it was anybody else's business. I didn't want to see the day turn into a media event.

By the end of the day, I could see that Mickey didn't have much time left. After I took Moose Skowron to the airport, I went home and got Joyce and went back to the hospital. I told her that if she wanted to see and talk with him again, this might be her last opportunity.

A couple of days later, on Saturday, I arrived at the hospital about 6:00 P.M. and found Merlyn there, alone, with Mickey. She told me that he had not been out of bed the entire day. Not a good sign. As she and I talked, I could hear that Mickey's breathing was very labored and his lungs seemed to rattle. Seeing that his eyes were set, I knew he really didn't have long now. Merlyn knew it, too. She asked me to help with arrangements for VIP seating at Mickey's funeral. It felt strange to be discussing the final arrangements for a dear friend as he lay nearby, but I knew it needed to be done.

When I got home that night, as sad as I've ever been, I told Joyce I didn't think Mickey would make it through the night. And about four hours later, he breathed his last—at 1:10 A.M., Sunday morning, August 13.

Just as at Howard Cosell's funeral, Mickey Mantle's was attended by a Who's Who of celebrities. Bob Costas presided, Bobby

Richardson provided the eulogy, and Roy Clark sang. Among those attending at Lovers Lane United Methodist Church in Dallas were Texas Governor George Bush and Laura Bush, Stan Musial, Bobby Bragan, Billy Crystal, Reggie Jackson, Joe Pepitone, Tony Kubek, Tom Tresh, Yogi Berra, Whitey Ford, Hank Bauer, and Moose Skowron. The service was beautiful, Bob Costas was magnificent, and Roy Clark added the special touch that Mickey would have loved.

A great athlete, and a great man, was laid to rest.

A lot has been written about Mickey Mantle over the years, not all of it good. But I can assure you that the good in Mickey far outweighed anything you may have heard to the contrary. A seventeen-year-old jumping from small-town America to superstardom in New York City is no easy climb. Although he may have been clumsy along the way, he did handle it.

And, after so much pain and so many tears, Mickey was finally reunited with those who had left him so early in life.

Murphy Martin, upper right holding ABC microphones, on morning walk with former president Harry Truman in April 1964. It was during these walks that Truman questioned the role of Dr. Martin Luther King, Jr., in the civil rights movement.

President Johnson with Secretary of State Dean Rusk and other world leaders at the funeral of Konrad Adenauer in Cologne, Germany, April 25, 1967. Murphy Martin accompanied the president on the trip and anchored coverage for the ABC Radio network.

Murphy and Joyce Martin with former president Richard Nixon at San Clemente party for POWs in 1978.

Talking with Vice President Hubert Humphrey prior to taping Face to Face with Murphy Martin *program at WFAA-TV in Dallas, 1968.*

Murphy and Joyce Martin with Governor Ronald Reagan and Nancy Reagan at POW dinner in Los Angeles.

With George H. W. Bush after completing half-hour interview at WFAA-TV, 1968.

Murphy and Joyce Martin with Dallas native and Las Vegas casino legend Benny Binion. Martin was one of the very few newsmen Binion ever granted an extended interview. Martin had been introduced to Binion by Chill Wills.

An interview with Bob Hope during one of his many visits to Dallas.

Murphy Martin and John Wayne have a laugh prior to taping Face to Face program at WFAA-TV in Dallas.

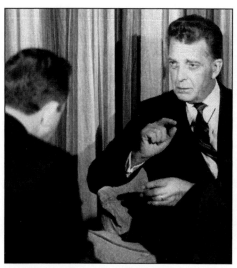 

Murphy Martin interviews longtime NBC-TV news anchor Chet Huntley just after he retired. The interview was taped in Dallas.

Melvin Belli and Murphy Martin have a laugh prior to taping an interview at WFAA-TV, 1968.

Martin doing another of his several interviews with Howard Cosell, this one in the studios of WFAA-TV after Howard completed his book Cosell.

Interviewing members of the Hell's Angels in 1968.

An interview with Texas Governor William P. Clements.

Martin interviews astronaut John Glenn.

Martin interviewing President William Tolbert of Liberia at WFAA-TV in Dallas, 1968.

Murphy Martin (left) interviewing William F. Buckley on WABC-TV in New York City, 1965.

In the home of longtime Dallas Cowboys Coach Tom Landry and wife Alicia. This interview focused on Landry's faith rather than football.

Martin with longtime Dallas Cowboy Coach Tom Landry and Mary Crowley, founder of Home Interiors and Gifts, at annual sales conference in Dallas.

Interviewing Mickey Mantle following his 500th home run hit on Mother's Day, May 14, 1967, in Yankee Stadium. Mantle would not talk with other members of the press until he completed the interview with his ABC-TV friend.

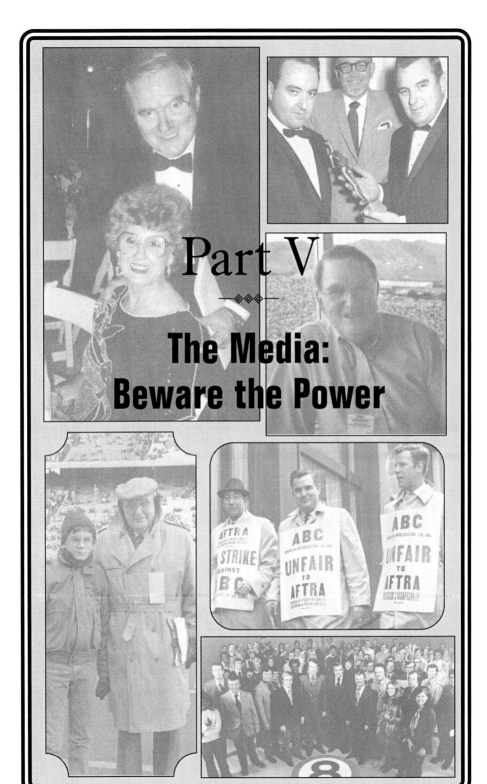

Part V

The Media:
Beware the Power

CHAPTER 12

Television: Then and Now

> *"Conservatives believe the government does too much and should withdraw from our life, and liberals believe government still has a larger role to play: to arbitrate, to preserve rights and so on. I believe, as the liberals, that the government still has a larger role to play."*
> —HOWARD K. SMITH, FORMER ABC-TV NEWS ANCHOR

I believe that television is the most powerful social instrument yet devised. In its early days, it even acted as a unifying force in American society. With only three major networks, Americans were unified by the shows they watched; after all, there were only three options on any given night. With the advent of more local stations, cable networks, the booming Internet, movies, it's no longer the unifying force it once was. It is, nevertheless, a prominent, if not the preeminent, source for information, including news, today.

I have actively participated in, or closely observed, television news since 1960. In those early days, most people who staffed television news rooms came from print or radio journalism, with little or no college training in the world of television journalism. As televisions made their way into more and more American homes, the anchor position became a seat of honor, prestige, and, later, power. Names like Edward R. Murrow, Howard K. Smith, Harry Reasoner, Ron Cochran, David Brinkley, and Chet Huntley became household words.

After a brief stint in the anchor job at WFAA-TV in Dallas, ABC-

TV hired me in February of 1963 to anchor the late night news in the spot that is filled so capably today by *Nightline* and Ted Koppel, who started at the network the same year I did. At that time, there were only a handful of network anchors: Huntley-Brinkley at NBC, Walter Cronkite at CBS, and Ron Cochran handled the early news program while I anchored the late night at ABC. Looking back now, some forty years later, I can see the changes that have taken place in the industry with a more objective eye. Some of those changes have been for the better; some for the worse.

Since its inception, television news has dominated American life, telling us what to eat, what to drink, what to drive, who and what to support, who to vote for. There is not a single element of our lives, in America particularly, that is not affected by this developing monster called television news.

According to recent surveys, however, the number of television sets in use is dwindling as people find other ways to occupy their time—the Internet, video games, and the resurgence of the theater box offices. That, coupled with the advent of the number of cable news networks, means that fewer people are watching the three basic networks for their news even in a time of rising population. Yet despite the dilution, the masses still depend on television news of some form or other for answers to the day's pressing concerns, be they the economy, terrorism, health issues, or whatever. That's no different than before. But what is different today?

In days past, the media had earned the trust of the viewing public. Viewers believed it if they saw it on the news. And see it, they did. The most expensive advertising rates, at one time, were those commercial spots within and adjacent to the news because the networks and advertisers knew that was when viewership peaked. But somewhere, somehow, there was a subtle shift in trust. It's hard to pin down the "when," but perhaps it was sometime in the '60s, in the time of the Vietnam War, when people started to question what they heard on television and radio and read in newspapers. Or perhaps it postdates that, arising out of Watergate. In any event, from there, it's all been downhill.

By 1989, according to opinion polls, public trust in the media had sagged to 54 percent, and it reached an all-time low of 32 percent during the post-election fallout from the 2000 presidential campaign. Things aren't much better today: A *USA Today*/Gallup

Poll in May 2003 showed public confidence in the media at an anemic 36 percent. And those numbers don't factor in the latest scandals at two of the nation's top newspapers, the *Washington Post* and the bellwether *New York Times*, where reporters have now admitted plagiarizing and fabricating major news stories.

In reality, it should be just the opposite. Technology today allows for instant reporting, with live pictures—and pictures don't lie, do they?—from anywhere in the world, including war zones such as Iraq. That's a far cry from coverage of the Vietnam War, when film had to be shot, shipped, processed, and edited, finally reaching the screen three days later in a form that might bear little actual resemblance to what was originally filmed. While Vietnam correspondents often had to rely solely on handouts from sources at the U.S. Embassy for accounts of fighting, today we see and hear directly from embedded reporters on the battlefields.

And the number of in-the-field reporters has vastly increased since those early days. Once upon a time, small market stations were lucky to have a staff of one or two, with a like number of camera crews. Even larger market stations, such as WFAA in Dallas, would have employed only eighteen to twenty people in the news department and two or three camera crews. Today, those same smaller market stations might employ news staffs of twenty-five to thirty, while each separate station in the larger markets such as Dallas, Atlanta, or Los Angeles might have news departments of up to 150 people and fifteen or more camera crews. In 2002 there were approximately 40,000 jobs nationwide in television journalism. More eyes and ears should increase accuracy, shouldn't it?

In those major market cities, it isn't unusual for television news anchors to make salaries of $1 million or more per year, while the network anchors in New York (Peter Jennings, Tom Brokaw, Dan Rather) make more than $10 million a year, with supporting casts made up with the likes of Ted Koppel, Barbara Walters, Diane Sawyer, and Mike Wallace not far behind.

So, along with the advent of new technology, more journalists, higher salaries, what else has changed, for better or worse? Well, for one thing, the *amount* of news presented has changed. In 1963 the thirty-minute nightly news broadcasts at ABC, NBC, and CBS contained twenty-two minutes of news and eight minutes of commercials. Today the average is nineteen minutes of news, eleven minutes of commercials. And, at both the network and local levels, you might actually find only six to eight minutes of the hard news of the day, with the rest of the time filled with magazine or feature stories.

Chalk up one change for the worse.

Another change to fit that category has to do with anchors ad-libbing their personal views on air. This practice seemed to blossom after the tragic events of 9/11, unavoidably, perhaps, as the network anchors spent hours on air with little new news to report or simply directing traffic from one reporter to another as bits and pieces of the unfolding story trickled in from different sources. To fill the time, they—inadvertently or otherwise—often told viewers their own personal thoughts.

During a visit to Dallas after 9/11, Peter Jennings told me that he had come under considerable viewer questioning because of remarks he made on air that fateful day. In particular, he had questioned why President Bush was not back in Washington after having been in Florida when the attacks occurred, but was instead moving from one military base to another. Without the benefit of whatever information the Secret Service might have had, Peter seemed to "lecture" the president on what actions to take. He concluded with something to the effect of "some presidents handle these crises better than others," the implication being that he believed President Bush was one of those "others."

I was shocked and astonished when I heard Peter that day. I had known Peter for better than thirty years and had watched over those years as he had worked hard, becoming, in my opinion, one of the best and most consistent anchors on the air since he had moved into the anchor chair in the early 1980s. But his conduct that dreadful day, in my opinion, was surprisingly out of character.

In post-9/11 conversations, I learned that Peter had also been taking heat because he had retained his Canadian citizenship rather than becoming an American citizen despite being at ABC since 1964. Others at the network told me Peter had chosen to remain a Canadian citizen because he felt it would hurt his late mother's feelings if he gave it up.

I tried calling Peter several times thereafter at ABC, hoping to pass along what I had been hearing out in the hinterlands about his words that day, but he never returned my calls. Sometime later, when ABC, at its owner-company Disney's instigation, made a run at getting David Letterman from CBS to replace the Ted Koppel *Nightline* spot, I wrote a letter to the editor at *USA Today* on March 15, 2002, in which I questioned Disney's efforts to displace Koppel. In that letter, I said, in part:

> [N]ow that Letterman is still a cash cow at CBS, ABC might better serve its viewers if executives cease and desist in trying to disturb Koppel and *Nightline* and take a long hard look at trying to guide Jennings back to the top anchor professional he once was ...
>
> Bottom line for ABC: Forget dumping Koppel and remind Jennings to return to his professional ways of just a short time ago.

I didn't intend the letter to be detrimental to Peter's talents; rather, I was suggesting how he might maximize those considerable talents to again become what he had once been, the best anchor on TV.

In July 2003, Jennings announced he had finally become an American citizen, while retaining his Canadian citizenship.

The question of biased reporting rears its head from time to time, usually advanced about every ten years or so by a new book on the subject. In 1971, Edith Efron came out with her book *The News Twisters*, in which she cited facts and figures to support her thesis that the television networks had supported Hubert Humphrey over Richard Nixon in the 1968 presidential election. According to her, the networks "actively slanted their opinion coverage against U.S. policy ... in favor of the black militants and against the white middle class majority ... [and] largely evaded the issue of the violent radicals." She concluded, "In summary, the presidential campaign of 1968 and its major issues were handled in a partisan fashion by all three networks."

The last "bias" book I read was one aptly titled *Bias* (Regnery Publishing 2002) by Bernard Goldberg. Goldberg's primary target? Dan Rather and CBS-TV, whom he accused of a liberal bias in news reporting. Goldberg, who had worked at CBS for a number of years, cited proof for his thesis in a statement made by Peter Jennings. Goldberg said, on page 213 of his book, "On July 4, 2001, there was a ray of sunshine. Peter Jennings told the *Boston Globe* 'Those of us who went into journalism in the '50s or '60s, it was sort of a liberal thing to do. Save the world.'"

The truth is, bias can wear many hats, none of them appropriate in the anchor chair. The role of an anchor is to deliver the news in an honest, accurate fashion. The viewer shouldn't be able to tell whether the anchor is a conservative or liberal, a Republican or Democrat or Independent. For years I listened to Walter Cronkite, a Democrat by his own admission, deliver the news and never knew his political persuasion by virtue of his anchoring work. And it was Cronkite, the most trusted man in America when he was at CBS, who once said in his book *A Reporter's Life* about a lot of news anchors, "I suspect that if television didn't exist, they would be in acting."

I suppose David Brinkley, who died in June of 2003, best summed up what a good anchor does: "Most of my life, I've simply been a reporter covering things and talking about it." Then he was reported to have said, "If I should start today, I probably couldn't get a job because I don't look like what people think an anchorman should look like."

I suspect that, with his wonderful writing skills and unique, punctuated delivery, David Brinkley would have no problem slipping into the anchor chair today, just as he did in 1956, when he teamed with Chet Huntley to form the most powerful network duo in television news history. In 1964, up against Walter Cronkite on CBS, Huntley and Brinkley got a whopping 84 percent of the viewers watching the Democratic National Convention in Atlantic City. And in 1965, a consumer research team found that Huntley and Brinkley were recognized by more adult Americans than either John Wayne or the Beatles.

But Brinkley's latter comment reflects on another part of the problem today, as I see it: the lack of journalism training. And by that I mean actual training in the craft of journalism—what journalism should be, instead of what it has become. I have heard more than one network news veteran complain that journalism schools were turning out undereducated graduates and that local stations exacerbated the problem by emphasizing cosmetics over news skills in their hiring and training practices. Perhaps that is because we live in a time when entertainment is considered by many to be as important as news, and celebrity is revered. Unfortunately, this way of thinking pervades many an executive office at television stations across the country.

Some executives still worried a bit, at least in the past, about the emphasis on cosmetics. Witness this telegram from the president and general manager of WFTV in Orlando, Florida, to Elmer Lower of ABC News in New York on the occasion of ABC's first nightly newscast in color in the mid-1960s:

> Congratulations on first Jennings color show. Here are our quick reactions to help you in shakedown period.
>
> - Set too blatantly colorful—too bright—not natural, too showy
> - China feature story good but too long for opener—belonged later
> - Too much "to do" over color show; Morgan spot weak
> - Even in ½ hour show, need more short stories for faster pace
> - Show seemed to run short. Also, too much credit time
> - Keep lipstick off Jennings. Not necessary
>
> We are delighted to see ABC's first effort in colorful news. Are sure these minor details will be solved quickly.

In television's early days, news people came up the hard way, learning and advancing through trial and error. To coin a cliché, they paid their dues. Later, television journalists came from colleges, trained in journalism theory, but little schooled in the actual practice. With the advent of technology, they had to work neither as long nor as hard as had their predecessors. In an instant gratification society, journalism leads the way.

Add to this the fact that local stations now can, and do, send their reporters to cover major stories worldwide, a far cry from the days when the locals had to rely on the networks for any stories outside the viewing radius of that particular station. The embedded reporters in Iraq are a prime example, their ranks filled by local stations from across the country, broadcasting side by side with their network and cable brethren and, bingo, instant celebrity at the local level.

Lost in the lack of journalism experience and the race for money and prestige is, among other things, judgment. During the '60s, when we were covering sometimes violent anti-war demonstrations (I think some never quite grasped the irony of violence at anti-war demonstrations), civil rights demonstrations, riots, assassinations, and space disasters, we were never at a loss for running story lines. Still, we judiciously weighed the facts, refusing to allow the medium to be used or manipulated, though sometimes that was unavoidable.

The thought process today in picking stories seems to be to find the most sensational—as Ross Perot said, getting himself in hot water with the media, the "gotcha" story. When stations have to compete with movies, video games, and the Internet for attention, the sensational bolsters the ratings, which bolsters the advertising revenues, which soothes the savage beasts in the executive offices. And so judicious weighing of facts sometimes gets sacrificed in the heat of the moment.

—◇◇◇—

> "Knowledge will forever govern ignorance—and a people who mean to be their own governors must arm themselves with the power that knowledge gives. A popular government without popular information or the means of acquiring it is but a prologue to a farce or a tragedy, or both."
> —PRESIDENT JAMES MADISON

I believe all of these things have contributed to the decline of public trust in the news media. On the flip side, I also believe that much of the public's distrust is unjustified. There are too many people today who prefer shrouds of secrecy, and their complaint is that television sheds light. Extremists of all persuasions abhor the sight of television news reporters. Even elected officials want the news disseminated on their terms. They call the news conference, they issue the press release, and they decide when and how television news reporters show them at work.

I find it interesting that critics of television news rarely express the same outrage at the conduct exposed as they do with the media for exposing it. The old admonition to not kill the messenger has its origins in ancient times, and criticism of the medium is nothing new. In the '60s, people enjoyed blaming the ills of the world on television news. Today, people derive that same pleasure. In the '60s, many felt television coverage of anti-war demonstrations gave the world a distorted view of America's support for its troops in Vietnam. In 2003 many felt television coverage of anti-war demonstrations gave the world a distorted view of America's support for its troops in Iraq.

Since 1960, television news has played an integral role in American life. Our world has grown much smaller because of it, and no part of the world has escaped the magic news screen. We have seen television news change life unnecessarily, such as when Dallas Police Chief Jess Curry bowed to the pressure and paraded the accused killer of John Fitzgerald Kennedy before the clamoring media, opening a window of opportunity for Jack Ruby.

We have also seen coverage of wars advance from mostly "handout" information from military sources to the day of embedded reporters traveling with the fighting forces. Was the embedded reporter a successful effort? Most reporters I have heard say it was, a sentiment echoed by military people from the Pentagon to Baghdad. It will surely play a part in the next military operation as well. After all, what would a story be without Geraldo Rivera?

I, for one, would like to find out.

For all its ills, the free press is one of the most important institutions in the world. Without a free press, you are one step away from censorship, and with censorship, you are one step away from dictatorship. So questions arise which today's journalists must answer: What does America want from its news sources today? Are Americans really losing trust in all news media, including television? What do they want from their anchors: straight facts only, or facts embellished by personal opinions?

The power of television today is unquestioned. Who can truly argue against the notion that, in recent years, television has played the biggest role of all in who is elected president? Despite all the other things competing for the viewers' attention, the power of television hasn't diminished over the years. In fact, it has increased. But it can and will diminish if people in positions of authority within the television news industry continue to abuse that power.

That's My Time;
Thank You for Yours

Over the years, I have had the good fortune to witness more history than any school could ever teach. I hope I have given you some new insights or new information on subjects of mutual interest. Unfortunately, neither time nor space permitted me to discuss all the interesting stories and people I have covered.

For instance, we could have discussed:

- Three Gemini space shots as pool reporter at Mission Control;
- The criminal trial of Billie Sol Estes, the Texas scam artist who became a millionaire using non-existent fertilizer storage tanks and grain storage facilities in West Texas;
- The slaying of civil rights workers in Mississippi;
- The trial of Byron De La Beckwith for the murder of Medgar Evers;
- Political campaigns from the left and right;
- The kidnapping of Mafia kingpin Joe Bonanno; and
- Walking a picket line with Peter Jennings and Howard Cosell.

I also could have filled a second book with other stories of people from the world of sports, business, politics, and entertainment. Folks like Arthur Temple, Jr., the East Texas timber baron who built a model small city from what used to be a sawmill town in Diboll, Texas. Like Jackie Robinson, Nancy Reagan, Senator Everett Dirksen, Stanley Marcus, Charley Pride, Gen. Robbie Risner, Gen. Alexander Haig, Senator Lloyd Bentsen, Senator John Tower,

William Scranton, astronauts Frank Borman and John Glenn, the Duke of Windsor, Ku Klux Klan leader Robert Shelton, Speaker of the House Jim Wright, Jimmy Stewart, Charlton Heston, Wayne Newton, Roger Miller, the Beatles, Rock Hudson, Jimmy Dean, Ken Curtis, Hugh O'Brien, Toots Shor, Jack Valenti, Adlai Stevenson, Richard Daley, Adam Clayton Powell. The list goes on and on.

In closing, though, there is one more story I want to revisit briefly: The first visit to the United States by a Pope, when Giovanni Battista Montini, Pope John VI, made a whirlwind, one-day visit to New York City on October 4, 1965. Though he was just in the city for thirteen and a half hours, more than three million people saw him in person as he made public statements during stops at the United Nations, a meeting with President Johnson at the Waldorf Towers, a Mass for Peace at Yankee Stadium, and a brief visit with other religious leaders at Holy Family Church on East 47th Street.

I had been assigned as pool reporter for all three networks that day, reporting from what was called a "crash unit," a vehicle that followed immediately behind the Papal entourage. Utilizing a mobile camera, I gave periodic reports as we moved from Kennedy Airport into New York City, passing through Harlem, down through Central Park, and eventually to Cardinal Spellman's residence, which served as home base for the Pope during his brief visit.

As I look back on that assignment, I can't help but think how small our world really is. So small that a church leader can fly from one continent to another and, in a world torn asunder by hatred and ideological differences, can reach millions "in person"—and tens-of-millions more on television—in less than a day. And I can't help but realize how journalists have that same capacity to reach millions with the stories they report every day.

In the old days, they called those who spread the news "town criers." But over the last forty years, we have needed more than a lamp and a loud voice to keep our audiences informed. In the twenty-first century, armed with new television technology, we have made American citizens the best-informed people in the world. In a world where man can orbit the earth faster than most of us can get in and out of an airport, the challenges facing journalists continue to grow. But despite the changes, the basic requirements of every story still haven't changed: who, what, when, why, and where.

Television news allowed me to live the American dream. As I

look back with great respect for good journalists and the hundreds of people who helped make my career better, let me share some of the indelible things I have learned:

- The reward of a thing well done is to have done it.
- Bravery is not the absence of fear but the mastery of it.
- Someone once described a hero as being no braver than an ordinary man—but a hero is brave five minutes longer.
- Remember that no one can make you feel inferior without your consent.
- Injustice anywhere is a threat to justice everywhere.
- He who keeps his fears to himself shares his courage with others.
- Character is not made in crisis; it is only exhibited then.
- When you can do the common things of life in an uncommon way, you will command the attention of the world.
- Cherish all your happy moments; they make a fine cushion as you grow older.

There was never a dull moment reliving the four decades that reshaped America, and I hope you have enjoyed sharing my *Front Row Seat*. From my own cushion of happy journalism moments, as I said thousands of times at the end of news broadcasts, "That's my time; thank you for yours."

Murphy Martin (center), Howard Cosell (left), and Peter Jennings (right) walk the picket line during a three-week strike by all network news employees in 1965.

Murphy Martin of ABC-TV interviews Dr. Robert Gilruth about fuel-cell problem in Gemini Four space flight in June of 1965. The interview took place in Mission Control.

Martin interviews Mrs. Ed White, wife of astronaut Ed White, during Gemini Four space flight for ABC-TV on June 4, 1965.

Murphy Martin promo picture for Channel 8, WFAA-TV in Dallas.

Staff of WFAA-TV surrounds four anchors in front from left to right: Verne Lundquist, sports, Don Harris, news, Murphy Martin, news, and Jack Van Roy, weather.

Murphy Martin holds Katie Award from Dallas Press Club for Best Documentary of the Year as Bob Gooding and Fred Hatton look on.

Murphy Martin receiving Katie Award from Dallas Press Club, presented by Dorothy Malone, for producing "Ten-Thousand Miles to Hell," a documentary on the Vietnam War. Bob Gooding was the reporter and Fred Hatton the cameraman on the trip.

Murphy Martin with grandson Clay Martin at Cotton Bowl Game in 1984.

Murphy Martin and wife Joyce with Jerry Jones, owner of the Dallas Cowboys, just prior to Martin's retirement ceremony as Voice of Texas Stadium in 1998.

Murphy Martin in press box at Sun Bowl in El Paso prior to announcing Dallas Cowboy pre-season game in 1997.

Murphy Martin, 1998.

Murphy Martin and wife, Joyce Royal Martin, at Dallas social event, 1997.

Mrs. and Mrs. Murphy Martin and Mr. and Mrs. Robert Oswald.

A native of Lufkin, Texas, Murphy Martin served as a news anchorman for more than twenty-five years, including a five-year stint at ABC-TV in New York. He was the first network anchor to originate an entire television news program via satellite from Europe. While with ABC, Martin replaced John Cameron Swayze as anchor of fifteen weekly network radio newscasts carried by more than 500 ABC stations in America and hosted ABC's weekly *Issues and Answers* program on numerous occasions. He co-anchored the ABC Radio Network's coverage of both the Democratic and Republican National Political Conventions in 1964 and was ABC's man on the scene in Austin, Texas, on election night when fellow Texan Lyndon Johnson swept away Barry Goldwater.

In addition to anchor experience at the network level, Martin anchored television news for WABC in New York, where his sports reporter was a former lawyer named Howard Cosell. He also served three tenures as anchor at ABC affiliate WFAA-TV in Dallas, the leading news station in the Southwest at the time. His first stint was from 1961 to 1963, when he was plucked away to the ABC-TV network anchor spot and had only been there ten months when John F. Kennedy was gunned down in Dallas.

While at ABC, Martin worked with young reporters Peter Jennings and Ted Koppel before returning to WFAA in Dallas in 1968. He took a leave of absence in 1970 to head up Ross Perot's

United We Stand organization, seeking the release of American POWs in North Vietnam, then returned to WFAA in 1972 as lead anchor on the nightly news. In 1975 he left to open his own television consulting business, and later spent another tenure with Perot in his 1992 presidential campaign.

Murphy Martin now works as a motivational speaker and has written, produced, and directed numerous marketing and new product videos. Still golden-throated, he has voiced hundreds of television and radio commercials and for twenty-four years, as a hobby, served as the stadium voice of the Dallas Cowboys, and also worked two Super Bowls as stadium announcer for the National Football League.